Gothic Literature

Sue Chaplin

Longman
is an imprint of

Harlow, England • London • New York • Boston • San Francisco • Toronto
Sydney • Tokyo • Singapore • Hong Kong • Seoul • Taipei • New Delhi
Cape Town • Madrid • Mexico City • Amsterdam • Munich • Paris • Milan

This book is dedicated to my family, especially my cousin Julie Spencer.
Sue Chaplin

YORK PRESS
322 Old Brompton Road, London SW5 9JH

PEARSON EDUCATION LIMITED
Edinburgh Gate, Harlow, CM20 2JE. United Kingdom
Tel: +44 (0)1279 623623 Fax: +44 (0)1279 431059
Website: www.pearsoned.co.uk

First edition published in Great Britain in 2011

© Librairie du Liban *Publishers* 2011

The right of Sue Chaplin to be identified as Author of this Work has been
asserted by her in accordance with the Copyright, Designs and Patents Act 1988.

ISBN 978–1–4082–6666–3

British Library Cataloguing in Publication Data
A CIP catalogue record for this book can be obtained from the British Library

Library of Congress Cataloguing in Publication Data
Chaplin, Susan, 1967-
  Gothic literature / Sue Chaplin.
    p. cm. -- (York notes companions)
  Includes bibliographical references and index.
  ISBN 978-1-4082-6666-3 (pbk. : alk. paper) 1. Gothic fiction (Literary genre),
English--History and criticism--Handbooks, manuals, etc. 2. Gothic fiction (Literary
genre), American--History and criticism--Handbooks, manuals, etc. I. Title.
  PR830.T3C47 20011
  823'.0872909--dc22

                          2011003150

10 9 8 7 6 5 4 3 2
14 13

Phototypeset by Carnegie Publishing Ltd, Lancaster
Printed in Great Britain by Ashford Colour Press Ltd, Gosport, Hants

Contents

Contents

Part One
Introduction

A study of Gothic literature must acknowledge from the outset that what counts as 'Gothic' within literature, or within any other cultural domain, has proved difficult to define. When we encounter certain early examples of the Gothic – the fictions of Ann Radcliffe and Matthew Lewis, for example, discussed in Parts Two and Three below – this might not seem to be the case. These fictions can appear rather formulaic; they appear to conform to certain quite specific generic conventions: notably, the setting (often in southern Europe, featuring a haunted castle or abbey); the evocation of (or at least an allusion to) the supernatural; and a recognisable Gothic villain and a persecuted victim, usually female. In the late eighteenth century, it was indeed the case that certain forms of Gothic literature adhered so readily to these conventions that they lent themselves first of all to accusations of plagiarism, and secondly to satire. Jane Austen's *Northanger Abbey* (published in 1818, but written in the 1790s) parodies contemporary Gothic through its representation of a naive heroine so immersed in formulaic, sensationalistic Gothicism that she interprets her experiences in terms of the Gothic conventions with which she is familiar. (Thus, she concludes that Northanger Abbey must be haunted, and that its owner, General Tilney, must be a Gothic villain harbouring a dreadful family secret, possibly the murder of his wife.) Even during this period, however, Gothic literature was beginning to reveal a capacity for diversity and mutability that has characterised Gothicism ever since.* 'Gothic' is indeed a slippery term and to begin to understand the complex terrain of literary Gothicism it is necessary to return to its ambiguous point of origin in a text that exemplified, in the manner of its production as well as its content and style, the peculiar resistance of the Gothic to easy categorisation.

Gothic fiction has its mid-eighteenth-century origin in a literary forgery written by an author described by the critic Robert Miles as a 'trickster'.[1] Horace Walpole's *The Castle of Otranto*, published first on Christmas Day 1764, was presented as a text printed in Naples in the sixteenth century (though of much earlier origin) and recovered from a library in the north of England by its 'editor', William Marshall. The first edition of this first Gothic novel thus complicates its origin, obscuring the identity of its author and presenting a bizarre supernatural narrative as an authentic historical artefact. Encouraged by the enthusiastic critical reception of his 'little piece', Walpole published a second edition of the novel some months later, this time admitting his authorship and seeking to justify his venture in terms of bold literary experimentation: the blending of old romance with the conventions of the emerging eighteenth-century realist novel.

The critical response to this second edition was much less positive, however; the text that had been lauded by the *Monthly Review* as a work of genius on its first appearance was condemned as 'preposterous' several months later by the same magazine. Walpole's Gothic story clearly touched a raw nerve; it revealed a contemporary fascination with, and enjoyment of, the superstition and violence of Europe's medieval past that was permissible if the text was a product of that unenlightened past, but not if authored by a respectable

* William Beckford's *Vathek* (featuring a Caliph who bargains with the devil) and William Godwin's *Caleb Williams* (in which the protagonist is driven to despair by the obsessive persecution visited upon him by his former employer) are two examples of Gothic narrative from this period that do not conform to the conventions parodied by Austen. Both texts are considered in Parts Three and Four below.

English gentleman in 1764. The conflicted origin and critical reception of the novel thus reflected mid-eighteenth-century anxieties concerning questions of literary authenticity, authorial good faith and generic stability. At the moment of its origin, Gothic literature emerged as a mode of writing capable of undermining cultural, historical and literary conceptualisations of past and present, civilisation and barbarism, old romance and new literary realism.

The capacity of the Gothic to frustrate straightforward categorisation and even to undermine its own generic coherence has persisted over the centuries since Walpole published his faked Gothic 'original'. Indeed, critics of the Gothic have increasingly emphasised over recent decades the extent to which literary Gothicism uniquely resists clear-cut historical and literary classification. Unlike, for instance, Romantic or Victorian literature, there is no historical period to which the Gothic can be assigned; forms of Gothic literature (and, since the early twentieth century, Gothic cinema) have proliferated since the 1760s, and Gothicism has undoubtedly come to constitute one of the most prevalent and commercially successful modes of fiction and film in the early twenty-first century (consider, for example, the success of Stephenie Meyer's *Twilight* saga and its film adaptations). Moreover, whilst the Gothic often does conform to certain conventions that make it identifiable in certain forms (evocations of the supernatural, for instance, and the presence of human and non-human 'monsters' such as vampires, zombies and serial killers), a great many texts that have been designated 'Gothic' contain no obvious elements of the supernatural or the monstrous. Texts such as William Godwin's 1794 *Caleb Williams*, Charlotte Perkins Gilman's 1892 short story 'The Yellow Wallpaper' and Daphne du Maurier's 1938 *Rebecca* have been positioned as 'Gothic' (and are indeed positioned as such in this volume), yet generically they appear far removed from novels such as Robert Louis Stevenson's 1886 *The Strange Case of Dr Jekyll and Mr Hyde* and Bram Stoker's 1897 *Dracula* (both of which are considered in Part Three below). These two late nineteenth-century novels are, in turn, radically different from many of the Gothic fictions of the century before. Have critics therefore defined the Gothic too widely? Or is it paradoxically the case that, as Anne Williams puts it, 'the attempt to define the Gothic challenges everything we thought we knew about genre as a critical concept'?[2]

One solution to this difficulty might be to rely upon the notion of 'reader-response'. Reader-response theory in literary criticism seeks to interpret literature in terms of the reader's experiences of a given text. From this perspective, it might be argued that what defines the Gothic is the response it provokes in the reader: fear. The problem with this approach is that it relies on a highly variable emotion that is dependent at least to some extent upon shifting historical and cultural contexts. For example, a novel that relies for its effect upon a contemporary reader's immersion in a culture that constructs certain social groups as 'Other' (Catholics in 1790s Protestant England, for example, or the indigenous populations of British colonies in the late nineteenth century – see Part Four: 'Nation and Empire') is likely to lose some of its impact upon a reader who is differently situated historically and/or culturally. Moreover, whilst certain phenomena might universally be relied upon to provoke fear (such as the threat of violence or death), the representation of such phenomena in an artistic work (in a fictional account of the First World War, say) is no more reliable as a criterion for defining Gothicism as the presence of a ghost and a haunted castle.

Recent work in Gothic criticism has argued that the Gothic ought not to be defined in terms of its emotional or aesthetic effect, or even regarded as a literary 'genre' at all (that is to say, as a class of texts conforming to particular conventions of content and/or style). Rather, it should be considered as a 'mode' of writing[3] that responds in certain diverse yet recognisable ways to the conflicts and anxieties of its historical moment and that is characterised especially by its capacity to represent individual and societal traumas. The Gothic from Horace Walpole to Stephen King might thus be said to concern itself with forms of psychological and cultural disturbance (emanating out of specific historical contexts) that cannot receive easy articulation through other modes of artistic expression. Even works that lack an overt element of supernaturalism or monstrosity thus deserve the designation 'Gothic' by virtue of their narration of trauma through instances of psychological 'hauntings', or the depiction of extreme mental states productive of a certain kind of existential 'monstrosity'. Hence, the representation in Godwin's *Caleb Williams* of an obsessive psychological persecution that drives its victim towards mental breakdown places that novel firmly within a Gothic mode of writing that expresses, with or without the presence of spectres or monsters, an experience of profound dislocation, alienation and despair. In the words of Robert Miles, the Gothic has become since its mid-eighteenth-century origins a 'coherent code for the representation of fragmented subjectivity'.[4]

This volume examines the development of Gothic literature, in its diverse forms, from the mid-eighteenth to the early twenty-first century. Part Three focuses upon key texts and authors within the Gothic tradition and is arranged in broadly chronological order. The first three chapters consider the origin of the Gothic in the eighteenth century, its productive, if often rather tense, relationship to the Romantic movement in the 1790s and early-nineteenth century, and the new forms of Gothicism that emerged in the Victorian period (in the work of Emily Brontë, Edgar Allan Poe and Robert Louis Stevenson, for example). The last three chapters address varieties of twentieth- and twenty-first-century Gothic in Britain and America, beginning with an analysis of the transition from the Gothic of the Victorian *fin de siècle* to the more modern horror narratives of the influential American author, H. P. Lovecraft. Of these, the last two are devoted to twentieth-century American and British Gothic respectively; both chapters acknowledge points of continuity and comparison between the British and American traditions of Gothicism (the influence of Bram Stoker on American horror writer Stephen King, for example), whilst also emphasising those features that distinctively characterise historically and culturally specific modes of the Gothic in America and Britain. Thus, 'Twentieth-century American Gothic' discusses American 'Southern Gothic' as negotiating particular tensions in the southern states of the USA that arose, predominantly though not exclusively, out of the legacy of nineteenth-century slavery, twentieth-century racial segregation and deeply embedded forms of political and cultural racism. 'British Gothic in the Late Twentieth Century' considers, amongst other works, the dystopian fictions of J. G. Ballard which in various ways 'Gothicise' the contemporary British urban landscape, and the ghost stories of Susan Hill and Sarah Waters that draw heavily upon, and in certain ways rework, the conventions of eighteenth- and nineteenth-century Gothic narratives.

Part Four is organised thematically rather than chronologically and focuses upon key critical debates and theoretical perspectives within Gothic studies. This section in some instances revisits texts discussed in Part Three (Horace Walpole's *The Castle of Otranto* and Mary Shelley's *Frankenstein*, for example,) in order to consider how such key Gothic narratives can be interpreted according to different critical and theoretical approaches. Other Gothic novels and short stories not previously discussed (or discussed only briefly) in previous chapters are examined thematically in terms of their relation to significant critical terms, concepts and theories: narrative instability, the Gothic body, female Gothic, and nation and empire. These chapters tend to prioritise certain theoretical developments that have especially influenced the themes and concepts under discussion: psychoanalytic theory in relation to the Gothic body, for example, and postcolonial theory in relation to nation and empire.

Finally, although the chief focus of this guide is Gothic literature rather than film, the importance of cinema to contemporary conceptualisations of Gothicism is acknowledged at various points. From Alfred Hitchcock's 1960 *Psycho* to Eli Roth's 2005 *Hostel*, some of the most iconic and controversial cultural productions of the last fifty years owe their celebrity to a combination of new cinematic techniques of horror and a literary tradition of Gothicism that goes back over 200 years.

Sue Chaplin

Notes

1   Robert Miles, 'Abjection, Nationalism and the Gothic', in Fred Botting (ed.), *The Gothic: Essays and Studies* (Cambridge: English Association, 2001), p. 61.
2   Anne Williams, *Art of Darkness: A Poetics of Gothic* (Chicago, IL: Chicago University Press, 1995), p. 15.
3   See Alex Warwick, 'Feeling Gothicky?', *Gothic Studies*, 9:1 (2007), p. 6.
4   Robert Miles, *Gothic Writing, 1750–1820: A Genealogy* (Manchester: Manchester University Press, 1993), p. 2.

Part Two
A Cultural Overview

The term 'Gothic' entered into English culture in the mid-eighteenth century and rapidly acquired a range of complex and often contradictory connotations. Unlike other cultural and artistic movements of the period, such as Neoclassicism (against which the Gothic in many ways reacted) and the influential mid-eighteenth-century 'literature of sensibility' (with which the early Gothic is closely aligned), it is difficult to identify the Gothic with a coherent set of cultural practices or aesthetic principles. Although it is certainly true that Gothic fiction in the first forty years of its development did adhere often rigidly to certain stock conventions (indeed, the incessant repetition of these conventions by authors who came close to plagiarising each other contributed to the hostile critical reception of the Gothic in the late eighteenth century – see Part Three: 'Eighteenth-century Gothic' and 'Romantic-era Gothic'), it is also the case that from the moment of its origin the literary Gothic had an extraordinary capacity for generic mutation. Within one hundred years of the publication of the first Gothic novel, Horace Walpole's *The Castle of Otranto* (1764), an emerging tradition of literary Gothicism (often working alongside or within other genres and movements) had already generated texts as diverse as William Godwin's *Caleb Williams*, William Beckford's *Vathek*, Coleridge's long poem *Christabel* and Mary Shelley's *Frankenstein*.

In order to understand the historical and cultural development of the Gothic, it is essential to try to establish what it is that unites these diverse works. In this respect, the turbulent political context of the mid-to-late eighteenth century is a key reference point: it is within the context of the emergence of conflicted modern forms of national and colonial power in Europe, and their consolidation and contestation during the following century, that the Gothic came to acquire its ambiguous, often contradictory and sometimes transgressive associations.

From 'Visigoths' to Eighteenth-century Gothic

The most straightforward historical understanding of 'Gothic' in the eighteenth century was based upon the fifth-century defeat of the Roman Empire by the north European tribe known as the Visigoths. Because of the cultural, political and aesthetic association of Rome with order, reason and refinement (evident in the Neoclassicism of the early eighteenth century, which sought to appropriate the aesthetic principles of Ancient Rome in the service of a new imperial civilisation – a new 'Rome', as it were), the Visigoth destroyers of Rome came to be understood as a savage, illiterate, irrational people. The 'Gothic' was thus posited as the antithesis not only of Rome, but of a European Enlightenment that regarded Rome as its model.

This historical conceptualisation of the Gothic, however, reflected only one contemporary interpretation of the term. In Whig political ideology,* the Gothic came to acquire quite a different connotation. Its historical meaning, first of all, started to shift to refer not so much to the Visigoths, as to all Germanic peoples including the Anglo-Saxon forebears of the English. At a time when the origin of the English nation, and the legitimacy of

---

* There were two main political parties in this period: the Whigs (associated broadly with the emerging middle class) and the Tories (associated more with the interests of the landed gentry).

9

its system of laws, was still a subject of debate after the turbulent events of the previous century (the English civil war, the restoration of the monarchy), the 'Gothic' Anglo-Saxons came to be imbued with an almost mythic status as the true originators of the country's ancient constitution. In particular, the Anglo-Saxon 'Gothic' origin of the English body politic allowed Whigs to distance the English nation from French Norman influence. In this context, Gothicism was associated not with barbarism, but with a freedom-loving people who were the true ancestors of the English; the nation was thus to look for its political beginnings not in the events of 1066 – the invasion of William the Conqueror – but further back, to an ancient system of rule forged by the Anglo-Saxons that continued to be reflected in English law even though its origin had become obscured. The most famous and influential expression of this Gothic political ideology came from the legal philosopher William Blackstone. His *Commentaries on the Laws of England* (1765–9) was the first attempt fully to codify English common law and it remained a foundational text of law for well over a century. Here, Blackstone speaks of English law as a 'Gothic castle':[*] it had, Blackstone argued, promoted freedom, justice and political stability throughout the ages and it was worthy of reverence and preservation, although it might need gradual improvement in order to render it appropriate to more modern times. A stronger association of the Goths with freedom and justice is found in James Thomson's poem 'Liberty' of 1735/6:

> Untamed
> To the refining subtleties of slaves,
> They brought a happy government along;
> Formed by that freedom which, with secret voice,
> Impartial Nature teaches all her sons ... (Part IV, ll. 962–4)

---

[*] The term 'Gothic' refers also to a distinct architectural style that flourished in Europe in the medieval period, and that enjoyed renewed popularity in mid-to-late eighteenth-century England.

These sources point towards a much more positive historical evaluation of the Gothic which served a particular political function in the mid-to-late eighteenth century in creating a coherent narrative of national origin. Other cultural engagements with Gothicism proved just as fruitful in terms of consolidating an emerging sense of English national identity in the period.

The Influence of Shakespeare

The notion of a uniquely English literary tradition was beginning to take shape in this century and central to its formation was the figure of William Shakespeare, whose plays, the tragedies especially, had a marked influence on Gothic fiction. Elizabeth Montagu's 'An Essay on the Writings and Genius of Shakespeare' (1769) presented Shakespeare as the key figure within a tradition of English folklore and romance that was more Gothic than Classical; indeed, Montagu described Shakespeare as England's 'Gothic bard', thus establishing a close aesthetic and cultural association between England's pre-eminent playwright (as he was fast becoming) and modes of Gothicism both ancient (the medieval Gothic and chivalric romances) and new (the Gothic fictions that began with Walpole's *The Castle of Otranto* in 1764). As is discussed in Part Three below, Horace Walpole, in the composition of *The Castle of Otranto*, drew upon the various nuanced meanings acquired by the Gothic during this century: he presents the first edition of the text as a genuine medieval manuscript, thus capitalising upon his culture's appetite for medieval artefacts and the romance associated with them (an appetite that he shared); he also, crucially, cited Shakespeare as his model in the preface to his second edition (see Part Four: 'Narrative Instability and the Gothic Narrator'). For Walpole, Shakespeare represents a key stage in the development of the English literary tradition; he is a writer capable of marrying tragedy with comedic interludes, and of expertly combining elements of the supernatural and the fantastical with psychological realism. Walpole makes it clear that this is precisely his intention in composing what the second edition describes on its title page as a 'Gothic story' (a designation omitted from the first edition, where the narrative is entitled simply 'The Castle of Otranto – a Story'). Walpole, in one sense, uses Shakespeare as a bridge between ancient folk literature and new forms of fiction in the eighteenth century that were committed to an aesthetic of literary realism: his new Gothic romance will, he hopes, achieve a blending of what is most valuable in each literary form through adherence to the precedent provided by William Shakespeare. Indeed, Walpole's commitment to the Shakespearean model is evident in the structure of his novel: its five chapters mimic the five-act form of a Shakespearean tragedy.

The influence of Shakespeare on Gothic fiction if anything intensified in the later decades of the eighteenth century as the status of the playwright continued to grow. The critic Edward Malone produced a multi-volume edition of Shakespeare's plays in 1790 and prefaced it with the following observation:

> It is remarkable that in a century after our poet's death, five editions of his plays were published; which probably consisted of not more than three thousand copies ... on the other hand, from the year 1716 to the present time, that is, in seventy-four years ... above thirty thousand copies of Shakespeare have been dispersed through England.[1]

Shakespeare's shaping of Gothic fiction in the 1790s is especially evident in the work of Ann Radcliffe. The late eighteenth-century critic Nathan Drake referred to Ann Radcliffe as 'the Shakespeare of Romance'. Radcliffe's work often evokes Shakespeare through quotations from his plays that are used to mark the development of certain themes in her work. In her 1790 novel *A Sicilian Romance*, for example, Radcliffe provides an epigraph to the work taken from Hamlet: 'I could a tale unfold.' These are the words, of course, that the ghost of Hamlet's father speaks to Hamlet as he prepares to relate the dreadful circumstances of his death and Claudius's usurpation of his throne. Radcliffe's epigraph prepares her readers for a tale which they are given to understand will be similarly harrowing and which will involve (though in a different context) instances of misrule, sexual and political corruption and the restoration of a proper genealogy of power (see, further, Part Four: 'Nation and Empire').

Contexts of the Gothic in the Late Eighteenth Century

In terms of the development of the literature of the Gothic and its relation to wider cultural contexts, the novelist and critic Clara Reeve in the 1770s followed Elizabeth Montagu in seeking critically to articulate and examine an emerging national literary tradition that was grounded not in the aesthetic principles of Classicism, but in romance and folklore. Reeve's *The Progress of Romance* (1785) is an important work that crystallises many of the most crucial and contested issues within contemporary literary criticism. Reeve acknowledges the tension between romance and the developing form of the novel. Whereas romance was frequently condemned (as was Gothic fiction) for its fantastical elements, Reeve declares her preference for what she terms 'heroic Romance' over realist fictions which, she believed, promoted moral laxity through their depiction of social life in even its most debauched aspects. Reeve's recuperation of medieval romance had a significant influence upon the development of Gothic fiction in its earliest forms, especially the Gothic romance popularised by Ann Radcliffe in the 1790s. The Gothic romance could indulge a contemporary fascination with the fantastical and with a past that could easily be denigrated as barbaric, whilst at the same time referring the reader to a chivalric moral code likely to 'excite men to great and generous actions', as Reeve puts it. Moreover, Reeve's implicit approval of certain feudal forms of social arrangement that supported chivalric codes of honour had considerable appeal during a politically unstable period (leading in France to the revolution in 1789) in which old orders of feudal power were disintegrating. This combination of nostalgia, fantasy and a rather conservative moral didacticism is apparent in Reeve's own Gothic romance, *The Old English Baron* (1778). This work owes a considerable debt to Horace Walpole and the debt is acknowledged by Reeve in her preface to the novel. Reeve deviates from Walpole, however, in her reluctance to imitate what she regarded as the absurd supernatural excesses of *The Castle of Otranto*. Whilst the supernatural does figure in this text, and as in Walpole its function is to expose and rectify a crime against the proper lineage of a noble family, it is muted indeed compared with Walpole's extravagant apparitions. This caution with regard to an excessive evocation of the supernatural in Gothic fiction was taken to further lengths by Ann Radcliffe in whose work the supernatural is invariably alluded to, only ultimately to be explained away (see Part Three: 'Eighteenth-century Gothic').

The 1790s, the decade in which Radcliffe published all her major work, was the high-point of the eighteenth-century Gothic romance. The relation between the Gothic and its political contexts, which had been apparent in the fifty years before, becomes especially marked in the period after the French Revolution. This period was characterised by anti-French and anti-Catholic sentiment in the British establishment which persisted (and which was reflected in certain Gothic fictions of the time – see Part Three: 'Eighteenth-century Gothic' and Part Four: 'Nation and Empire') until the end of the Napoleonic wars in 1815. Notions of the 'Gothic' were incorporated, moreover, into the dominant political discourses of the period. The 'Gothic' Anglo-Saxon constitution was invoked as the antidote to dangerous revolutionary aspirations, on the one hand; on the other, the revolution was figured as a traumatic 'Gothic' event and Gothic novelists themselves were castigated as 'terrorist novel writers' (see Part Three: 'Eighteenth-century Gothic'). William Godwin, meanwhile, described the British establishment as a corrupt 'Gothic' entity; its laws were a 'Gothic unintelligible burden' upon the nation.[2] In terms of the fiction of the period, the observation of the French aristocrat the Marquis de Sade in 1800 that Gothic novels were beyond doubt the consequence of 'revolutionary shocks felt throughout the whole of Europe' acknowledged the correlation between this new, controversial literary form and the political anxieties of the period.[3] The Gothic enabled writers and readers to articulate and explore traumatic political violence whether perpetrated by revolutionaries or the *ancien régime*.

As has been suggested, Gothic literature in the 1790s was associated predominantly with the writer Ann Radcliffe whose novels were not only best-sellers, but often better received critically than many other examples of the genre at this time. Radcliffe's novels are usually set in the past and, like Walpole's and Reeve's, they tend to turn upon a mystery pertaining to lineage, identity and inheritance. Frequently, though, it is the heroine of the Radcliffean romance, rather than the male protagonists of Walpole and Reeve, who encounters various persecutions as she moves towards the resolution of this mystery and (in *A Sicilian Romance* and *The Italian*, for instance) it is a mystery relating to the identity of the heroine's mother that is foregrounded. The prioritisation of female bloodline, and the violent persecutions suffered by women within patriarchal structures of power, have led critics to see in Radcliffe a concern with feminine subjectivity and female victimisation that became the hallmark of what has been termed 'female Gothic' (see Part Four: 'Female Gothic'). Here, the haunted, violent Gothic space – the castle, monastery or even the home – becomes the location of female struggle against various forms of patriarchal domination. This is not to say, however, that Radcliffe can unequivocally be set alongside contemporary proto-feminist writers such as Mary Wollstonecraft; Radcliffe's heroines are invariably incorporated back into the patriarchal family, albeit a family that has been re-ordered according to a less feudal, more democratic and companiable model.

Radcliffe's Gothicism was sufficiently influential in this decade to generate a considerable number of inferior, deeply formulaic imitations and Jane Austen's *Northanger Abbey* (1818) famously satirised the style and content of this genre. Through her gullible protagonist Catherine Morland, moreover, Austen satirised the readers of Gothic novels who were assumed to be, in the main, naive and suggestible young women without the intellectual capacity to discern fact from fiction. Although Austen's satire is relatively benign, and indeed she does differentiate Radcliffe from her inferior imitators, the work reflects a common cultural assumption made in much literary criticism of the moment: Gothic fictions were pernicious because they tended to inflame the imagination, and could potentially corrupt the morals of their young, female, middle-class readers. This critical debate concerning the potentially dangerous effect of Gothic fiction upon vulnerable minds reached a new pitch of anxiety with the publication in 1796 of Matthew Lewis's tongue-in-cheek homage to Radcliffe, *The Monk*. Lewis significantly reworked the Radcliffean Gothic in order to make explicit the violence and debauchery that was only ever implicit in Radcliffe. Excoriated in the press by, amongst others, the poet Samuel Taylor Coleridge, the novel was condemned as blasphemous and obscene (see Part Three: 'Romantic-era Gothic'). It nevertheless served to take the Gothic in a new aesthetic direction: the text introduced a new variety of Gothic writing into an already complex cultural mix. Lewis's representation of extreme violence (the rape and murder, for example, of an almost impossibly virtuous and naive young woman by a monk who also happens to be her brother) gave rise to a new form of Gothicism that came to be termed 'horror'. Radcliffe herself, in response to Lewis's travesty (as she saw it) of her work, introduced the distinction between 'horror' and 'terror' in Gothic writing. Horror exposed the reader to graphic depictions of violence and supernatural intervention; terror, which for Radcliffe was the superior Gothic aesthetic, produced its effect through subtle stylistic techniques that suggested without ever overtly displaying objects and scenes of dread (see Part Three: 'Eighteenth-century Gothic'). This distinction still broadly persists over 200 years later and has passed over into Gothic cinema; one might compare, for instance, the 'terror' techniques exemplified in Hitchcock's psychological thrillers with the graphic violence typical of 'horror' cinema from the late 1960s onwards.

Gothic Fiction and the Romantic Movement

Another context for the development of the Gothic in the late eighteenth and early nineteenth centuries is provided by the movement that became known as Romanticism. Part Three: 'Romantic-era Gothic' discusses the significant, but often rather tense, relationship between Gothic and Romantic literature during this period. The Romantic movement in Britain has been associated primarily with poets such as William Wordsworth, Samuel Taylor Coleridge, William Blake and Percy Bysshe Shelley who placed considerable emphasis upon the importance of spontaneous imaginative expression in the composition of poetry. In 1800, for example, Wordsworth published an influential essay which accompanied a collection of poetry by himself and Coleridge, the *Lyrical Ballads* (first published in 1798). Here, Wordsworth defined poetry as 'the spontaneous overflow of powerful feeling'. This stress upon 'feeling' as the defining characteristic of poetry aligns Romanticism with Gothic fictions that sought also to express and provoke in the reader 'powerful feeling', though in a different literary context. Gothic fiction was considered by many Romantic poets to be an inferior expression of 'feeling' whereby sensationalist and supernatural elements combined to produce an excessive, ungovernable emotion far removed from the high intellectual aspirations of the Romantic movement. Nevertheless, there were significant points of overlap between Gothicism and Romanticism with much Romantic poetry (works by Coleridge and Byron that are discussed below, for example) containing distinct Gothic elements.

German literature especially influenced the interface between the Gothic and early Romanticism; the German *Schauerroman* ('shudder novel') was a genre of horror story, often more graphic than the English variety, that influenced Matthew Lewis and that was avidly read by Coleridge. Coleridge's long poems of the late 1790s, *The Rime of the Ancient Mariner* and *Christabel* (see Part Three: 'Romantic-era Gothic' for a detailed analysis), are Gothic in style and content. Other Romantic poets, notably Keats and Byron, also produced work strongly influenced by literary Gothicism (Byron's *The Giaour* and Keats's *Lamia*, for example). Indeed, it is possible to regard the Gothic in this period as defined to some extent by an often subversive reworking of the Romantic aesthetic that, in turn, infiltrates Romanticism itself. Central to this understanding of what might be termed Gothic Romanticism is the considerable contemporary aesthetic and cultural influence of the notion of the sublime. A full discussion of the significance of the sublime in this context is reserved for Part Three; the point to be made here is that the sublime, associated often in Romanticism with a transcendental Nature that facilitates the creative and spiritual development of the individual, appears in the Gothic as a form of grotesque materiality that threatens the annihilation of the self. This subverted, abject Gothic sublimity find its exemplary expression in Mary Shelley's *Frankenstein* (1818), considered in Part Three where it is posited as a 'bridging' text between the Romantic era and the Victorian Gothic. Shelley's text can be regarded as originating a new form of literary Gothicism that prioritises an uncanny bodily monstrosity, a form that became increasingly influential as the Gothic moved further into the modern period. In later novels, such as Robert Louis Stevenson's *The Strange Case of Dr Jekyll and Mr Hyde* (1886) and Bram Stoker's *Dracula* (1897), the body itself becomes the site of haunting and the agent of transgression, as opposed to some exterior space (the Gothic castle of Walpole's *The Castle of Otranto*) or some spectral apparition (the 'bleeding nun' in Matthew Lewis's *The Monk*). The idea of the 'Gothic body' is further considered in Part Four of this volume; in particular, the considerable influence of psychoanalytic theory over critical analyses of the Gothic and its representations of the body is considered in detail.

Nineteenth-century Contexts

The Gothic in the nineteenth century underwent a variety of generic transformations. The Gothic short story became especially influential largely through the work of Edgar Allan Poe and Sheridan Le Fanu, though Charles Dickens's *A Christmas Carol* (1843) is certainly one of the most enduring supernatural tales of the period. Through the work of Poe, Charles Brockden Brown, Nathaniel Hawthorne and others, the Gothic emerged in America as a multi-faceted literary form that articulated from diverse narrative perspectives that nation's political, social and cultural tensions, especially with regard to race and religion (see Part Three: 'Nineteenth-century Gothic'). In the nineteenth century, the Gothic also revealed its capacity to infiltrate and almost to become parasitical upon other genres. The stock conventions associated with the literary Gothic in the eighteenth century began to fade from view; the Gothic developed new tropes, motifs and conventions that reflected a transformed social, political and cultural landscape, whilst still displaying a kind of family resemblance to its eighteenth-century antecedents. Indeed, one could argue that what assured the survival of Gothicism most decisively during this period was its influence upon other genres of literature. Sensation fiction was as popular during the early-to-mid-Victorian period as Gothic romance had been in the 1790s and sensation fiction was heavily dependent upon tropes, themes and motifs developed first in Gothic fiction. Charlotte Brontë's *Jane Eyre* (1847) is ambiguously situated between realism and Gothicism, and Charles Dickens's fiction frequently incorporates distinctly Gothic elements. (Consider the figure of Miss Havisham in *Great Expectations*; the depiction of London's criminal underworld in *Oliver Twist*; the treatment of a sinister, labyrinthine legal system in *Bleak House*.) The development of detective fiction in this period likewise owed a great deal to literary Gothicism. (Consider Poe's 'The Murders in the Rue Morgue' and, of course, Arthur Conan Doyle's fiction.) These Gothic interventions into other genres of literature are discussed in Part Three: 'Nineteenth-century Gothic', and it will be seen that during this period the mutable quality of the Gothic became, paradoxically, one of its characteristic features; 'paradoxically' because the very quality of mutability is what makes it so difficult to 'characterise' the Gothic, to identify its defining qualities as a literary category.

It has been frequently observed by critics that the Gothic tends to acquire particular cultural force during periods of social and political upheaval. Thus, the Gothic increased considerably in popularity in the aftermath of the French Revolution, and one hundred years later, during the Victorian *fin de siècle*, Gothic fictions again assumed a certain cultural authority in terms of their capacity to symbolise the anxieties of this turbulent historical moment (see Part Three: 'From the *Fin de Siècle* to Modern Gothic'). Throughout the nineteenth century, processes of industrialisation, urbanisation and imperial expansion had radically transformed British society and the nation's sense of its identity at home and abroad. The presence in all major British cities of a deprived industrial working class crammed into insanitary slums caused considerable unease amongst a middle class that recognised in this urban underclass a significant threat to bourgeois social and political stability. The city slums are frequently 'Gothicised' in this period and not only within fictions that are overtly, generically Gothic: see George Gissing's *The Netherworld* (1889), for example, and Arthur Morrison's *A Child of the Jago* (1896). Other social and political developments that generated the sort of tensions and anxieties that one finds reflected in *fin de siècle* Gothic include the campaign for female emancipation, especially female suffrage; the influence on Britain of other cultures as the empire expanded; the Darwinist challenge to religion as the theory of evolution through natural selection became widely known. The extended commentary in Part Three: 'From the *Fin de Siècle* to Modern Gothic' considers Bram Stoker's *Dracula* as an exemplary *fin de siècle* Gothic novel that represents in complex ways these various late nineteenth-century developments and discontents.

Gothic Fiction and the Freudian 'Uncanny'

Gothic fictions of the Victorian *fin de siècle* often turn upon monstrous representations and transformations of the body: Stoker's *Dracula*, for example, is one of a number of Gothic texts that have been opened up to diverse psychoanalytic interpretations over recent decades. Indeed, throughout the twentieth century there was a close, almost symbiotic relationship between psychoanalysis and Gothicism and it is arguably the case that many of the foundational principles of psychoanalytic theory as it began to be developed by Sigmund Freud in the early twentieth century were anticipated by Gothic fiction as early as the mid-eighteenth century. It could be said, further, that Gothic fiction and Freudian theory are both products of certain modern configurations of power and sexuality, and that both of these discourses – Gothicism and psychoanalysis – explore and interrogate these aspects of modernity in similar ways. It is therefore no coincidence to find that Freud's most influential essay as far as Gothic criticism is concerned, namely 'The Uncanny' (1919), was in part a critical reading of E. T. A. Hoffmann's Gothic short story, 'The Sandman' (1816).

Freud acknowledges that the 'uncanny' in common parlance is understood to be related to terror or dread. He notes the peculiar etymology of the German term *unheimlich* and its close relation to its apparent antonym, *heimlich*. The latter means homely and familiar, but in the German it has shades of meaning that merge into its opposite; thus the uncanny is, or can be associated with, that which is familiar to us in spite of the dread that it evokes. Freud examines this odd conflation of the 'homely' with the 'unhomely' in terms of his theory of psychological development, especially his understanding of the infantile Oedipal drives that the child must represses in order to become a functioning adult. The origin of these repressed drives within the complex nexus of family relations helps explain why, for Freud, that which is most familiar to us can easily become a source of the uncanny. In Hoffmann's Gothic tale, a child in bed at home is tormented by the monstrous figure of the sandman who threatens to remove the child's eyes. Freud interprets this as symbolising for the child the repressed fear of castration, a fear that emanates out of the boy's Oedipal relationship with his father and mother; the boy fears castration by the father as a punishment for the boy's sexual desire for the mother. As many critics have since argued, the Gothic has become one of the key means in Western culture whereby unconscious desires and fears are symbolised; the nightmare scenarios of Gothic fiction and film play out the guilt, desires and drives associated since Freud with that archetypal Gothic family narrative: the Oedipus complex (discussed further in Part Four: 'Gothic Bodies').

The critic Steven Bruhm makes an important point in this respect when he observes that in Gothic fictions, 'the Freudian machinery is more than a means for discussing narrative; it is in large part the subject matter of the narrative itself'.[4] A notable feature of twentieth-century Gothic is the way in which it seems deliberately to stage what Freud called 'the return of repressed'. In the mid-twentieth-century fiction of H. P. Lovecraft, for example, protagonists frequently encounter shapeless monsters that emerge from some subterranean space; the protagonist is often rendered speechless, almost catatonic, by the spectacle; and the narrative at times breaks off completely as if the symbolic structures of the conscious world (the ego, civilisation) are collapsing. These crises are rarely unequivocally resolved by Lovecraft; even when the protagonist escapes back to civilisation, there is the sense that he (it is invariably a he) has been indelibly marked by the experience, and in some narratives the monster pursues the man into his safe, 'homely' space either to send him mad or destroy him. Lovecraft's deeply uncanny monster narratives anticipate later developments in Gothic horror and science fiction; in the *Alien* film series, for example, the infiltration by the Alien firstly of the Mother ship, then of the bodies of crew and finally of the heroine Ripley herself can be interpreted, like Lovecraft's fiction, in terms of psychoanalytic theories of the uncanny. Part Four: 'Gothic Bodies' considers in detail such representations of monstrosity and their cultural and theoretical implications.

Gothic in the Early Twentieth Century

Throughout the twentieth century, the Gothic continued to draw extensively upon the tropes and conventions of earlier narratives, as well as proliferating into new forms. In the early 1900s, however, Gothic fiction was not quite as visible as it had been in the later years of the previous century. Part Three: 'From the *Fin de Siècle* to Modern Gothic' considers some of the reasons for this, whilst also presenting the arguments of recent critics to the effect that the Gothic did have a distinct presence in the period associated with literary Modernism, a presence that tended to be downplayed in the literary criticism of the early twentieth century. The horror stories of M. R. James and H. P. Lovecraft, which are considered in Part Three, are indebted in many ways to the supernatural tales of the previous century (to the work of Edgar Allan Poe, for example), but they manifest a definite affinity with aspects of literary Modernism in their portrayal of an existential alienation that seemed increasingly to characterise the Modernist *Zeitgeist*.

Certain genres of cinema, most notably German Expressionism, began in the early twentieth century to form an important cultural expression of Gothicism. Expressionism rose to prominence in the 1920s with the work of F. W. Murnau (who directed the seminal adaptation of Bram Stoker's *Dracula* – *Nosferatu* – in 1922), Fritz Lang (see *Metropolis*, 1927, and *M*, 1931) and Robert Wiene (see *The Cabinet of Dr Caligari*, 1920). These films reflect some of the same political and cultural tensions that were finding expression elsewhere in the Modernist movement (and it should be added that there is a distinct Gothic thread in many key Modernist texts: for example, the vivid vampiric imagery in T. S. Eliot's *The Waste Land*, 1922). These films convey an almost overwhelming sense of individual and social alienation in the face of the seemingly inhuman and dehumanising processes of modernity that manifested themselves most starkly in the First World War of 1914–18.

From Modernism to Postmodernism

During the course of the twentieth century the Gothic was adopted more and more as a form through which contemporary political conflicts and anxieties could be negotiated and represented in often radical and transformative ways. Parts Three and Four consider from various different perspectives, for example, female and postcolonial narratives that use Gothic themes and tropes to portray and interrogate gender and racial oppression (see 'Female Gothic' and 'Nation and Empire'). Many of Angela Carter's novels and short stories rework patriarchal fairy tales and folklore that position women as either the passive victims of murderous violence (the wives in the Blue Beard tale, for example), or as the monstrous instigators of violence against the young (the wicked stepmother is a key archetype here, of course). In a different context, Jean Rhys's *Wide Sargasso Sea* stages a radical postcolonial rewriting of Charlotte Brontë's *Jane Eyre*. In Brontë's novel, Jane discovers just before her marriage to Edward Rochester that Rochester is in fact already married to a Creole woman named Bertha Mason. Like the wicked women of patriarchal fairy tales, Bertha is thoroughly 'Gothicised': she is insane and represented as impure, animalistic and inescapably 'other'. Rhys's 1966 novel places Bertha at the centre of the narrative and gives her a voice and a history. As discussed in Part Three, Rhys's postcolonial Gothic is one of a number of twentieth-century rewrites of earlier Gothic texts that in various ways prioritise the voice of the racial or sexual 'other'.

Critical appraisals of twentieth-century Gothic have emphasised, though, that the Gothic continues to defy not only easy literary categorisation, but also interpretation according to straightforward cultural and political paradigms. The Gothic cannot easily be positioned as either unequivocally radical or conservative; its multiple cultural and political engagements are far too complex and ambiguous. The Gothic can and frequently has been appropriated for radical political ends, from William Godwin's anti-establishment fiction in the 1790s (see Part Three: 'Eighteenth-century Gothic') to Carter's female Gothic of the 1970s (Part Four: 'Female Gothic'). Other forms of Gothicism, however, have been read as deeply conservative responses to the political upheavals of their moment and this has been especially true of horror film, from its origins in the 1930s through to the 'slasher' genre of the late twentieth and early twenty-first centuries. Whilst this volume focuses primarily on Gothic literature (and Part Three: 'Twentieth-century American Gothic' contains a detailed analysis of American horror fiction in the late twentieth century), Gothic horror cinema provides a key cultural context for the development of the Gothic in this period. Robin Wood and Mark Jancovich, two influential critics of the horror genre, observe how 1950s America horror film generally depicted threats external to the nation that reflected specific Cold War anxieties: for alien, read communist.[5] Horror film since has frequently narrated the invasion of a normative space – the middle-class, white community or family – by monstrous 'others' that emanate from beyond the boundaries of this safe place. These monsters – zombies, vampires, murderous ghosts, aliens and so on – can be read in terms of Freud's theory of the uncanny: they stage the return of the repressed into the (un)homely space of the conventional family group, though here the uncanny should be understood in cultural as well as individual psychological terms. Wes Craven's seminal horror film *A Nightmare on Elm Street* (1984) narrates the return to an ordinary, relatively privileged suburban community of a prolific child-killer, Freddy Krueger; the murderer comes back as a ghost that manifests itself through the nightmares of the community's teenagers, ultimately transgressing the boundary between nightmare and reality by emerging out of the dreams to commit actual killings. The film – and this is often the case with American horror cinema – posits these violent events as the consequence, at least in part, of a catastrophic failure of adults (especially fathers) to protect their children. The authority of the father as head of the conventional nuclear family collapses and this can be seen to reflect deep cultural anxieties in late twentieth-century

America as to the integrity of the traditional family and the position of the father within it.[*] It is telling that *A Nightmare on Elm Street* closes with a happy suburban scene as a mother waves to her children from the doorstep of her home; at the very last moment, however, the mother is dragged violently back through the door of the house by an unseen force, presumably Freddy Krueger. The monster continues to haunt the home and the father remains powerless to protect his wife and children.

Another iconic late twentieth-century horror film that deserves consideration from this perspective is *The Exorcist* (1973). William Friedkin's film (based on William Blatty's 1971 novel) is graphically violent and in so far as this is invariably a feature of contemporary horror (in fiction as well as film) it reveals a certain continuity in the Gothic tradition from the 1790s to the 1970s and 1980s. Part Three: 'Eighteenth-century Gothic' considers the opposition that opened up in the 1790s between two varieties of Gothic writing: 'terror' (associated with the work of Ann Radcliffe) and 'horror' (associated with Matthew Lewis's *The Monk*). Horror has always eschewed the subtleties of the technique of terror, preferring to revel in graphic depictions of violence against victims positioned as especially vulnerable: young people and, in particular, young females. In Lewis's *The Monk* (1796), the young virginal Antonia is raped and murdered; in *The Exorcist* the pubescent Regan is possessed by a demon which, in probably the most notorious scene from the film, rapes its victim with a crucifix. The extent of the violence visited upon young females in this sub-genre of Gothic film and fiction has led to accusations of misogyny; these works are understood to reflect a deep male hostility (a hostility that is cultural and political, encoded within the power structures of patriarchal society) towards women and their sexuality.[†] Moreover, even when the violence of the slasher

---

[*] This is also a key concern of horror fiction in this period: see, for example, the work of Stephen King discussed in Part Three: 'Twentieth-century American Gothic' and Part Four: 'Gothic Bodies'.

[†] Again, this is reflected also in horror fiction in ways that have proved controversial: see the discussion of American horror in Part Three: 'Twentieth-century American Gothic'.

film is not directed exclusively against females, it is frequently visited upon sexually active teenagers engaged in some form of trangressive activity, an attempt to define themselves against adult authority (see, for example, *Night of the Living Dead*, 1968, and *Halloween*, 1978). Again, then, horror film can be seen to be marked by anxieties concerning the absence of proper paternal authority; one way of reading the violence suffered by the young is as punishment for their rebellion against conventional patriarchal codes of sexual behaviour that retain considerable ideological power in contemporary America.

An equally popular variety of contemporary Gothicism, and one that again appropriates and reworks older Gothic forms, is what might be termed 'Vampire Gothic'. These narratives, in fiction, film and recently as television drama, often have a distinctly postmodern, subversive twist. Part Three: 'Twentieth-century American Gothic' considers Anne Rice's *Interview with the Vampire* (1976) as an archetypal postmodern vampire text. In this novel, Rice plays with and subverts the conventions associated with vampire fiction from the early nineteenth century onwards; the narrator is a rather disaffected vampire who tells his story to a journalist almost in the manner of a modern celebrity in search of public vindication. Crucially, this psychologically tortured creature is presented as a sympathetic, if not entirely reliable, narrator and the tendency of a text or film to portray the 'monster' as victim is a key feature of postmodern Gothic that nevertheless turns back to a central theme of earlier Gothic narratives: the ambivalent and often alienated existential status of the 'human'. There is often a tension in Gothic narratives between what counts as human and what counts as monstrous, inhuman or subhuman; the dividing line between humanity and its monstrous 'other' is rarely secure. In Robert Louis Stevenson's *The Strange Case of Dr Jekyll and Mr Hyde* (considered in detail in Part Three: 'Nineteenth-century Gothic') the seemingly respectable Dr Jekyll slides all too easily into his other self, Hyde, and strategies of 'doubling' in Gothic fiction often work to collapse, or at least to question, the opposition between the human and the monster (see Part Four: 'Gothic Bodies'). In Rice's novel, the vampire Louis can be read as 'doubling' the journalist who listens to his story (significantly, the journalist wishes to become like Louis by the end of the narrative), and thus Louis might be said also to double the reader who is positioned (through the narrative intervention of the journalist) to empathise with Louis. The important term here is empathy. The monster is posited as having a distinctly 'human' quality and, indeed, in postmodern Gothic, the 'monster' is sometimes portrayed as implicitly possessed of more 'humanity' than the humans around him: the monster is self-reflective, often compassionate and willing to assume responsibility for even its worst actions, whereas the 'human' is frequently figured as irrational, animalistic, irresponsible, self-alienated, 'monstrous'. As Fred Botting observes, 'Excluded figures once represented as malevolent, disturbed or deviant monsters are rendered more humane while the systems that exclude them assume terrifying, persecutory and inhuman shapes.'[6]

Two modern television dramas exemplify Botting's point: *Being Human* in the UK and *True Blood* in the USA. These dramas feature typical Gothic 'monsters' (a werewolf, ghost and vampire in *Being Human* and a community of vampires in America's deep South in *True Blood*). In each instance, the 'monsters' form communities that mirror mainstream society, and in various ways interrogate its values. They seek to fit into the wider culture, either by passing as human (in *Being Human*) or by positioning themselves as an oppressed minority fighting for recognition of their civil rights (*True Blood*). As Botting suggests, these excluded figures are no longer presented as absolutely 'other' to the human community; in so far as they manifest a propensity towards violence, madness and deviance, they do so in a manner that suggests these tendencies are by no means the preserve of monsters who have negated their humanity. These monsters are the victims of a traumatic affliction that is both physical and existential, and they are often tragically aware of their own self-alienation. The human community, meanwhile, is displayed as deeply dysfunctional not least because, unlike the monsters it persecutes, this community is blithely unaware of the extent of its own monstrosity.

Postmodern Gothic has taken other forms in the late twentieth and early twenty-first centuries that do not necessarily prioritise monstrosity, the supernatural or the visceral, graphic violence of contemporary horror. The work of writers such as J. G. Ballard and Alasdair Gray in Britain, and Mark Danielewski and Bret Easton Ellis in the USA (see Part Three: 'British Gothic in the Late Twentieth Century' for a discussion of Ballard's dystopian fiction; Part Four: 'Narrative Instability and the Gothic Narrator' for a consideration of Gray, Danielewski and Ellis) has a Gothic aspect that has come to receive increased critical scrutiny over recent years. These writers examine the conditions under which culture, subjectivity and political institutions take shape in Western post-industrial, postmodern capitalism. In Ballard and Ellis, in particular, an obsessive, alienating consumerism becomes the dominant force in the lives of protagonists who have little connection to anything but commodities. In postmodern Gothic, stable reference points often dissolve entirely as uncanny virtual realities, simulations and nightmares come to constitute the postmodern condition. In so far as this is the case, it can be argued that Gothicism has become the definitive mode of cultural engagement with the traumas of modernity and postmodernity: in the words of Angela Carter, 'We live in Gothic times.'[7]

Notes

1   Cited in Angela Wright, 'In Search of Arden: Ann Radcliffe's William Shakespeare', in John Drakakis and Dale Townshend (eds), *Gothic Shakespeares* (London: Routledge, 2008), p. 111.

2   William Godwin, *Enquiry Concerning Political Justice* (1794; London: Penguin, 1985), p. 476.

3   Marquis de Sade, 'Ideas on the Novel' (1800), quoted in Angela Wright, *Gothic Fiction* (London: Palgrave, 2007), p. 64.

4   Steven Bruhm, 'The Contemporary Gothic: Why We Need It', in Jerrold E. Hogle (ed.), *The Cambridge Companion to Gothic Fiction* (Cambridge: Cambridge University Press, 2002), p. 262.

5   See Mark Jancovich (ed.), *Horror: The Film Reader* (London: Routledge, 2002).

6   Fred Botting, 'After Gothic: Consumption, Madness and Black Holes', in Hogle (ed.), *The Cambridge Companion to Gothic Fiction*, p. 286.

7   Afterword to *Fireworks: Nine Profane Pieces* (London: Virago, 1974).

Part Three
Texts, Writers and Contexts

Eighteenth-century Gothic: Walpole, Radcliffe and Lewis

Part Two considered how the term 'Gothic' came to acquire multiple, often conflicting meanings in the eighteenth century. It became synonymous with a certain literary and cultural barbarism at odds with the Neoclassicism* of the early 1700s; at the same time, however, it came increasingly to signify a vital point of reference for writers and political commentators concerned to establish for the nation a unique origin, history and culture against the southern European influences that shaped the Classical revival. The Goths were rehabilitated, and mythologised, as a freedom-loving, northern European tribe who were posited as the ancestors of an emerging Protestant, democratic tradition. Of course this was largely an exercise in myth-making rather than history, but it had the important ideological function of cementing a fresh, national, political and cultural identity that differentiated England from Catholic Europe, particularly France.† In the literature and literary criticism of the mid-eighteenth century, this absorption of Gothicism into a wider narrative of national identity took the form of a re-appraisal of

---

* Neoclassicism was an early eighteenth-century artistic movement so called because it re-invoked the style associated with the Classical civilisations of Ancient Greece and Rome.
† England was at war with France from 1756 to 1763, a key period in the formation of this Gothic myth of national origin.

literatures associated prior to this point with a certain primitivism: tales of chivalry and romance aligned with an ancient English (or Celtic) tradition of folklore and myth began to assume an increasing cultural prominence in the 1750s and 1760s. Gothicism was certainly still represented as 'the old-fashioned as opposed to the modern, crudity as opposed to elegance', and so on,[1] but these qualities were given a positive inflection; they came to signify, according to this new version of the nation's history, the values of an indigenous heritage against an overly sophisticated, artificial European culture that had been imposed from without. Key texts of this mid-eighteenth-century period include Thomas Warton's *Observations on the Faerie Queene of Spenser* (1754), Bishop Richard Hurd's *Letters on Chivalry and Romance* (1762) and Thomas Percy's *Reliques of Ancient Poetry* (1765). These works reveal a new interest not only in ancient romance, but in English writers of more recent origin who were understood to have emerged out of this tradition. As Richard Hurd observes:

> The greatest geniuses of our own and foreign countries, such as Ariosto and Tasso in Italy, and Spenser and Milton in England, were seduced by these barbarities of their forefathers, were even charmed by the Gothic romances. Was this caprice and absurdity in them? Or, may there not be something in the Gothic romance peculiarly suited to the views of a genius, and to the ends of poetry?[2]

The re-appraisal of the literary, cultural and historical value of the Gothic romance occurred simultaneously with the validation of William Shakespeare as the quintessential English genius, and Shakespeare was regarded as an important model for early Gothic novelists: he was the poet and dramatist most closely associated with 'sublime terror', a key component of the emerging Gothic aesthetic (see below). These re-appraisals of the past also triggered some bold gestures on the part of writers eager to capitalise upon the nation's appetite for romances of antiquity: James Macpherson published *The*

Poems of Ossian in the 1760s, claiming that they were derived from an ancient Gaelic manuscript which had come into Macpherson's possession and which he had translated. Although based closely on the Gaelic ballad tradition, *The Poems of Ossian* was a forgery – but also a European literary sensation and its publication provides an important point of reference for the publication in 1764 of Walpole's *The Castle of Otranto* which is considered in detail in the extended commentary below.

The cultural and literary privilege afforded to Gothic romance in this period also owed a great deal to a wider philosophical and artistic shift away from the scientific rationalism of the Enlightenment and from what might be described as the literary rationalism of Neoclassicism. The work of Alexander Pope exemplifies the Neoclassical commitment to well-ordered poetic form and diction that ought, he argued, to be derived from Nature's 'Rules'; the emphasis is upon an imagination disciplined by Reason as can be seen in the following lines from *An Essay on Criticism* (1711):

> First follow Nature, and your Judgment frame,
> By her just Standard, which is still the same:
> Unerring Nature, still divinely bright
> One clear, unchang'd and Universal Light ...
> Those Rules of old discover'd, not devis'd,
> Are Nature still, but Nature methodis'd,
> Nature, like Liberty, is but restrain'd
> By the same Laws which first herself ordain'd.

By the mid-eighteenth century, such concerted Enlightenment conformity to 'Nature's Laws' was falling out of favour. In philosophy, David Hume asserted that feeling, as opposed to reason, was the basis of all human experience and judgement including – controversially – moral judgement (see *An Enquiry Concerning Human Understanding*, 1748). In literature, emotionality came to be celebrated in the 'novel of sensibility',* a genre which influenced

---

* See especially Samuel Richardson's *Pamela* (1740) and *Clarissa* (1748).

Gothic fiction considerably and in which the sentimentality of the protagonist is aligned not with an undisciplined, irrational excess of feeling, but with the most exemplary virtue. Emotion in the 1740s and 1750s was also privileged as especially creative, even though it was seen often to tend towards melancholy, or even morbidity. In the 1740s, a number of poetic works flew in the face of Neoclassical rationalism to initiate the 'grave yard' school of poetry.* These meditations on death and despair, together with evocations of the supernatural that anticipate the conventions of later Gothic fictions, contributed significantly to the establishment of what might be described as the first Gothic counter-culture at least a decade before the publication of the first 'Gothic story': Horace Walpole's quirky novella, *The Castle of Otranto* (1764).

Gothic Fiction: Revolution and Reaction

Following the publication of Walpole's *The Castle of Otranto* (discussed in more detail in the extended commentary below), the development of Gothic fiction was slow in the 1770s and 1780s. Indeed, as Emma J. Clery has observed, the broader genre of the novel itself slipped into decline in these decades; the publication of new works of fiction in any genre fell by two-thirds in the 1770s, for example.[3] Three notable exceptions to this general lull in the production of Gothic tales are Clara Reeve's *The Old English Baron* (1778), Sophia Lee's *The Recess* (1783) and William Beckford's *Vathek* (1786). Reeve's novel follows Walpole's in attributing the term 'Gothic' to her narrative; she subtitles it 'a Gothic Story'. The details of the plot also closely follow Walpole's earlier work: a young peasant named Edmund is discovered to be the proper heir of Castle Lovel which (like Walpole's Otranto) has been misappropriated from its rightful owners. Critics David Punter and Glennis Byron point out that 'Reeve is usually credited with

---

* See Edward Young's *Night Thoughts* (1742–5), Robert Blair's *The Grave* (1743), James Hervey's *Meditations Among the Tombs* (1747) and Thomas Gray's *Elegy Written in a Country Church Yard* (1751).

introducing the motif of the haunted chamber';[4] she has Edmund spend a night in a deserted, haunted wing of Castle Lovel wherein he receives visions that suggest his status as rightful heir. Reeve, however, keeps supernatural visitations to an absolute minimum in her text, a gesture that caused Walpole to dismiss it as too rationalistic for a 'Gothic Story'.

Sophia Lee's *The Recess* combines elements of Gothicism with aspects of the developing genre of the historical novel (a genre that Sir Walter Scott brought to maturity in the early nineteenth century). The text recounts the lives of two fictional daughters of Mary Queen of Scots, Matilda and Ellinor, who are forced to spend their childhood hidden in the vaults of a ruined abbey (the 'recess' of the novel's title) since, as heirs of Mary, their lives are in danger under the reign of Elizabeth I. When they leave the recess as young women, they suffer various forms of persecution, imprisonment and exile, and the novel departs from earlier Gothic romances in moving beyond Europe to Jamaica to where Matilda is removed (and imprisoned) by a tyrannical plantation owner, Mortimer. The novel is also innovative in terms of its narrative technique: it takes the form of a memoir written by the dying Matilda and it includes extracts from Ellinor's diary, providing an alternative narrative perspective. Thus, the text anticipates later Gothic novels which develop often complex modes of multiple narration. See, for example, Charles Maturin's *Melmoth the Wanderer* (1820) and Mary Shelley's *Frankenstein* (1818) discussed in the following chapter and in Part Four.

Beckford's *Vathek* departs further from the precedents provided by Horace Walpole and Clara Reeve. Beckford produced what Emma J. Clery describes as 'the first fully-fledged orientalist tale of terror'.[5] The protagonist is the Caliph Vathek who is devoted to the excessive pursuit of pleasure.* He is tempted by a demon named the 'Giaour' who grants him strange powers that increase Vathek's wealth and power. The price, however, is Vathek's damnation; he is finally transported to the 'Halls of Eblis' (Eblis being the name of Lucifer in Islam) where he confronts riches

---

* A caliph is an Islamic spiritual and political leader.

beyond his wildest imaginings before being condemned to 'an eternity of unabating anguish'. The theme of the Satanic bargain became a key motif in Gothic literature during the Romantic period influencing fictions such as Matthew Lewis's *The Monk* and some of the Gothic poetry of Lord Byron (discussed more fully in the following chapter).

Following the lull of the 1770s and 1780s, the Gothic exploded in popularity during the turbulent decade after the French Revolution and, in his examination of contemporary 'novels [of] sorcery and phantasmagoria', the Marquis de Sade* attributed the phenomenon to the 'revolutionary shocks' convulsing Europe throughout the 1790s.[6] It is not possible, though, to attribute to Gothic writers a unified political commitment, whether pro- or anti-revolutionary. In certain romances, the early work of Ann Radcliffe for example, the conventions of the Gothic initiated by Walpole are used to present feudalism as a benign hierarchical order, so long as power is exercised by men of virtue (see *The Castles of Athlin and Dunbayne*, Radcliffe's first novel published in 1789, and Clara Reeve's *The Old English Baron*, considered above). The critic James Watt describes such novels as 'loyalist romances' which offer a vision of a chivalric, heroic society in which medieval feudal militarism is tempered by an eighteenth-century, bourgeois sensibility.[7] These works offer an alternative to exploitative, aristocratic feudal government, on the one hand, and the perceived excesses of French radicalism, on the other. In Radcliffe's 1789 romance, the tyrannical Lord Malcolm resembles the destructive and dysfunctional Manfred in Walpole's *The Castle of Otranto* and his rule is likewise illegitimate. Malcolm is ultimately deposed by Osbert, Radcliffe's version of Walpole's hero Theodore, except that Osbert is much more effective as a man of decisive action and military prowess. Written in the year of the Revolution, Radcliffe's narrative is a much less equivocal affirmation of the merits of the *ancien régime*: Osbert is not a man disabled by melancholy as he ascends the throne and (unlike Otranto,

---

* The Marquis de Sade was a controversial French noble man who is most famous for the novels, *Justine* (1787) and *120 Days of Sodom* (1785).

which is, in a sense, destroyed by the ghosts of its feudal past) the two castles still stand as daunting monuments to patriarchal, aristocratic power.

Other writers of this decade appropriated Gothic techniques in order to contest the *ancien régime* and expose its injustices. William Godwin's *Caleb Williams* (1794), Eliza Fenwick's *Secresy, or the Ruin on the Rock* (1795) and Mary Wollstonecraft's unfinished novel *Maria, or The Wrongs of Woman* (published posthumously in 1798) do not deploy any evocations of the supernatural (not even in the subtle, suggestive manner of Radcliffe); nor do they locate their narrative in the feudal Middle Ages. Nevertheless, these novels reproduce the Gothic's heightened sense of dread, its themes of persecution, incarceration and excessive, irrational violence, and its depiction of a deep, brooding paranoia. In so far as these novels are set in England in the 1790s, they have the effect of 'Gothicising' English systems of law and governance: the contemporary establishment, as opposed to the medieval castle and its Gothic tyrant, becomes an object of dread. Fenwick's novel describes the fate of a young mother of an illegitimate child at the hands of a cruel, persecutory legal system, and the title of the text clearly evokes the Gothic conventions of the time: the 'ruin on the rock' is a crumbling, Gothic edifice, but it alludes also to the 'ruin' of the heroine at the hands of contemporary English law. Wollstonecraft's novel deals similarly with the deadly persecution of women not at the hands of feudal tyrants, but through the machinations of an unjust late eighteenth-century legal system that is represented as 'Gothic' – as sinister, irrational and persecutory. Godwin's novel likewise interrogates contemporary political structures and juridical processes that remain essentially feudal in nature and that tower over the hapless protagonist Caleb like the giants' castles alluded to by Richard Hurd in his 1762 analysis of Gothic romance, considered above.*

---

* Hurd's *Letters on Chivalry and Romance* specifically associates the fantastical giants of old romances and Gothic fictions with aristocratic over-lords perceived as terrorising their subjects.

Moreover, conservative commentators in this period explicitly aligned Gothic fiction with revolutionary impulses imported from France that were seen to pose a substantial threat to the English body politic after 1789. Two essays, published in 1793 and 1797, aptly illustrate this point. The 1793 piece, suggestively entitled 'The Terrorist System of Novel Writing', was published anonymously in the *Monthly Review*; it laments that English culture has seen fit to imitate:

> the SYSTEM OF TERROR, if not in our streets, and in our fields, at least in our circulating libraries, and in our closets. Need I say that I am adverting to the wonderful revolution that has taken place in the *art* of novel-writing, in which the only exercise for fancy is now upon the most frightful subjects, and in which we reverse the petition in the litany, and riot upon 'battle, murder, and sudden death'.[8]

The author evokes here the French 'Terror' initiated by Robespierre (to whom the essay refers explicitly elsewhere); he regards the Gothic as the product of a literary 'revolution' that threatens to debauch the judgement and morals of its readership. The second essay, 'Terrorist Novel Writing', returns to this theme four years later. Like the earlier writer, this anonymous commentator lambasts Gothicism as artistically, intellectually and morally impoverished; moreover, it is politically pernicious since its depictions of tyranny and bloodshed seek, like the French, to *'make terror the order of the day'*.[9]

1797, the year of publication of 'Terrorist Novel Writing', was also the year of publication of Ann Radcliffe's last major work, *The Italian*. Radcliffe dominated literary Gothicism in the 1790s.[*] She was, indeed, one of the best-selling authors of the period, and the writer of 'Terrorist Novel Writing' undoubtedly had Radcliffe in

---

[*] She published five Gothic novels during her life: *The Castles of Athlin and Dunbayne* (1789), *A Sicilian Romance* (1790), *The Romance of the Forest* (1791), *The Mysteries of Udolpho* (1794) and *The Italian* (1797). Her final work, *Gaston de Blondeville*, was published posthumously in 1826.

mind as he castigated the corrupting tendencies of Gothic fiction; the Gothic techniques he describes in this essay were, by 1797, inextricably associated with the Radcliffean romances that had enjoyed an almost unprecedented popularity for the past decade. This might seem paradoxical given that Radcliffe's romances often appeared to celebrate the political and social structures of feudalism (albeit modified by certain eighteenth-century, middle-class values). It would, however, be a simplification of Radcliffe's complex and often conflicted works to regard them as overtly and invariably conservative. The tropes and themes of Gothic fiction, beginning with Walpole, frequently interrogate the dominant political ideology of the day even when they appear to conform to a conventional, conservative vision of the body politic. In Radcliffe's novels, for example, tyranny appears on the face of it to be associated with alien regimes of power, most notably with southern, Catholic Europe.[10] Nevertheless, in the context of England in the 1790s, Radcliffe's depictions of political, patriarchal violence press close to home – a fact undoubtedly appreciated by the anxious author of 'Terrorist Novel Writing'.

The beleaguered heroines of Radcliffe's most famous novels – *The Mysteries of Udolpho* and *The Italian* – face dilemmas that were hardly alien to women in eighteenth-century England. In *The Mysteries of Udolpho*, for example, Emily finds herself orphaned and under the control of the murderous Montoni. Emily is forced to move from her childhood home, La Vallée, an idyllic, fertile enclave amidst the mountains that is symbolically associated with maternal nurture. She is transferred (and the passive voice is entirely appropriate – Emily has no power whatever to control her destiny) to Montoni's rugged, brooding castle; this location is an ultra-masculine environment that poses a real threat to the physical safety of the heroine. Although Radcliffe's work conforms explicitly to Gothic conventions in a way that Fenwick's and Wollstonecraft's, for example, do not, the oppressive, patriarchal environment in which Emily's drama unfolds could be transferred to eighteenth-century England; the law would hardly be more inclined to redress the injustices suffered by Emily at the hands of her male guardian and thus there is an implicit connection between Radcliffe's Gothic and the more overtly radical fictions of the day. Radcliffe's novel, moreover, turns upon a mystery pertaining to female lineage – the identity in particular of Emily's aunt, the Marchioness de Villeroi, murdered by her husband to facilitate his marriage to a member of the Udolpho family. This is a lineage easily obscured by patriarchal culture and law, and the novel recounts numerous instances of the ease with which men such as Montoni and the Marquis de Villeroi are able to efface female identity and appropriate their property. Emily's recovery of her lineage through the female line liberates her from Udolpho, restores Udolpho to its rightful heirs and allows her to claim as her own the estate of her aunt. It also facilitates her return (with her husband Valancourt, an exemplary man of sensibility) to La Vallée, the 'feminine' space of her childhood. In this respect, Radcliffe subverts a crucial aspect of early Gothic romance: the restoration of order does not depend upon the restoration of male lineage (the revelation of Theodore as the true heir of Otranto, for example), but upon the revelation and validation of female histories that bring about the liberation of the heroine from tyrannical patriarchal control.*

The argument here, then, is that Radcliffe can be read as contesting the same structures of power that are subjected to a much more explicit interrogation in the work of 1790s radicals such as Fenwick, Godwin and Wollstonecraft. Thus, whilst it has been common critical practice to read Radcliffe's Gothic fiction either as distanced from the politics of the decade, or as a resolutely conservative response to events,[11] critics more recently have sought to emphasise the social and political complexities and nuances of her work. Claudia Johnson contends that the mechanisms of persecution that operate within the walls of the Radcliffean Gothic castle obliquely evoke an institutional violence much closer to home: 'From the vantage point of eighteenth-century England', she observes, 'torture was hardly a remote affair.'[12] Legislation in the 1700s (known as England's 'bloody code') had created over 500 new capital

---

* This theme is considered further in Part Four: 'Female Gothic'.

offences and the repeal of 'habeas corpus' (the right in law not to be imprisoned for an indefinite period without charge) in the 1790s legitimised politically motivated incarcerations that effectively placed detainees beyond the scrutiny of the judicial process. A key concern of Radcliffe is the relation between institutions of power and institutionalised violence and David Punter is one of several critics to describe Radcliffe's Gothicism as an 'intense, if displaced, engagement with political and social problems'.[13]

'Terror' and 'Horror': Ann Radcliffe and Matthew Lewis

From a critical perspective, it is significant that the Gothic in the 1790s became associated, in the conservative imagination at least, with the term 'terror' as a signifier of political violence. It is interesting because this term acquired quite a different aesthetic meaning in the same period. Gothic fiction began in this decade to develop the generic complexities with which it has been associated ever since. Through the work of Radcliffe and the young Matthew Lewis, the Gothic developed two modes of expression that continue to influence the genre to this day: Gothic 'terror' and Gothic 'horror'. The idea that a certain pleasure could be derived from contemplating objects of dread or situations of suspense had been developed earlier in the century[*] and in the 1790s this aesthetic of 'terror' came to be associated with the work of Radcliffe.

Ann Radcliffe never explicitly depicts objects of dread; she evokes the supernatural obliquely only to ultimately explain it away and eschews any direct representation of violence. These are the hallmarks of the aesthetic of 'terror'; narrative tension builds by means of subtle suggestions of impending violence and the representation of obscure figures, possibly spectral, that flit amongst the shadows. Thus, in Radcliffe's second novel, *A Sicilian Romance* (1790),

---

[*] See Edmund Burke's *A Philosophical Enquiry into the Origin of Our Ideas of the Sublime and the Beautiful* (1757), considered in more detail in the following chapter, and Anna Laetitia Aikin's *On the Pleasure derived from Objects of Terror* (1773).

unexplained sounds and glimmering lights emanate from a quarter of the castle that has been shut up for years, terrifying two young sisters who are under virtual house arrest in their father's home. The insinuation is that the noises are of supernatural origin, and at this point in Radcliffe's career readers would not have been so familiar with her technique that they would have expected her ultimately to explain these obscure phenomena away. On the contrary, readers' expectations would have been guided by novels such as Walpole's *The Castle of Otranto* and Clara Reeve's *The Old English Baron* in which the sort of events Radcliffe presents here usually are manifestations of the supernatural. Radcliffean terror, however, diffuses tension by resolving all mysteries rationally; in *A Sicilian Romance*, the strange occurrences that terrify the sisters are the result of their mother having been imprisoned by her husband who declared her dead in order to marry again (illustrating once more the extent to which the Radcliffean Gothic turns upon questions of female identity and male tyranny). Probably the most famous instance of Radcliffe's 'explained supernatural', though, occurs in *The Mysteries of Udolpho*. The text focuses the reader's attention upon a black veil behind which there is presumed to be something dreadful – possibly even the dead body of the mysterious woman whose identity seems to be at the heart of the mysteries of Udolpho. Emily approaches the veil in a state of profound terror; Radcliffe ratchets up the suspense as Emily reaches for the veil and draws it back. Whatever is revealed causes Emily to collapse in fright, though what this dreadful object is remains hidden from the reader. Only at the end of the novel is it disclosed that this object of terror is a wax mannequin.

Some readers were becoming rather impatient with Radcliffe's refusal to satisfy their expectations, to disclose something truly terrible or supernatural.[14] The Scottish novelist Walter Scott, who was otherwise an ardent admirer of Radcliffe, confessed that 'the reader feels tricked' by the artificial machinations of Radcliffean terror.[15] Another writer frustrated by Radcliffe's technique was Matthew Lewis who read *The Mysteries of Udolpho* avidly and, in response to it, wrote probably the most notorious Gothic novel of the decade: *The Monk* (1796). *The Monk* is part homage to, part satire of the Radcliffean Gothic; Lewis's aim was to deliver precisely those moments of violence and supernaturalism that Radcliffe scrupulously avoids. The result was a novel deemed to be so violent and, indeed, blasphemous, that it was excoriated in the press and ultimately banned. As the following review suggests, the fact that Matthew Lewis was a member of parliament fuelled the anxiety surrounding this spectacularly gruesome text:

> A legislator in our own parliament, a member of the House of Commons of Great Britain, an elected guardian and defender of the laws, the religion and the good manners of the country, has neither scrupled nor blushed to depict and to publish to the world, the arts of lewd and systematic seduction, and to thrust upon the nation the most open and unqualified blasphemy against the very code and volume of our religion. And all this, with his name, style and title, prefixed to the novel or romance called THE MONK.[16]

The protagonist of this novel is a popular and charismatic monk, Ambrosio, who becomes embroiled in a kind of Faustian pact with a demonic woman, Matilda, who appears to him initially in the form of a young novice monk. Ambrosio is drawn to this boy – the attraction is implicitly sexual – and eventually Matilda reveals herself to be female. She agrees to help Ambrosio seduce the young, virginal Antonia and the novel closes with the rape and murder of Antonia by the monk (who happens to be her brother). The novel also relates the attempted elopement of a nun, Agnes, with her lover, Raymond, and this episode delivers one of the most vivid depictions of the supernatural in the fiction of this period. Agnes resolves to elope by disguising herself as the ghost of a nun who is supposed to haunt her convent. According to the legend, the 'bleeding nun' was brutally murdered following a breach of her vow of chastity. Her situation thus mirrors that of Agnes and, sure enough, when Raymond collects 'Agnes' from the convent in the middle of the night, he ends up embracing the ghost of the bleeding nun itself. The plot concerning this couple produces a moment that is shockingly gruesome even by twenty-first-century standards: Agnes, having given birth to an illegitimate child, ends up in a dungeon cradling the worm-infested corpse of her infant:

> My slumbers were constantly interrupted by some obnoxious insect crawling over me. Sometimes I felt the bloated Toad, hideous and pampered with the poisonous vapours of the dungeon, dragging his loathsome length across my bosom: Sometimes the quick cold Lizard roused me leaving his slimy track upon my face, and entangling itself in the tresses of my wild and matted hair: Often have I at waking found my fingers ringed with the long worms, which bred in the corrupted flesh of my Infant. At such times I shrieked with terror and disgust, and while I shook off the reptile, trembled with all a woman's weakness.[17]

This passage displays the key characteristics of what became known as 'horror' Gothic. It is explicit in its depiction of death and degradation, and replete with abject material detail (the lizard tracks on the face, the worms coiled around the fingers).

It is the refusal to leave any detail unspecified, to leave anything to the imagination of the reader, which so antagonised Ann Radcliffe. In 1797, she wrote a novel in response to Lewis which reaffirmed the aesthetic of terror: *The Italian*. The novel features a corrupt monk, Schedoni, who plots to murder the heroine, Ellena. The novel was reviewed in the following year by Nathan Drake. Drake's praise here of Radcliffe's treatment of Schedoni's attempted assault on Ellena can be read as an implicit condemnation of Lewis's treatment of his monk Ambrosio's assault on Antonia:

> The attempt of Schedoni to assassinate the amiable and innocent Ellena whilst confined with banditti in a lone house

on the seashore is wrought up in so masterly a manner that every nerve vibrates with pity and terror, especially at the moment when about to plunge a dagger into her bosom he discovers her to be his daughter: every word, every action of the shocked and self-accusing Confessor, whose character is marked with traits almost superhuman, appal yet delight the reader, and it is difficult to ascertain whether ardent curiosity, intense commiseration or apprehension that suspends almost the faculty of breathing, be, in the progress of this well-written story, the most powerfully excited.[18]

Radcliffe wrote her own essay on Gothic terror, 'On the Supernatural in Poetry' (published posthumously in 1826). Like Drake, Radcliffe asserts the artistic and, implicitly, the moral superiority of terror over horror and in so doing she attributes to horror the corrupting qualities associated by some contemporary critics with Gothic romance *per se*. Radcliffe's essay also reveals the crucial connection between terror writing and the eighteenth-century aesthetic of the sublime (considered in more detail in the following chapter). Evoking Shakespeare and Milton as precedents for her utilisation of terror in fiction (and thus cleverly situating herself within a developing tradition of English literary greatness), Radcliffe argues through two fictional interlocutors that terror depends to a large extent upon the generation of obscurity and uncertainty with regard to objects of dread and, as Radcliffe's interlocutors agree, obscurity is the hallmark of the sublime. Here, Radcliffe is indebted to Edmund Burke's influential *A Philosophical Enquiry into the Origin of Our Ideas of the Sublime and the Beautiful* (1757). Her essay mentions Burke by name and her fiction constantly puts into play Burke's conceptualisation of the sublime in terms of 'terror' and of 'terror' in terms of 'obscurity'. Burke observes that, 'To make anything very terrible, obscurity seems in general to be necessary. When we know the full extent of any danger ... a great deal of the apprehension vanishes'. Radcliffe's Mr W— in the 1826 essay echoes precisely this notion with his assertion that, 'they must be men of very cold imaginations with whom certainty is more terrible than surmise'; in making this judgement, he aligns the Radcliffean Gothic, and its aesthetically sensitive readers, with one of the most influential aesthetic theories of the eighteenth century.

By the end of the eighteenth century, then, the Gothic had developed into a complex blend of different stylistic techniques and become implicated in a range of contemporary political and aesthetic discourses. In particular, the Gothic in the 1790s and early nineteenth century acquired an important aesthetic and cultural relationship with the dominant literary movement of the period: Romanticism. The next chapter considers how this cross-over influenced both Gothicism and Romanticism, and how the Gothic began to acquire that capacity for generic self-transformation that has characterised it for the two centuries since.

Extended Commentary: Walpole, *The Castle of Otranto* (1764)

The Castle of Otranto established many of the conventions, tropes and themes that came to characterise the Gothic romance in the late eighteenth century. Evocations of the supernatural are vivid and extravagant, much more so, in fact, than in certain later fictions which tended to minimise or explain away supernatural interventions (see the work of Clara Reeve and Ann Radcliffe). The novella begins with Manfred, the Prince of Otranto, about to oversee the marriage of his youngest son, Conrad, to the noblewoman Isabella. Before the nuptials can take place, however, Conrad is killed in a most fantastical manner: a giant helmet falls from the sky and crushes him. This helmet resembles, in gigantic form, a helmet belonging to the former ruler of the principality, the 'Good Alfonso'. From this point, it becomes apparent that the present ruling family of Otranto, headed by Manfred, is implicated in a perversion of the legitimate governance of the principality. Manfred, aware of his increasingly precarious position, becomes obsessed with the perpetuation of his bloodline as he seeks to avoid the fulfilment of an ancient, mysterious prophecy pertaining to the true heir of Otranto. Manfred becomes increasingly murderous and rapacious in his desire to cling to power; he plans to divorce his wife and marry the fiancée of his dead son in order to secure another male heir, and he ends by mistakenly murdering his own daughter before the ghost of Alfonso – again in gigantic form – finally appears to identify Otranto's legitimate prince. This text thus prioritises – as later Gothic fictions invariably do – the problematics of inheritance and legitimate bloodline. It produces tension and terror through the persecution by a powerful male of vulnerable younger people, usually female. Evocations of the supernatural, moreover, are frequently tied to the theme of perverted authority and disturbed lineage: spectral apparitions may be read as providential signs that aid the restoration of legitimate bloodlines. The ghost of Hamlet's father functions similarly in Shakespeare's tragedy, of course, and Shakespeare was an important precedent for Walpole in the writing of this text.[*]

The Castle of Otranto also established the close correlation between the literature of terror and the literature of sensibility, associated with writers such as Samuel Richardson, Tobias Smollett and Henry MacKenzie, which aimed at the credible representation of emotion in virtuous, sensitive individuals (usually women) subjected to difficult, often extreme circumstances. Walpole wished to unite the psychological realism and emotional force of such fiction with the fantastical elements of old romance and, whilst the supernatural exoticism of Otranto removes it from the domain of a more domesticated eighteenth-century realism, its main characters have everything in common with the heroes and heroines of the eighteenth-century novel of sensibility. Like the popular novels of Richardson published in the 1740s, *The Castle of Otranto* features women of virtuous sensibility who are the subject of persecution at

---

[*] Walpole discusses the influence of Shakespeare on his work in his preface to the second edition of the novel in 1765. The first and second prefaces to *The Castle of Otranto* are considered in Part Four: 'Narrative Instability and the Gothic Narrator'.

the hands of a domineering male who treats these women as chattels to be controlled and exploited. The suffering of these young women, and the style of its representation, conforms to the conventions of the novel of sensibility, but the Gothic, beginning with Walpole, sets these women within locations far removed from the middle-class English home. Ruined abbeys, convents, caves, dark forests and rugged mountain landscapes become the settings for persecutions that are entirely out of the ordinary and that are designed to elicit not only heightened emotion, but terror in the protagonist and the reader.

These wider social and political contexts associated with the discourse of sensibility provide a significant point of access into the political and cultural engagements of Walpole's novella and of later Gothic fictions. Structures of political power in the eighteenth century underwent important reconfigurations as the country moved towards a modern commercial capitalist economy and the establishment of an entrepreneurial middle class. The culture of sensibility was implicated in these shifts as the new middle class sought to establish an authority and identity for itself. Sensibility – the emphasis upon an emotive empathy that in theory anyone could cultivate (not least by reading the literature of sensibility) – had the effect of democratising virtue. Qualities such as generosity, courage and fairness were no longer the prerogative of those of noble birth, but of men and women of sentiment; these heroes and heroines of sensibility might well happen to be of noble birth, but their lineage is no longer the guarantee of their virtue. Indeed, in novels of sensibility and in Gothic romance, aristocrats are frequently the villains of the piece. *The Castle of Otranto* reveals the politics associated with the discourse of sensibility at this historical moment: Theodore (who initially appears to be a peasant, but who bears a marked physical resemblance to the ancient ruler of Otranto, Alfonso) is revealed as the rightful heir of Otranto, but his fitness to rule the principality rests implicitly upon his possession of a benevolent sensibility that differentiates him sharply from Manfred. Thus, whilst the restoration of the proper feudal right to rule appears to affirm the legitimacy of that mode of governance, the emphasis upon sensibility as the true locus of personal and political virtue undermines somewhat the feudal commitment to governance based exclusively on blood and land.

Indeed, this Gothic novella in various ways contests an aristocratic system of personal and political values that is shown, by means of Walpole's complex manipulation of symbols, to be dangerously dysfunctional. To appreciate the text's diverse and ambivalent responses to its political moment, it is important to acknowledge the rather conflicted political position of Walpole himself. Walpole was the son of the Whig Prime Minister, Robert Walpole, who held office from 1730 to 1742. Horace Walpole was himself a Whig parliamentarian for twenty-eight years. The Whig party was the party of the new commercial middle class (the class for which 'sensibility' came to serve such an important ideological function in the mid-eighteenth century) and it often set itself against the perpetuation of aristocratic privileges in political and economic life. The Walpoles were an aristocratic family, however, and thus the political struggles of this period had a particular personal resonance for Horace Walpole. Nowhere is this more evident than in the Whig opposition to aristocratic rights of inheritance from which Walpole stood to benefit, but which, as a Whig, he contested. Property law in the eighteenth century sought to protect the integrity of the aristocratic family estate by limiting the extent to which land could be sold out of the family by younger generations; it was often said that the law exerted a 'dead hand' over the free exchange of property and this worked against the economic interests of the middle class. From this perspective, the following extract from one of Horace Walpole's letters written in March 1765 is illuminating. Walpole describes a dream which he identifies as providing the inspiration for *The Castle of Otranto*:

> I waked one morning in the middle of last June from a dream of which all I could recover was that I had thought myself in an ancient castle (a very natural dream for a head filled like

mine with Gothic story) and that on the uppermost banister of a great stair case I saw a gigantic hand in armour. In the evening, I sat down and began to write, without knowing in the least what I intended to say or relate. The work grew on my hands, and I grew fond of it – add that I was very glad to think of anything rather than politics – in short I was so engrossed in my tale, which I completed in less than two months, that one evening I wrote from the time I had drunk my tea, about six o' clock, till half an hour after one in the morning, when my hand and fingers were so weary, that I could not hold the pen to finish the sentence, but left Matilda and Isabella talking, in the middle of a paragraph.[19]

This correspondence is of critical interest for a number of reasons. It presents *The Castle of Otranto* as a form of poetic dream-text and Walpole seems to have written it almost in a trance. From a psychoanalytic point of view (though of course this vocabulary was not available to Walpole in the 1760s), it might be said that the novel appears to have emerged out of the author's subconscious and it might be expected to express (as Gothic fiction is often said to do) the repressed conflicts and anxieties of the writer. An indication that this might indeed be the case is provided by a seemingly throw-away comment in the above extract: Walpole says that he was very glad of the distraction provided by his dream, and the novel that resulted from it, because it stopped him from thinking about politics. The dream and the novel seem, though, to manifest precisely those political anxieties that Walpole tries to downplay in his letter. The giant hand of the dream (the 'dead hand' of English property law) could be seen to signify the remnants of an aristocratic power that threatened the Whig understanding of political and economic liberty in the eighteenth century. The hand translates into the surreal giant body parts of the spectre of Alfonso which appear to signal to Manfred that his illegitimate rule of Otranto is coming to an end.

The text may therefore be read as a form of political allegory, and in the mid-eighteenth century there was already a precedent for reading Gothic romance with a view to uncovering its veiled political content. Richard Hurd, in his *Letters on Chivalry and Romance* (1762), had contended that medieval romance represented the oppressive extent of feudal authority in the fantastical form of giants and ogres: 'Every Lord was to be met with, like a Giant, in his stronghold, or castle'. In *The Castle of Otranto*, Manfred's seemingly unlimited, oppressive power over his subjects (he has the authority to compel Isabella to marry him, for instance, even though the marriage would technically be incestuous) figures him symbolically as the tyrannical ogre of fairytale preying on the vulnerable. More disturbing, though, are the appearances of the ghost of Alfonso who appears not only as a giant, but for a large part of the novel as a dismembered giant. The novel's complex symbolism thus reveals aristocratic power to be dysfunctional to a quite surreal extent. Alfonso is certainly depicted as a benign feudal lord in one respect (his usual moniker is 'the Good Alfonso' and the subjects of Otranto clearly have affection for his memory), but his spectral appearance in gargantuan form undermines the notion that the structure of governance he represents (and that is restored by his heir, Theodore) is some sort of enlightened kingship. This is reinforced spectacularly in the novel's closing pages as the spectre of Alfonso re-appears – this time physically intact – to announce that Theodore is the rightful ruler of Otranto: he appears again as a giant whose massive form shatters half of the castle. The feudal stronghold that Theodore inherits is thus a ruin, and Theodore ascends the throne in a state of mourning for his beloved Matilda, murdered accidentally by her father, Manfred.

The dysfunction that appears to define systems of power (Manfred's and Alfonso's) in this novel is also suggested by the fact that the signs (supernatural and otherwise) that confront Manfred, supposedly to suggest to him that his rule of Otranto is approaching its end, are often indecipherable and thus ineffective. For example, Theodore bears a strong physical resemblance to Alfonso that is repeatedly noted, but its significance in terms of Theodore's alignment with Alfonso and his supernatural appearances is scarcely articulated. What is more, Manfred's own inability to interpret what is signified by the 'divine' portents – beyond the fact that they threaten his rule – cannot be attributed purely to his wilful blinding of himself to the obvious: the spectral signs of 'true' authority do not make themselves clear, nor do they establish for Alfonso or his heirs a secure source of power. They reveal, in fact, nothing as to the origin of the right of Alfonso's bloodline to rule Otranto; the foundation of this right to power is lost to history and asserts itself in the text only by means of references to Alfonso as 'good', and through the force of an ancient prophecy which is concerned as much with the illegitimacy of the usurper as it is with the legitimacy of Alfonso. Indeed, the one moment in the text at which Manfred does confront a sign that promises to reveal to him the nature of the circumstances in which he finds himself is one that again fails to deliver any possibility of interpretation. Acting as if to support the ghost of Alfonso in impressing upon Manfred the peril he is in, the portrait of Manfred's grandfather breaks free of its frame; in spite of Manfred's protestations, however, it refuses to speak. Unlike the appearance to Hamlet of the ghost of his father, which this moment evokes, the apparition reveals nothing to Manfred. It gestures to Manfred to follow it only to shut him out of the chamber into which it disappears. Manfred is left, once more, frantic and unknowing and it is important to remember that it was not Manfred who usurped the throne of Otranto, he merely inherited it. In the following passage, Manfred begs the spectre to reveal whatever secret it holds; the apparition, however, will not even allow Manfred to name the crime for which it was responsible and which now condemns Manfred to rule Otranto in fear and guilt:

> Do I dream? cried Manfred returning, or are the devils themselves in league against me? Speak, infernal spectre! Or, if thou art my grandsire, why dost thou too conspire against thy wretched descendant, who too dearly pays for – Ere he could finish the sentence the vision sighed again, and made a sign to Manfred to follow him. Lead on! cried Manfred; I will follow

thee to the gulph of perdition. The spectre marched sedately, but dejected, to the end of the gallery, and turned into a chamber on the right hand. The prince, collecting courage from this delay, would have forcibly burst open the door with his foot, but found that it resisted his utmost efforts. Since hell will not satisfy my curiosity, said Manfred, I will use the human means in my power for preserving my race; Isabella shall not escape me.[20]

Manfred's response to this incomprehensible apparition is to continue to pursue his incestuous plan to marry Isabella, a plan that tragically misfires when Manfred ends up accidentally killing his daughter. Manfred's murder of Matilda reveals another aspect of this text's complex cultural and political engagements. Manfred's relations with the women in his family reveal the oppressive and dysfunctional quality not only of aristocratic, but of masculine power. Manfred's wife, Hippolita, is the very model of a submissive wife, to the extent that she is prepared to countenance divorce to facilitate Manfred's incestuous marriage to Isabella. This marriage is incestuous, according to the laws of the time, because Isabella was betrothed to Conrad, Manfred's son. Manfred's capacity to insist on this incestuous union reveals that his power as the head of his family is absolute; he regards his wife as eminently disposable since she is too old to provide him with a new heir, and Isabella as a mere chattel to be appropriated at will. Gothic fiction after *The Castle of Otranto* was to continue to foreground the destructive power dynamic that characterised the patriarchal family, often figuring the father, or father-figure, as a 'Giant' with terrifying control over his domestic 'stronghold'. This theme acquired a particular political charge after the French Revolution as Gothic fiction negotiated various anxieties concerning the status, perpetuation and contestation of ancient regimes of monarchical, patriarchal power.

Notes

1   David Punter and Glennis Byron, *The Gothic* (Oxford: Blackwell, 2004), p. 8.
2   Quoted in Punter and Byron, *The Gothic*, p. 8.
3   Emma J. Clery, 'The Genesis of "Gothic" Fiction', in Jerrold E. Hogle (ed.), *The Cambridge Companion to Gothic Fiction* (Cambridge: Cambridge University Press, 2002), p. 32.
4   Punter and Byron, *The Gothic*, p. 159.
5   Clery, 'The Genesis of "Gothic" Fiction', p. 34.
6   Marquis de Sade, 'Ideas on the Novel' (1800), quoted in Angela Wright, *Gothic Fiction* (London: Palgrave, 2007), p. 64.
7   James Watt, *Contesting the Gothic: Fiction, Genre and Cultural Conflict* (Cambridge: Cambridge University Press, 1999).
8   Quoted in Wright, *Gothic Fiction*, p. 20.
9   Quoted in Wright, *Gothic Fiction*, p. 24.
10 The anti-Catholicism of Radcliffe's work, and of Gothic fiction generally, has been extensively discussed by critics – see, for a summary of various critical perspectives, Wright, *Gothic Fiction*, ch. 4.
11 See David Durant, 'Ann Radcliffe and the Conservative Gothic', *Studies in English Literature*, 22 (1982), pp. 519–30.
12 Claudia Johnson, *Equivocal Beings: Politics, Gender and Sentimentality in the 1790s* (Chicago, IL: Chicago University Press, 1995), p. 121.
13 David Punter, *The Literature of Terror*, vol. 1, *The Gothic Tradition* (London: Longman, 1996), p. 54. See also Robert Miles, *Ann Radcliffe: The Great Enchantress* (Manchester: Manchester University Press, 1995).
14 Maggie Kilgour, *The Rise of the Gothic Novel* (London: Routledge, 1995), p. 129.
15 Ibid.
16 Thomas Mathias, *The Pursuits of Literature* (1797), quoted in Wright, *Gothic Fiction*, pp. 19–20.
17 Matthew Lewis, *The Monk* (Oxford: Oxford University Press, 1995), p. 415.
18 Quoted in Wright, *Gothic Fiction*, p. 46.
19 Horace Walpole, Letter to Revd William Cole, 9 March 1765, in W. S. Lewis (ed.), *The Yale Edition of Horace Walpole's Correspondence* (New Haven, CT: Yale University Press, 1937), pp. 73–4.
20 Horace Walpole, *The Castle of Otranto* (Oxford: Oxford University Press, 1996), p. 24.

Romantic-era Gothic: Coleridge, Byron and Mary Shelley

The critic Robert Hume, writing in 1969 in the journal *PMLA*, identified a close correlation between Gothic literature of the early nineteenth century and the Romantic movement, though he acknowledged also that this relation was somewhat controversial:

> That Gothicism is closely related to Romanticism is perfectly clear, but it is easier to state the fact than to prove it tidily and convincingly. There is a persistent suspicion that Gothicism is a poor and probably illegitimate relation of Romanticism, and a consequent tendency to treat it that way. There are some, indeed, who would like to deny the relationship altogether.[1]

Hume's contention was in fact disputed in the same issue of the *PMLA* in a companion piece by Robert Platzer that was titled as a 'rejoinder' to Hume. For Platzer, whilst it was possible to observe certain general points of crossover between Romanticism and Gothicism, the two movements lacked any real unity of origin or influence and remained essentially distinct in terms of their specific generic forms and key thematic and aesthetic concerns. The disagreement between Hume and Platzer is evidence of a wider critical dispute, before and since the 1960s, regarding the interpretation of these contemporaneous movements, and this dispute could be said to reflect tensions between the two movements that persisted throughout the nineteenth century in various forms.[2] Romanticism did incorporate various aspects of literary Gothicism during this period and many of the central figures of the Romantic movement (notably Coleridge, Mary and Percy Shelley, Byron and Keats) were avid readers of Gothic literature. However, Gothicism was nothing if not controversial and, as considered in the previous chapter, it tended to be associated with a popular, 'low' form of culture that was at odds with some of the aesthetic and intellectual aspirations of Romanticism; Hume's essay cited above evokes this very point in describing Gothic as an 'illegitimate relation' of the more respectable discourse of Romanticism. Thus, whilst it is possible to speak of a certain 'Gothic Romanticism' emerging out of the turbulent post-revolutionary period, it is vital also to consider the extent to which the Gothic was positioned against Romanticism and how this fraught relationship of mutual influence and antagonism influenced both movements. The middle sections of this chapter seek to signal the proximities and conflicts that characterise the interface between Gothic and Romantic literature, examining the work of Romantic writers who sought to appropriate and disavow the Gothic aesthetic from the 1790s onwards. The subject of the extended commentary is one of the most famous of all Gothic novels, a text that is also deeply implicated in (and in many ways critical of) the artistic and intellectual priorities associated with Romanticism: Mary Shelley's *Frankenstein* (1818).

Sensibility and the Sublime

The mid-eighteenth-century discourse of sensibility, discussed in the previous chapter, forms a crucial backdrop to the emergence of Romanticism in the 1780s and 1790s. As the critic Gary Kelly has observed, the prioritisation of individual sentiment, of a finely-tuned empathic response to social life, is articulated first in the literature of sensibility, and then appropriated by the key figures of early

Romanticism as one of the defining aspects of their aesthetic; indeed, as Kelly points out, many twentieth-century critics have described the literature of sensibility as 'Pre-Romanticism'.[3] When Wordsworth asserted in the preface to the *Lyrical Ballads* (1798, one of the founding documents of early Romanticism co-written by Wordsworth with Samuel Taylor Coleridge) that poetry was to be understood as 'the spontaneous overflow of powerful feeling', he articulated an artistic principle indebted to the literary, social and psychological precepts of the earlier literature of sensibility. [4]

Another point of connection between early Gothic literature and Romanticism turns upon late eighteenth-century interpretations of the concept of the sublime. It is notoriously difficult to define the sublime exactly (indeed, the notion is marked by a certain indeterminacy that resists easy categorisation – rather like the Gothic itself) but in aesthetic terms it came to be associated from the early eighteenth century onwards with a sense of grandeur and magnitude that had the power to inspire transcendence of mind, or terror. The sublime re-entered European aesthetic discourse at the end of the seventeenth century following a French translation of an essay by an ancient Greek philosopher, Longinus; this essay, 'On the Sublime', associated the concept with that style of elevated rhetoric that had the capacity almost to transform the mind of the listener – to take the listener out of his or her ordinary reality. In 1704 the critic John Dennis published an important essay entitled *The Grounds of Criticism in Poetry* in which he, too, aligned the sublime with an elevating, almost transformational style of poetry able to reproduce rhetorically the awe-inspiring grandeur of certain natural landscapes. Later in the century, the sublime came to be associated with a power that was natural, or divine, and that enabled the human mind to reach its full, transcendental potential. John Baillie in 1747 observed: 'That object can only be called sublime which disposes the mind to this enlargement of itself, and gives her a lofty conception of her own powers.'[5] In *A Philosophical Enquiry into the Origin of Our Ideas of the Sublime and Beautiful* (1757), Edmund Burke asserted that the sublime is always 'some modification of power';[6] this is a power that originates in nature, or in God, and it has the capacity to inspire 'terror'. Burke's definition of the sublime had a profound influence on late eighteenth-century Gothic fictions, notably those of Ann Radcliffe. Radcliffe was especially concerned to capture in her prose the visual effects associated with a certain genre of landscape painting of the seventeenth and eighteenth centuries, a genre associated especially with the wild mountain landscapes of the Italian painter Salvator Rosa. For example, in one of Rosa's famous paintings, *The Passage of St Gothard*, a group of travellers (appearing tiny against the dramatic mountain landscape) clings to a mountain pass above a precipitous drop. It is this type of scene that Radcliffe sought to recreate in fictions such as *A Sicilian Romance*, *The Mysteries of Udolpho* and *The Italian*. In these fictions, moreover, the power of the sublime is often related to the inner workings of the protagonist's consciousness in a manner that anticipates the psychological function of the sublime in Romantic writing. In Romantic poetry, the emphasis is not so much on the landscape, as on the effect that the landscape has on the poet's imagination. The same emphasis is seen in the following extract from Radcliffe's *A Sicilian Romance* (1790). The passage begins with the sublimity of a wild and dramatic mountain landscape and proceeds to record its deeply spiritual effect on the mind of a character called Madame de Menon (the guardian of two sisters, Julia and Emily, who are the heroines of the narrative):

> A group of wild and grotesque rocks rose in a semi-circular form, and their fantastic shapes exhibited nature in her most sublime and striking attitudes. Here her vast magnificence elevated the mind of the beholder to enthusiasm ... The scene inspired madam with reverential awe, and her thoughts involuntarily rose from nature, to nature's God.[7]

The sublime as manifested through nature has a spiritual dimension for Radcliffe that is clearly related in this passage to the character's experience of the sublimity of the Christian God. In later Romantic poetry, the correlation between sublimity and the conventional representation of God in and through nature is often more ambivalent, but this passage from Radcliffe can still usefully be compared with the following from Wordsworth's 'Lines Written a Few Miles above Tintern Abbey' (1798) which evoke the sublime as a 'sense' related to a spiritual power in nature and the 'mind of man':

> … And I have felt
> A presence that disturbs me with the joy
> Of elevated thoughts, a sense sublime
> Of something far more deeply interfused,
> Whose dwelling is the light of setting suns,
> And the round ocean, and the living air,
> And the blue sky, and in the mind of man –
> A motion and a spirit that impels
> All thinking things, all objects of all thought
> And rolls through all things. (ll. 94–103)

A comparison between Radcliffe's and Wordsworth's writings of the early Romantic period reveals the shared investment of Gothic fiction and Romantic poetry in a spiritual, sublime power that appears to facilitate a union of the mind with nature and the divine. As Burke's *A Philosophical Enquiry into the Origin of Our Ideas of the Sublime and Beautiful* of 1757 suggested, however, and as Radcliffe's essay 'On the Supernatural in Poetry' (1826) made clear, the sublime was also an important component of the Gothic aesthetic of 'terror' (see the previous chapter) and this introduced a certain tension into the relation between the Gothic and Romanticism. By virtue of its use specifically to generate terror in the reader, the sublime was related in Gothic fiction to a certain emotional response that proved central to the Gothic's popularity and notoriety in the late eighteenth century: Gothic terror, and the unstable emotional affectivity associated with it, was deemed likely to corrupt the minds of the nation's young readers, especially female readers. Romanticism, on the other hand, developed in opposition to this Gothic aesthetic a Romantic sublimity that privileged a rarefied, transcendental imagination capable of mediating between the individual and the divine: imagination becomes almost in itself a sublime power 'lifting up itself', says Wordsworth, 'before the eye and progress of my song' (Book VI of *The Prelude*).[8] For Coleridge, in his critical essay *Biographia Literaria* (1817), imagination is 'a reflection in the finite mind of the eternal act of creation of the infinite I AM',[9] and Coleridge sharply distinguishes between the power of imagination and the lesser power of 'fancy' which was often the term used to disparage the superficial, sensationalistic musings of Gothic fiction. What is more, the Romantic theorisation of imagination places it firmly within the literary domain of poetry, not fiction. Romanticism has invariably been defined in terms of the work of a small number of poets working between (approximately) the 1790s and the 1820s. Although this rather restrictive definition of the movement was challenged extensively by critics in the late twentieth century, it remains the case that for over 200 years Romanticism was considered a movement in poetry, not fiction, and poetry during this period acquired an elevated cultural status that set it against the literary and cultural practices associated with 'low' popular culture – including the production and consumption of Gothic fiction.

The Gothic against Romanticism

In 1797, Wordsworth published a five-act tragedy entitled *The Borderers*. The play was concerned with the border wars between England and Scotland that preceded the 1707 Act of Union* and it evoked certain elements of early Gothicism: the ancient castle, the Gothic villain, themes of persecution, paranoia and violence. Matthew Lewis's play *The Castle Spectre* was a successful Gothic drama of 1797 and in the same year Coleridge wrote his own quasi-Gothic tragedy *Osorio* (later known as *Remorse*). These Gothic dramas were greatly influenced by the Romantic movement in Germany, and especially by a particular variant of German Romantic

---

* This Act of Parliament joined Scotland with England to form Great Britain.

literature known as *Schauerroman* ('shudder novels', made famous by
Schiller). These ghost stories often contained more explicit, and
more violent, evocations of the supernatural than their English
counterparts and Coleridge was quite open in stating his fascination
with such Gothic tales. The following extract from a letter by
Coleridge to his close friend and fellow poet Robert Southey (later
to become poet laureate) positions Coleridge as a typical wide-eyed
reader of Gothic romance overawed by the terrible suspense of
Friedrich Schiller's 1781 drama, *The Robbers*:

> 'Tis past one o'clock in the morning – I sate down at twelve
> o'clock to read the 'Robbers' of Schiller – I had read chill and
> trembling until I came to the part where Moor fires a pistol over
> the Robbers who are asleep – I could read no more – My God!
> Southey! Who is this Schiller? This convulser of the heart?
>
> Did he write his tragedy amidst the yelling of fiends? –
> I should not like to be able to describe such characters –
> I tremble like an aspen leaf – upon my Soul, I write to you
> because I am frightened – I had better go to Bed. Why have
> we ever called Milton sublime? That Count de moor – horrible
> Wielder of heart-withering Virtues - ! Satan is scarcely
> qualified to attend his Execution as Gallows Chaplain.[10]

The emotions Coleridge describes here will be familiar to anyone
who has ever been compelled to read (or watch), into the early
hours of the morning, a terrifyingly suspenseful, gruesome Gothic
novel (or film). The piece captures exactly the Gothic effect of
sublime terror – and note that here Coleridge not only designates
this quality of Schiller's work 'sublime', but compares it favourably
to the work of Milton who was considered by the Romantics to be
the pre-eminent poet of the sublime. The extract also reproduces,
albeit somewhat ironically, those stylistic techniques of Gothic
fiction which it appropriated in part from the novel of sensibility:
the punctuation consists in the main of dashes and exclamation

marks that signify the emotionally wrought state of the writer, and the writer breaks off at one point to address the reader in heightened emotional terms – 'My God! Southey! Who is this Schiller?' Coleridge is no doubt over-emphasising his over-awed reaction for comic effect; both he and his friend Southey were 'knowing' readers of this type of fiction able to relish, but also to parody its style. Nevertheless, if this extract is placed within its wider cultural and literary context it is possible to appreciate not only why Gothicism was so popular amongst a diverse readership in this period, but why it proved so problematic for the writers associated with Romanticism

Schiller's play positions Coleridge as a reader somewhat disordered mentally by the contrivances of the narrative and this subject position is, in this period, explicitly gendered feminine. Coleridge aligns himself here (again somewhat ironically, though the irony itself can be read as a defence against a genuinely unsettling terror) with those young girls evoked by the critic Thomas Mathias who take Gothic romances to their closets only to become virtually hysterical under their influence (see the previous chapter). Critics from the 1980s onwards have identified a specifically gendered dimension to the construction of Romanticism against literary genres associated with femininity.[11] Gothic fiction was perceived to be read overwhelmingly by women. It was considered to be an inferior literary mode that could not accommodate what were posited as the higher intellectual aspirations of Romanticism. There was in addition a significant class dimension to this re-alignment of literary values in the Romantic period. Developments in print technology in the eighteenth century had democratising potential as a wider range of texts became available to a much wider readership. Thus, whilst certain readers might have lacked the education to appreciate works written in – or heavily alluding to – Latin and Greek, they could certainly relish, as Coleridge and other classically educated readers clearly did, the Gothic tales of the moment. The extract from Coleridge's letter reveals, then, that Gothic fiction was a potentially radical, democratising force uniting the lower-class daughters of tradespeople with the educated readers of John Milton in a shared appreciation of such 'convulsers of the heart' as Schiller.

But this, precisely, was the problem. Romanticism was a movement that prioritised a notion of original genius entirely at odds with the fluid literary practices of Gothicism. Gothic fictions influenced each other to the extent that they were often condemned as plagiaristic (this indeed was one of the charges levelled against Matthew Lewis's *The Monk* by Coleridge), but the notion of plagiarism is inseparable from the emergence of a Romantic aesthetic that valued above all else a commitment to individual, non-derivative genius. The critic Fred Botting identifies at the heart of Romanticism a conceptualisation of the self that is resolutely individualistic and idealistic, but which is nevertheless 'shadowed' by despair; Gothic threatens to expose the 'shadow' behind this idealised, transcendental self; Gothic is 'a writing of excess' that 'shadows the despairing ecstasies of Romantic idealism and individualism'.[12] Wordsworth's initial flirtation with Gothicism in 1797 thus gives way to his excoriation of 'frantic novels' and 'sickly German tragedies' in the 1800 edition of the *Lyrical Ballads*; Coleridge's absorption in German Gothic does not prevent him from lambasting Lewis's *The Monk* as obscene and plagiaristic in the *Critical Review*; and Byron's own deeply Gothic sensibility does not hinder him from aligning Gothicism with intellectually degenerate femininity and devilism in *English Bards and Scottish Reviewers* (1809). Thus, in spite of their shared origins and influences, the culture of the Romantic movement forced a divide between Gothic and Romanticism; the division did not succeed in eliminating the Gothic entirely from Romanticism, but it certainly succeeded in presenting Gothicism for some 200 years as 'the poor and probably illegitimate relation of Romanticism'.[13]

The Gothic in Romanticism

Gothic literature in this period existed predominantly in the form of prose fiction, but from the 1740s onwards there was a distinct Gothic sensibility apparent in certain genres of poetry: James

Macpherson's *The Poems of Ossian* of the 1760s played upon a contemporary fascination with the exoticism and mystery of the past, for example, whilst the 'graveyard' poets anticipated later Gothic and Romantic concerns with mortality, with the nature of body and spirit, and with states of emotional trepidation, or melancholy that were considered conducive to creativity (see the previous chapter). In 1796, moreover, a translation of the German poem *Lenore* by Gottfried Bürger appeared in the *Monthly Magazine*. The poem was a ballad which narrated the tale of a woman carried away at midnight by her dead lover whose demise she has foreseen in 'frightful dreams'. This supernatural narrative was as successful as the romance fictions of the time and it triggered something of a fashion for 'spook balladry'.[14] Matthew Lewis published Gothic ballads in the late 1790s and Coleridge early in his career wrote poetry in this German Gothic style: see 'The Mad Monk' (1800).[*]

It is through Coleridge – that avid consumer of the German 'shudder novel' – that the often uneasy interconnection between Gothicism and early Romanticism becomes most apparent. Indeed, Coleridge's early career can be seen as something of a lightning rod for the tensions, fractures and productive negotiations that characterised the relation between the Gothic and Romanticism in the late 1790s and early nineteenth century. Coleridge co-wrote with William Wordsworth one of the key works of the early Romantic movement: the collection entitled the *Lyrical Ballads*. Wordsworth's preface to the second edition of the *Lyrical Ballads* served as something of a manifesto for a new literary project that emphasised the creative importance of spontaneous feeling in the composition of poetry. Nevertheless, Wordsworth resolutely disavowed Gothicism and this brought him into a degree of conflict with his co-author, Coleridge. Although Coleridge had his own anxieties concerning Gothic romance, he believed, unlike Wordsworth, that the supernatural and the fantastical had a definite place in poetry (see his

---

[*] Interestingly, Coleridge refused to have this poem published in a collection that included work by Matthew Lewis, which again signals his anxiety about too close an association with Gothicism.

essay *Biographia Literaria*, 1817) and his longest contribution to the collection, *The Rime of the Ancient Mariner*, was a Gothic ballad containing evocations of the supernatural as vivid and chilling as anything in the romances of Schiller and Lewis.

The Rime of the Ancient Mariner is one of Coleridge's best known poems and, as Steve Jones points out, 'contemporary readers would have immediately recognized [the poem] as fashionably "romantic" in the German style, a kind of Gothic horror ballad then popular in the magazines'. Jones cites an anonymous review of the work from 1819 which specifies the poem's relationship to the context provided by German Romanticism and the popularity in the 1790s of the German horror story:

> [This poem] appeared at a time when, to use a bold but just expression, with reference to our literary taste, '*Hell made holiday*,' and '*Raw heads and bloody-bones*' were the only fashionable entertainment for man or woman. Then Germany was poured forth into England, in all her flood of sculls and numsculls: then the romancing novelist ran raving about with midnight torches, to shew death's heads on horseback, and to frighten full-grown children with mysteries and band-boxes, hidden behind curtains in bedrooms ...[15]

The poem contains some of the most overtly Gothic scenes in Romantic-era poetry. It narrates the misadventures of a mariner who curses himself and his ship when he shoots an albatross thought by the crew to be a good omen. As a result of the curse, the mariner enters a fantastical, nightmarish world in which he encounters a ghostly ship that brings death to all the crew except for him. In this stanza, death appears as a fiendish woman who resembles the vampiric Christabel in Coleridge's other highly Gothic poem of the same period:

> Her lips were red, her looks were free,
> Her locks were yellow as gold:

Her skin was as white as leprosy,
The Night-mare Life-in-Death was she,
Who thicks man's blood with cold. (Part III, ll. 48–52)

The Rime of the Ancient Mariner was included in the *Lyrical Ballads*, but Coleridge's equally Gothic poem, *Christabel*, was not. This narrative of a vampiric female who preys upon a vulnerable, virginal young girl is one of the most striking instances of the Gothic in Romanticism.

It was common in this period for authors to write prefaces to their work in which they sought to justify and explain their project to the reader. Coleridge's preface to *Christabel* posits it as an experiment in verse form that attempts to move poetry away from the rule-bound rigidity of the early eighteenth century. Neoclassical verse tended to privilege the 'heroic couplet' – the closest thing in English to classical Latin verse – which reproduced a scheme of ten syllables and five stresses per line. Coleridge insists that *Christabel* is 'founded on a new principle' that utilises old Anglo-Saxon verse forms that were organised only according to the stresses in a line; there was no requirement as to the number of syllables a line must contain. Anglo-Saxon verse thus gave the poet much more flexibility in so far as lines could be of any length so long as they contained the required number of stresses. In *Christabel*, Coleridge ensures that lines contain four stresses only, but he varies line length frequently and this contributes to the overall sense of dislocation and confusion that is central to the poem's evocation of terror (see the discussion of the opening lines of the poem below). Moreover, the authority afforded here by Coleridge to Anglo-Saxon verse evokes those earlier eighteenth-century recuperations of a 'Gothic', Germanic past in the formulation of a new national identity (see the previous chapter). The preface thus positions this poem within a tradition of literary Gothicism that looks to an ancient English/Gothic past for its vindication.

Christabel is also replete with the tropes and themes of earlier Gothic literature from Walpole to Radcliffe and Gottfried Bürger.

The narrative problematises a feudal order of power that from the outset is presented as ineffectual, if not dysfunctional. The protagonist, Christabel, is the daughter of Sir Leoline whose name evokes the kingly authority to be expected in a feudal patriarch. However, Leoline's authority seems to be severely compromised; his castle is protected by a 'toothless mastiff bitch', he 'is in weak health' and Christabel is apparently at liberty to leave the castle alone in the middle of the night to mourn her lost lover. The language and imagery of the opening stanza generates a sense of confusion and obscurity on a number of levels; nothing can be clearly identified and defined, sights and sounds are misrecognised or else are too ambiguous to be accounted for at all:

> 'Tis the middle of the night by the castle clock,
> And the owls have awakened the crowing cock;
> Tu-whit! Tu-whoo!
> And hark, again! The crowing cock,
> How drowsily it crew ...
> Is the night chilly and dark?
> The night is chilly, but not dark –
> The thin grey cloud is spread on high,
> It covers but not hides the sky ...
> The night is chill, the forest bare –
> Is it the wind that moaneth bleak? (ll. 1–45)

These opening lines are a poetic exercise in the production of Gothic terror and they illustrate the importance of Coleridge's new scheme of using Anglo-Saxon verse form in this Romantic–Gothic context. Each line has only four stresses, but line length varies considerably and Coleridge uses such variation to generation certain 'shocks' in the narration of events. The first two lines are relatively long, twelve and eleven syllables respectively, but they are followed by the short, sharp evocation of the owl's hooting: 'Tu-whit, Tu-whoo!' This four-syllable, alliterative and onomatopoeic line, with stresses falling on each syllable, breaks the flow established by the longer, more regular lines that precede it; it is a rather jarring intervention in the narration of events that are about to become weirdly distorted. The owl hoots at the same time as the cock crows, throwing the poem into temporal disorder. Why would a cock crow at midnight? The night is chill, but 'not dark' since there is a full moon; nevertheless, the light of the moon affords no clarity because strangely it is 'small and dull' and grey cloud covers the sky. This scene of sinister obscurity outside the walls of the feudal stronghold is the location of the appearance to Christabel of a beautiful woman dressed in white; this is Geraldine, the demonic woman who will corrupt the household of Leoline, beginning with his daughter. Geraldine poses as a woman in distress and Christabel invites her into the castle and into her own closet (there are strong intimations of vampirism here; Geraldine must be invited over the threshold – carried over, in this instance). The first half of the poem concludes with Geraldine's ambiguous seduction of Christabel. Again, the language is unclear; Geraldine reveals a strange physical deformity (apparently a missing or mutilated breast, but this is not made explicit) and she mutters a spell over her sleeping victim the purpose of which is not wholly evident. Nevertheless, the implication is that Geraldine will claim Christabel as one of her own and this is emphasised here through the poem's appropriation of the Gothic motif of the absent mother. Christabel's mother is dead and here Geraldine must exorcise the protective spirit of the mother before she can begin her assault on the daughter: 'Off, woman, off! This hour is mine –/ Though thou her guardian spirit be/ Off, woman, off! – tis given to me' (ll. 204–6).

In the second part of the poem, Geraldine turns her attention to the rest of the household, and the success with which she infiltrates the family anticipates the demonic charm that characterises the figure of the vampire in later Gothic fictions, such as Le Fanu's *Carmilla* (1872) and Stoker's *Dracula* (1897). Moreoover, prophetic and symbolic dreaming occupies a central place in the poem, as it does elsewhere in the Gothic tradition before and after the Romantic period. Leoline's bard, Bracy, relates his dream of a snake attacking a dove; the relevance of this dream to the situation facing Leoline could hardly be clearer, but, rather like Manfred in *The Castle of Otranto*, Leoline is wilfully blind to such providential signs and his fate appears sealed as he turns away from his daughter and accepts Geraldine into the bosom of his family.

'Second-generation' Romanticism

It is significant that the figure of the vampire, a staple of later literary Gothicism, should be evoked so vividly by Samuel Taylor Coleridge, a founder of English Romanticism who in many ways shared his culture's hostility towards Gothicism. Probably the most famous poetic representation of the vampire in this period,[*] though, was published by an author with a more overt admiration for Gothicism: Lord Byron. Byron belongs to what critics have termed the 'second generation' of Romantic poets who came to prominence in the second decade of the nineteenth century. Moreover, Byron has given his name to a certain influential Romantic and Gothic archetype: the 'Byronic hero'. This figure (which provides the model for Emily Brontë's Heathcliff in *Wuthering Heights*, discussed in the following chapter) is invariably represented as possessing a charisma and brooding sexual power that borders on the malevolent. It derives its association with Byron from Byron's own chequered personal history; he had many affairs, including an incestuous liaison with his sister, and was described famously by Lady Caroline Lamb as 'mad, bad and dangerous to know'. Byron himself deployed this archetypal figure of the charismatic anti-hero in two highly Gothic poems, *The Giaour* and *Manfred*.

Byron praised Horace Walpole as 'the father of the first romance, and the last tragedy in our language, and surely worthy of a higher place than any living writer, be he who he may'.[16] In 1813, Byron

---

[*] In terms of prose fiction, a key vampiric narrative of this period is John Polidori's *The Vampyre* (1819) which is considered in Part Three: 'From the *Fin de Siècle* to Modern Gothic' in relation to the development of vampire fiction before Bram Stoker's *Dracula* (1897).

produced his own Gothic poem, *The Giaour: A Fragment of a Turkish Tale*. This narrative deploys many of the conventions of Gothic romance: it is a tale of love, vengeance and violence the protagonist of which is an unrepentant killer portrayed as demonic and, ultimately, vampiric. The Giaour is a Romantic anti-hero – a 'Byronic hero' – whose depiction here resembles John Milton's representation of Satan in the poem *Paradise Lost*. Milton's Satan was taken as the model of charismatic evil by Gothic and Romantic writers, as is clear from Byron's portrayal of the Giaour here:

> Dark and unearthly is the scowl
> That glares beneath his dusky cowl
> The flash of that dilating eye
> Reveals too much of times gone by –
> Though varying – indistinct its hue,
> Oft will his glance the gazer rue –
> For in it lurks that nameless spell
> Which speaks – itself unspeakable – (ll. 832–9)[17]

Byron's poem brings into sharp focus other aspects of early literary Gothicism and its rather tense relation to Romanticism. It reveals an ongoing contemporary interest in antiquarianism and (like Walpole) Byron presents the work on its first publication as a discovered manuscript that carries a charge of exoticism by virtue of its association with the east. Byron thus distances the narrative from the contemporary reader by means of its location in a time and place that can simultaneously be disparaged and enjoyed as barbaric and superstitious. The first edition was accompanied by 'editor's' notes through which Byron comments extensively upon Islamic culture and attempts, as critic Michael Gamer observes, 'to debunk the very materials that he indulges in most strongly in the text of his poem'.[18] Byron therefore positions himself as a learned scholar of history and literature guiding the reader through this oriental tale and dismissing its Gothic absurdities even as he indulges them. Byron's Gothic Romanticism thus shares – and even exaggerates – the tendency of early Gothic to subvert the conditions of its own narration for reasons that are in large measure to do with the culture's anxiety towards and fascination with the Gothic's guilty pleasures.

In 1817, Byron published probably his most Gothic work, the long dramatic poem *Manfred*. This was never intended to be performed in the theatre; rather, Byron presents the poem in dramatic form in order to externalise the conflicts within the protagonist as he struggles with various supernatural entities in an attempt to contact the spirit of his sister, Astarte. Manfred remains in love with Astarte, a love that is clearly not purely fraternal; the allusion to incest evokes Byron's own personal history and introduces into the poem a theme that was already a well established component of the Gothic novel (Ambrosio's lust for his sister, Antonia, for example, in Matthew Lewis's *The Monk*). The poem also establishes Astarte as a Gothic 'double' of Manfred:

> She was like me in lineaments-- her eyes
> Her hair, her features, all, to the very tone
> Even of her voice, they said were like to mine;
> But soften'd all, and temper'd into beauty;
> She had the same lone thoughts and wanderings,
> The quest of hidden knowledge, and a mind
> To comprehend the universe: nor these
> Alone, but with them gentler powers than mine,
> Pity, and smiles, and tears-- which I had not;
> And tenderness-- but that I had for her;
> Humility-- and that I never had.
> Her faults were mine-- her virtues were her own--
> I loved her, and destroy'd her! (ll. 199–211)

From these lines, it would appear that Astarte is a feminine version of Manfred – a being entirely like him except for qualities of sensibility and gentleness that were culturally associated with womanhood in this period. It could be argued that Astarte represents a feminine component of Manfred's own psyche towards which

Manfred feels a considerable antagonism: he 'loves' Astarte, but 'destroys her'. The notion that the Gothic double represents a repressed aspect of the protagonist's self becomes increasingly prominent from the nineteenth century onwards[*] and Byron significantly anticipates this development in *Manfred*.

Manfred is possessed of considerable supernatural powers to the extent that even the most potent spirits regard him with respect as a 'man of no common order'. The poem begins with Manfred summoning spirits in the Alps – a typically sublime region for the Romantic poets. He is portrayed as an almost superhuman or supernatural figure – godlike, even – with power to control elemental forces:

> Mysterious Agency!
> Ye spirits of the unbounded Universe,
> Whom I have sought in darkness and in light!
> Ye, who do compass earth about, and dwell
> In subtler essence! ye, to whom the tops
> Of mountains inaccessible are haunts,
> And earth's and ocean's caves familiar things--
> I call upon ye by the written charm
> Which gives me power upon you-- Rise! appear! (ll. 28–36)

When the spirits appear they are in a position to grant anything that Manfred desires in terms of worldly wealth and power, but all that he seeks is death and reunion with Astarte. Byron thus twists the Gothic plot of the 'Faustian pact'[†] – the protagonist's bargain

---

[*] See the discussion in the next chapter of Poe's short story 'The Fall of the House of Usher' (in which Roderick Usher is 'doubled' by his sister) and Stevenson's *The Strange Case of Dr Jekyll and Mr Hyde*. See also Part Four: 'Female Gothic', for an extended consideration of the Gothic 'double'.

[†] The figure of Faust originated in German folklore. Faust was a man who sold his soul to the devil in return for unlimited knowledge and worldly power. English playwright Christopher Marlowe produced an influential version of this legend: *The Tragical History of Doctor Faustus* (1604). The German writer Johann Wolfgang von Goethe's rendition of the tale in *Faust* (1808) is a seminal text of European Romanticism.

with the devil that ultimately damns him – into a heroic narrative in which Manfred refuses all that the demonic spirits can offer in his quest to find Astarte and die with her. Her spirit, when it does appear, offers him no comfort; it prophesies Manfred's death and refuses to forgive him. He is desolate, yet faces death with courage and fierce rebellion against the prospect of his damnation. In the closing scenes an abbot attempts to reconcile Manfred to the church, but Manfred refuses this consolation; instead, he contemptuously denounces the demonic spirit that has come to claim his soul, insisting that he made no pact with the devil. He relied throughout on his own supernatural powers and thus he, not Satan, is responsible for his own destruction. His final speech is an extraordinary repudiation of the power of the devil:

> Back to thy hell!
> Thou hast no power upon me, *that* I feel;
> Thou never shalt possess me, *that* I know:
> What I have done is done; I bear within
> A torture which could nothing gain from thine …
> *Thou* didst not tempt me, and thou couldst not tempt me;
> I have not been thy dupe nor am thy prey,
> But was my own destroyer, and will be
> My own hereafter.-- Back, ye baffled fiends!
> The hand of death is on me-- but not yours!
> … [*The Demons disappear*] (ll. 386–401)

Unlike other characters in Gothic literature that fall victim to Satanic power (the Caliph in Beckford's novel *Vathek*, for example, and Ambrosio in Lewis's *The Monk*), Manfred will not submit to any authority but his own. He is one of the most powerful instances of the Gothic Romantic anti-hero – the 'Byronic hero' – in the literature of the period, refusing to become the mere puppet of Satan (or of God, for that matter) and asserting mastery over his destiny even in the face of death.

Another second-generation Romantic poet whose work displays distinct Gothic qualities is John Keats, a close associate of Lord Byron and Percy Bysshe Shelley. Keats's poem *Lamia* (1819) has points in common with Coleridge's *Christabel*: both poems feature monstrous women who possess considerable seductive powers. The term 'Lamia' refers to a mythological female creature supposed to prey on, even to suck the blood of, children. There is clearly, then, an association between Keats's Lamia and the vampiric Geraldine. Just as Geraldine is physically grotesque in spite of her great beauty (she has a deformed breast – see the discussion above), so Lamia is initially a monstrous woman/serpent who is made human by the god Hermes. She falls in love with the mortal Lycius and the two marry. When Lamia's true identity is revealed at their wedding feast, however, Lamia dies, and her death is shortly followed by that of the distraught Lycius.

Where Keats's poem differs from Coleridge's, however, is in its sympathetic treatment of the female protagonist. Geraldine is unequivocally evil, but Lamia is portrayed more as a victim than a villain. She was once a human woman, she claims to Hermes, and is now trapped in the body of a serpent. Her motivation for wishing to be remade in human form is to seek love, and whilst her beauty is enchanting it is not deadly. Her death and that of Lycius are caused by the appearance at the wedding feast of a man (Apollonius) who is determined to expose her: it is his naming of Lamia that destroys her and Lycius, who dies of grief and not because of any evil machinations on the part of his bride. Keats thus reworks the Gothic motif of the monstrous female, presenting what is essentially a tragic Gothic love story. Keats's Gothicism thus inhabits Romanticism perhaps more comfortably, less 'monstrously' one might say, than is the case with Coleridge.

Extended Commentary: Mary Shelley, *Frankenstein* (1818)

Mary Shelley produced in 1818 one of the most iconic of all Gothic texts; it is indeed one of those narratives (Bram Stoker's *Dracula* is another) that has acquired a life of its own since its publication, generating numerous adaptations from stage versions in the 1820s to dozens of film variations throughout the twentieth and twenty-first centuries. Not only has the novel attracted an extraordinary degree of cultural and critical attention, the circumstances of the text's composition have acquired an almost mythic status also. Mary Shelley was holidaying at Lake Geneva with her husband, Percy, and their friends Lord Byron and John Polidori. Byron challenged the group to a ghost story competition and Mary Shelley's preface to the second edition of her novel (published in 1831) describes how a dream that she had following Byron's suggestion gave rise to *Frankenstein*.

A great many cultural, political and literary contexts form the backdrop to this novel; it is, indeed, one of the most intertextual* of Gothic narratives comprised (rather like its monster) of bits and pieces from elsewhere, from contemporary discourses of science, radical politics, sensibility, theories of education and human development and, of course, Romanticism. The author engages with the revolutionary politics of the 1790s and, especially, with the radical theories of her father, William Godwin, and the mid-eighteenth-century philosopher Jean-Jacques Rousseau whose work had a considerable impact upon early British Romanticism. Rousseau believed that education and environment had a determining influence over human development and his ideas were reiterated, with some

---

* 'Intertextuality' refers to the formation of texts through the recitation and appropriation of previous literary works and cultural discourses. It is discussed in greater detail in Part Three: 'British Gothic in the Late Twentieth Century' and Part Four: 'Narrative Instability and the Gothic Narrator'.

variation, by Godwin. For Godwin, human nature was malleable, not fixed, and could be improved through enlightened systems of education and governance. In Mary Shelley's novel, the monster is 'born' into the world lacking any formative influences; his 'parent', Victor, woefully neglects his duty to educate and develop the character of his progeny and the result is a deeply alienated creature who lacks a grounding in the world into which Victor abandons him. The novel at various points (especially through the monster's own narrative and his emotional appeal to his creator) requests the reader's sympathy for a creature who is the product of forces beyond his control, who appears to possess an innate sensibility and capacity for intellectual advancement (he educates himself through his study of some of the classics of the European literary tradition and becomes an eloquent speaker), but who nevertheless lacks any social and cultural reference points to help him develop a fully socialised human subjectivity.

Indeed, some critics have extended this analysis to see in *Frankenstein* a political allegory pointing to the neglect and exploitation of a new labouring class brought into being for, and effectively 'monsterised' by, the emerging forces of modern capitalism.[19] The novel is set during the 1790s and therefore has as its immediate political reference point the French Revolution. Victor is a member of a wealthy bourgeois family and finds it easy to gather the material resources that he needs to carry out his experiments. The monster that he creates to serve him, but that he then callously abandons, revolts against the injustice of his servitude and abandonment. Karl Marx was later to express the tension between the dominant and oppressed economic classes of capitalist society in terms that are strongly evocative of Shelley's novel:

> Modern bourgeois society with its relations of production, of exchange and property, a society that has conjured up such gigantic means of production and of exchange, is like the sorcerer, who is no longer able to control the powers of the nether world whom he has called up by his spells.[20]

The novel can also be read as a critique of the Enlightenment emphasis on science and an exploration of the possibility that science might overreach itself in its attempts to control nature. A central theme of the novel is, indeed, the ambition, or hubris, of Victor; the text's subtitle is 'The Modern Prometheus' after the hero of Greek myth who tried to steal fire from the gods. Victor is a man of science consumed by the ambition to create life, to 'play God', and the very term 'Frankenstein' has become synonymous with scientific developments that appear to overreach themselves and to threaten the balance and integrity of life. (It is thus common to refer to various forms of genetic mutation as 'Frankenstein foods', 'Frankenstein babies' and so on.) The novel, then, can be read as part of a wider Romantic reaction against Enlightenment scientific thinking and the processes of technology associated with the Industrial Revolution. Victor's experiments with electricity bring his monster to life and Shelley's preface makes explicit the contemporary relevance of Victor's machinations: she writes of a conversation between her husband and Byron in which they discussed:

> [t]he experiments of Dr. [Erasmus] Darwin who preserved a piece of vermicelli in a glass case, till by some extraordinary means it began to move with voluntary motion ... Perhaps a corpse would be reanimated. Galvanism had given a token of such things: perhaps the component parts of a creature might be manufactured, brought together, and endued with vital warmth.[21]

This is, of course, the premise of *Frankenstein*, with the scientific musings of Percy Shelley and Byron given a macabre Gothic twist as Victor digs up corpses for body parts which he assembles in his 'charnel house' of a laboratory.

The novel, though, is not exclusively a critique of Enlightenment rationality borne out of the discourses of late Romanticism; it may be read, in fact, as a critical engagement with some of the central precepts of Romanticism itself. Victor is an arch-individualist, unconcerned with social and especially domestic life who seeks transcendence through his 'art'. He might be said to be in search of the ultimate experience of the sublime: a mastery of the very principle of life. Victor, then, may be defined as a Romantic, a man in pursuit of self-fulfilment through power over nature; his scientific genius is the corollary in this narrative of the Romantic imagination: 'The repetition in the finite mind of the eternal act of creation in the infinite I AM', as Coleridge described it in the *Biographia Literaria* (see above). Margaret Homans suggests a connection in this regard between Frankenstein and Wordsworth; both men, she argues, 'read nature [to impose on it] apocalyptic patterns of meaning that destroy it'.[22] A similar point might be made in relation to the character of Walton whose letters to his sister narrate part of the novel. At the beginning of the text, Walton writes from a ship bound for the Arctic in search of the elusive 'northern passage'. Jonathan Bate argues that Walton's voyage of discovery is part of a wider colonial project that sought dominion over other cultures and over the environment.[23] This colonial quest actualises a crucial aspect of the Romantic aesthetic: nature is viewed as the raw material that facilitates the self-realisation of the individual.

In this respect, Shelley's evocation of the sublime deserves further comment not least because it points towards certain key developments in the Gothic's treatment of the sublime as it moved further into the nineteenth century. In Romantic poetry, the sublime, working with and through poetic imagination, is often the motivation for spiritual transcendence and self-actualisation; in Shelley, the sublime is aligned with the destructive power first of Victor and then of the monster who becomes a killer and roams the Alps* like a fugitive. In the following key passage, Victor finds himself elevated emotionally and spiritually as he confronts Mont Blanc; the scene is clearly meant to evoke the dominant precepts of Romanticism, to the extent that an extract from Percy Shelley's poem 'On Mutability' (1816) is quoted. Victor then describes his own 'Romantic' response to the landscape from a high

---

* The Alps are the setting of much Romantic poetry concerning the sublime – see Wordsworth's *Prelude*, Book VI (published 1850), and Percy Shelley's 'Mont Blanc' (1816).

vantage point above the glacier fields of the Alps from which he 'overlooks the sea of ice ... Montanvert was exactly opposite, at the distance of a league; and above it rose Mont Blanc, in awful majesty ... my heart, which was before sorrowful, now swelled with something like joy' (pp. 64–5). The sublime here is associated, through the intrusion of the monster into this archetypal Romantic landscape, not with divine power and transcendence (which is how Victor initially conceptualises his experience), but with destructive compulsions and monstrosity. The monstrous sublimity that in this novel appears almost to parody the Romantic aesthetic of the sublime is anticipated in the earlier Gothic Romantic works of Coleridge and Byron. Coleridge's *Christabel* and Byron's *Giaour* are figures of sublime evil, figures that embody an abject, yet hypnotic material power evident in Geraldine's deformed breast, the Giaour's 'ghastly whiteness' and 'dark scowl', and so on. What Vijay Mishra has termed the 'Gothic Sublime' promises not transcendence and self-knowledge, but 'desecration' and the possibility of a total disintegration of self.[24] This dark potential within Romanticism is articulated through Gothicism in a manner that was to be influential upon the development of Gothic literature in nineteenth-century England and America – in the work of Emily Brontë, for example, and Edgar Allan Poe, whose work is discussed in the next chapter.

Notes

1   Robert Hume, 'Gothic Versus Romantic: A Revaluation of the Gothic Novel', *PMLA* (Publications of the Modern Language Association of America), 84 (1969), p. 282.

2   See Michael Gamer, 'Gothic Fictions and Romantic Writing in Britain', in Jerrold E. Hogle (ed.), *The Cambridge Companion to Gothic Fiction* (Cambridge: Cambridge University Press, 2002), pp. 85–104.

3   Gary Kelly, *English Fiction of the Romantic Period, 1789–1830* (London: Longman, 1989), p. 12.

4   Duncan Wu, *Romanticism: An Anthology*, 1st edn (Oxford: Blackwell, 1995), p. 495.

5   John Baillie, 'An Essay on the Sublime', in Peter de Bolla and Andrew Ashfield (eds), *The Sublime: A Reader in Eighteenth-century Aesthetic Theory* (Cambridge: Cambridge University Press, 1996), p. 87.

6   Quoted in de Bolla and Ashfeld, *The Sublime*, p. 137.

7   Ann Radcliffe, *A Sicilian Romance* (San Diego, CA: Icon Classics, 2008), p. 102.

8   Wu, *Romanticism*, p. 553.

9   Samuel Taylor Coleridge, *Biographia Literaria*, in Duncan Wu, *Romanticism: An Anthology*, 3rd edn (Oxford: Blackwell, 2005), p. 169.

10 Quoted in Gamer, 'Gothic Fictions and Romantic Writing in Britain', p. 88.

11 See especially Anne Mellor, *Romanticism and Gender* (London: Routledge, 1992).

12 Fred Botting, *Gothic* (London: Routledge, 1996), p. 1.

13 Hume, 'Gothic Versus Romantic', p. 282.

14 Marilyn Gaull, *English Romanticism: The Human Context* (New York: Norton, 1988), p. 269.

15 Steven E. Jones, 'Supernatural, or at least "Romantic": *The Ancient Mariner* and Parody', *Romanticism on the Net*, 15 (1999), accessed from http://www.erudit.org.

16 Byron's preface to *Marino Faliero* (1821), quoted in Gamer, 'Gothic Fictions and Romantic Writing in Britain', p. 88.

17 Lord Byron, *The Giaour* (1813), in *Byron's Poetry* (London and New York: Norton, 1978), p. 84.

18 Gamer, 'Gothic Fictions and Romantic Writing in Britain', p. 99.

19 See Warren Montag, 'The Workshop of Filthy Creation: A Marxist Reading of *Frankenstein*', in Ross C. Murfin and Johanna Smith (eds), *Mary Shelley's Frankenstein: A Case Study in Contemporary Criticism* (New York: St Martin's Press, 1991).

20 Karl Marx, *The Communist Manifesto* (Oxford: Oxford University Press, 2008), p. 27.

21 Mary Shelley, *Frankenstein* (London and New York: Norton, 1996), pp. 171–2.

22 Margaret Homans, 'Bearing Demons: Frankenstein's Circumvention of the Maternal', in Fred Botting (ed.), *Frankenstein: Contemporary Critical Essays* (London: Macmillan, 1995), p. 142.

23 Jonathan Bate, *The Song of the Earth* (Cambridge, MA: Harvard University Press, 2000), p. 49.

24 Vijay Mishra, *The Gothic Sublime* (New York: State University of New York Press, 1994), p. 187.

Nineteenth-century Gothic: Emily Brontë, Poe, Collins and Stevenson

An alternative title to this chapter might have been 'Victorian Gothic' since a number of critical studies use this designation to categorise and assess developments in Gothicism from the 1830s to the *fin de siècle*. This designation, however, has certain limitations; it imposes a rather artificial distinction between the Gothic of the Romantic era and that of the Victorian period, and implicitly it excludes developments in Gothicism outside Britain. The aim of this chapter is to emphasise the continuity between 'Gothic Romanticism' and the diverse forms of the Gothic that emerge later in the nineteenth century, whilst also acknowledging and assessing the changed historical contexts that encouraged the development of new expressions of Gothicism. The authors who are the main focus of the chapter are carefully chosen to facilitate coverage of key generic and cultural shifts during this century, amongst which are: the blending of elements of Gothicism with Victorian domestic realism, sensation fiction and the detective novel; the emergence of the Gothic short story as a popular and influential narrative form (examples of the Victorian ghost story are considered more fully in Part Four: 'Gothic Bodies'); the development of American Gothic; and the cultural significance of Gothic narratives of monstrosity, in particular the iconic Gothic novel of the 1880s, Robert Louis Stevenson's *The Strange Case of Dr Jekyll and Mr Hyde* (1886).

Domesticating the Gothic

Critics have observed that the mid-nineteenth century marks a shift away from the conventions that came to characterise Gothic fiction from the 1760s to the end of the Romantic period.[1] In particular, earlier Gothic narratives tended invariably to distance the location of its terrors from the contemporary middle-class reader. The scene of persecution, murder, haunting and so on was geographically and/or historically removed from eighteenth-century England, and Gothic villains and their victims were by this means 'othered' and exoticised. By the end of the Romantic period, however, Gothic terrors appeared to be coming closer to home. Texts such as James Hogg's *The Private Memoirs and Confessions of a Justified Sinner* (1824) and Maturin's *Melmoth the Wanderer* (1820)* are set in contemporary Scotland and Ireland respectively and both use Gothic devices of doubling, haunting and psychological persecution to interrogate aspects of contemporary political, social and religious life. These works also developed technical strategies that came to characterise Gothic storytelling in later decades: they both employ multiple narrative perspectives to relate events that can therefore be interpreted from various viewpoints. The notion that there is a single narrative 'truth' to be discerned in the reading of a novel becomes impossible to sustain in relation to most Gothic fictions.

Another transitional text that blends aspects of Gothic Romanticism with emerging forms of a more domesticated and psychologically interiorised Victorian Gothic is Emily Brontë's *Wuthering Heights* (1847). This novel is an unconventional love story detailing the deeply conflicted relationship between Catherine Earnshaw and Heathcliff, a foundling who is adopted into the Earnshaw family as a small child. The text is not 'Gothic' in the sense of, say, Matthew Lewis's *The Monk* (with its emphasis upon diabolical supernatural evil) but, as Gilbert and Gubar argue in their influential critical work *The Madwoman in the Attic* (1979), there are significant technical and thematic points of

---

* Both these texts are considered more fully in Part Four: 'Critical Theories and Debates'.

contact between this novel and earlier examples of the Gothic, most notably *Frankenstein*. In its use of different narrative voices to exclude and demonise Heathcliff, they assert that '*Wuthering Heights* might be a deliberate copy of *Frankenstein*'.[2] Heathcliff is referred to repeatedly as demonic or monstrous; he is an 'evil beast', an 'imp of satan' and 'a goblin'; his eyes are 'black fiends', his teeth 'sharp, white'; and Nelly Dean (who narrates a large proportion of the narrative) asks the loaded question, 'Is he a ghoul or a vampire?' Heathcliff is the embodiment in many ways of the Gothic villain or (and there is a strong correlation between the two) the Romantic, Byronic anti-hero who is simultaneously charismatic and monstrous. Nelly Dean's descriptions of Heathcliff often evoke Romantic-era characterisations of the vampiric male; in John Polidori's short story *The Vampyre* (1819), for instance, Lord Ruthven (a character thought to be based on Polidori's friend, Lord Byron)[3] is described as a charming man who infiltrates London high society and exerts an almost hypnotic effect upon those with whom he comes into contact; like Nelly's descriptions of Heathcliff, Polidori's text focuses upon the deadly charisma of Ruthven evident especially in the power of his 'dead grey eye'.[4] The critic James Twitchell has examined in detail the relationship between Heathcliff and the nineteenth-century figure of the vampire and concludes that whilst Heathcliff cannot be regarded as actually vampiric, he certainly 'acts as if he were a vampire' and in so doing enables Brontë to establish what is for Twitchell the text's dominant metaphor: 'one of parasite and host, oppressor and victim, vampire and vampirised'.[5]

Crucially, moreover, in terms of the development of a Victorian Gothic that domesticates the type of threat represented by the figure of the vampire, Heathcliff is adopted as a foundling into the middle-class Earnshaw family. Mr Earnshaw brings him back from Liverpool having apparently found him homeless and starving on the streets; there is no clue as to the child's origin or identity and immediately (through, again, the narration of Nelly Dean) the child is 'othered' by virtue of his appearance and incomprehensible speech:

We crowded round and, over Miss Cathy's head, I had a peep at a dirty, ragged, black haired child; big enough both to walk and talk – indeed, its face looked older than Catherine's – yet when it was set on its feet it only stared around, and repeated over and over again, some gibberish that nobody could understand. I was frightened and Mrs Earnshaw ready to fling it out of doors.[6]

Mr Earnshaw's return with the child, and his insistence that the boy be adopted into the family, especially antagonises the female members of the household. Mrs Earnshaw expresses revulsion towards the boy and has to be pretty much ordered by her husband not to put him out ('see here, wife ... you must e'en taken it as a gift of God'), whilst Nelly's response is to dehumanise and fear what she calls 'it'. As in *Frankenstein*, Mr Earnshaw and his 'monster', Heathcliff, are set against a domestic, feminine milieu that is threatened by the intrusion of this rootless creature. Here, furthermore, is another instance of Brontë appropriating earlier Gothic themes and transplanting them into a contemporary, middle-class English landscape. The question of familial authority and proper patriarchal lineage was central to eighteenth- and early nineteenth-century Gothic narratives in which supernatural interventions frequently worked to expose or initiate some fatal disruption within the proper hierarchy of the family. In Coleridge's *Christabel*, for example, Sir Leoline forsakes his daughter in favour of the vampiric interloper, Geraldine. In *Wuthering Heights*, Mr Earnshaw quickly establishes the foundling as his favourite child and names him Heathcliff after his dead son.[7] The Earnshaws' eldest son, Hindley, so resents this usurpation that he helps initiate a cycle of violence and revenge that spans two generations. Brontë's text therefore radically reworks the theme of dysfunction within the patriarchal family, relocating the threat of family disintegration and violence from the distant feudal past, or the exoticised landscapes of southern Europe, to contemporary England. Moreover, although the Earnshaw family home is to some extent 'othered' as a wild, Gothic space throughout the narrative, the capacity of Heathcliff to stretch his influence beyond this domain and into the much more conventionally bourgeois home of the Linton family exemplifies the Gothic's movement in this period from the exotic 'outside' of bourgeois culture to its 'inside': the vampire/monster/demon infiltrates the middle-class family.

The narrative structure of *Wuthering Heights* is also significant in its appropriation of earlier styles and its anticipation of later multiple-voice, 'framing' techniques; these techniques often have the unsettling double effect of distancing and rationalising the weird events that are narrated, whilst also rendering the material yet more disturbing by associating them with, and causing them to exert a considerable influence upon, figures posited as rational, authoritative and reliable. In the novel, the lawyer Lockwood and the housekeeper Nelly Dean fulfil this function; both of them maintain a distance from and a scepticism towards the seemingly unnatural occurrences which they relate. Their rational world-view is nevertheless undermined by the events they are required to narrate. Nowhere is this more apparent than in Lockwood's early confrontation with the ghost of the young Catherine Earnshaw as he sleeps as a guest in what used to be her room; Lockwood dreams that a young girl comes knocking at the window and grasps his hand. The 'dream' has such an aspect of reality to it that Lockwood is left profoundly disturbed and he is required henceforth to confront and narrate events wholly at odds with his solid, lawyerly, middle-class education. Similarly it is Nelly who, in spite of her self-professed 'common sense', first introduces the reader to Heathcliff's seemingly monstrous, possibly vampiric qualities. This narrative technique acquires greater complexity in Bram Stoker's *Dracula* (studied in detail in the following chapter) in which events are related by means of a variety of 'authoritative' documents associated with a rational, Victorian culture: doctor's records, a ship's log, newspaper reports and the letters of another lawyer, Jonathan Harker. Again, what can be seen here is a further aspect of the domestication of the Gothic: these narratives come to the reader not in the form of a rediscovered ancient manuscript, but through the first-hand account of 'reliable' witnesses (Lockwood, Nelly, Harker) or through familiar modern media – newspapers, journals, even, in *Dracula*, a voice recorder.

Gothic Fiction and the Sensation Novel

A key facet of the Gothic in the nineteenth century (and ever since) has been its capacity to adopt diverse generic forms and to infiltrate other modes of writing. *Wuthering Heights* incorporates elements of romance and domestic realism, as does Charlotte Brontë's *Jane Eyre* (1847). Dickens mixed realism with certain Gothic tropes and themes (the 'fallen woman', the ancestral home, conflicts and crimes within families, various forms of haunting, persecution and the tyrannical aspects of the legal system) in several of his novels and short stories.[*] The Gothic also developed an intimate relation in the 1860s and 1870s with one of the most popular fictional genres of the time: the sensation novel. This was primarily a novel of mystery turning, like many Gothic fictions, upon the presence and ultimate revelation of a secret that frequently pertained to a crime within a family – bigamy, illegitimacy, adultery or even murder. The emphasis on scandal, secrecy and often violence caused sensation fiction to be viewed with some critical suspicion, much as Gothic fiction had been in the 1790s. A critic writing in the *Spectator* magazine in 1861 on the subject of the 'enigma novel' observed, 'We are threatened with a new variety of the sensation novel, a host of cleverly complicated stories, the whole interest of which consists in the gradual unravelling of some carefully prepared enigma.'[8] The troubling aspect of these narratives was chiefly that the 'enigma' related to family secrets that, when exposed, threatened the Victorian ideal of the middle-class family as a place of security, purity and propriety – an ideal that was especially embodied in the figure of the good mother and wife. It was largely on account of its rather subversive sexual and domestic implications – its insertion of

*   See *Bleak House* (1852), *Great Expectations* (1860) and *A Christmas Carol* (1843).

an element of dark impropriety into an otherwise seemingly respectable domestic setting – that the sensation novel (dubbed the 'romance of vice' by the novelist Henry James in 1865) was so sensationalistic and thus so deeply compelling for a middle-class, broadly female readership. This new variety of fiction blended Gothicism, romance and domestic realism in order to articulate for these readers the conflicts and, indeed, the violence that often lay behind the Victorian idealisation of family life.*

One of the most successful sensation novels of the period – and one that reveals its close generic relation to Gothicism – was Wilkie Collins's 1860 best-seller, *The Woman in White*. From the point of view of narrative structure, the novel employs the technique closely associated with literary Gothicism from the Romantic period onwards: the plot unfolds from multiple perspectives, thus preventing any single narrative voice from holding sway over the reader's interpretation of events. The reader is, therefore, in the position almost of a jury or inquisitor to whom a variety of versions of events are presented, and is encouraged by this means to unravel the enigma and to appreciate also the provisional nature of any single determination of the 'truth'. It is even asserted at the outset in Collins's novel that: 'As the judge might once have heard it, so the reader shall hear it now.'[9] There is thus a clear correlation not only between sensation fiction and Gothic writing, but also between both of these genres and the detective novel (see the following section).

The novel's central character is Walter Hartright who is employed as an art teacher to the niece of the wealthy Frederick Fairlie. Walter and his student, Laura, fall in love; she, however, has been promised in marriage to Sir Percival Glyde, a friend of her uncle. In this respect, then, the novel follows the typical trajectory of romance fiction: an obstacle is presented to a couple's love and the narrative works towards the resolution of the couple's dilemma. The Gothicism of the text begins to emerge in the gradual unravelling of

---

* This ideal found one of its most influential contemporary articulations in Coventry Patmore's poem 'The Angel in the House' (1854), the 'Angel' being the chaste and nurturing wife and mother.

the key 'enigmas': the identity of a mysterious 'woman in white' and the various machinations whereby Sir Percival and his accomplice, Count Fosco, seek to deceive Laura Fairlie of her inheritance once she is married. Although the woman in white is no ghost (she is one Anne Catherick, an inmate of an insane asylum), the narration of her mysterious appearances does evoke a suggestion of the supernatural, much as Ann Radcliffe's Gothic fiction often attributes a spectral quality to certain apparitions without ever employing supernatural devices explicitly. The novel also employs, through this figure, the Gothic device of 'doubling': when Catherick escapes from the asylum and then dies following her recapture by Glyde and Fosco (she suffers heart failure, but it is clear that her persecution by these men is responsible for it), her identity is switched with that of Laura; Laura is confined in Catherick's place in order for Glyde to appropriate her wealth, and Hartright and Laura's half-sister, Marian Halcombe, eventually expose the crime.

The novel's Gothic elements – mysterious apparitions, doubling, the incarcerated woman, the physical and psychological persecution at the hands of a larger-than-life, diabolical villain (Count Fosco is undoubtedly one of the most memorable villains in nineteenth-century fiction) – combine to reveal the deep dysfunction at the heart of a seemingly respectable patriarchal family. Like Ann Radcliffe's Gothic romances of the 1790s, Collins's Victorian Gothic explores the various ways in which patriarchal institutions effaced the identity and agency of women, and Alison Milbank is one of several critics who have seen a deliberate appropriation of Radcliffe's 'female Gothic' in Collins's treatment of gender.[10] Collins, however, attributes to women, through the character of Marian Halcombe, a much more effective capacity for assertive, rational action than is found in the Radcliffean heroine. Indeed, it is in many ways Marian more than Walter who represents the rational focus of the novel:[11] her contribution to the narrative, for example, takes the form of clear-sighted daily diary entries, contemporaneous accounts that are clearly positioned by Collins to carry more authenticity – more legalistic weight, to re-invoke the juridical analogy Collins himself used in respect of this novel – than the later versions furnished from memory by most of the other characters. Her characterisation is complicated, however, by Collins's clear attempt to render her more masculine than feminine in personality and appearance, and in this respect the text does not move too far beyond contemporary gender stereotypes: Marian's rationality and assertiveness are posited as freakish and she thus emerges as something of a peculiar Gothic hybrid – a 'monster', almost. Note the emphasis in this passage on the piercing eyes (a near-universal feature of the villain, or even the vampire, in Gothic fiction) and on Marian's excess of thick, black hair:

> She had a large, firm, masculine mouth and jaw; prominent, piercing, resolute eyes; and thick, coal-black hair, growing unusually low down on her forehead. Her expression – bright, frank and intelligent – appeared, while she was silent, to be altogether wanting in those feminine attractions of gentleness and pliability, without which the beauty of the handsomest woman alive is incomplete. (p. 58)

The reception and circulation of the text, finally, illustrates another aspect of the generic hybridity associated with Gothicism. The previous chapter discussed the popularity of Gothic drama in the 1790s; the Gothic, melodramatic qualities of sensation fiction rendered it suitable for stage adaptation in the 1860s and 1870s and *The Woman in White* was adapted successfully for the theatre. Collins himself, in a preface to an earlier novel, stated that the 'extraordinary accidents and events' of his fiction drew from conventions associated with theatre. The mutability of the Gothic by the mid-nineteenth century is thus evident in the capacity of this one text to shift between literary genres of prose and drama, and between genres of prose fiction such as romance, domestic realism and the sensation novel.

The Gothic and Detective Fiction

Another important instance of the Gothic's generic diversity and hybridity is found in its close relation to the development of crime writing from the 1840s onwards in Britain and America. Indeed, the origin of the detective novel can clearly be seen before the mid-nineteenth century in the Gothic mysteries of Ann Radcliffe. Radcliffe's fiction did not formalise the conventions of detective writing in any overt sense, but her work introduced key elements of what might be termed mystery writing which the detective novel came to draw upon extensively. As Charles Rzepka observes, Radcliffe's most famous fiction of the 1790s, *The Mysteries of Udolpho*, is 'a detective story prototype'.[12] Here is an 'amateur detective', Emily St Aubert, confronted with certain enigmas that she must solve in order to free herself from incarceration and persecution at the hands of the archetypal Gothic villain, Montoni (whose elaborate contrivances anticipate the diabolical cunning of many villains of detective fiction). As in the later work of Poe and Collins, various events seem to evade natural explanation and, indeed, Radcliffe evokes suggestions of the supernatural to exacerbate terror and tension. Each of these mysteries ultimately receives a rational explanation, however, and Radcliffe's insistence upon providing sound, empirical justifications for her perplexing enigmas is certainly a precursor of the detective novel's mode of resolving its complex twists of plot.

The writer associated with the rise of detective fiction in America is Edgar Allan Poe, and the genre is often said to begin with his short story 'The Murders in the Rue Morgue' in 1841. This fiction introduces, in the form of Auguste Dupin, the character of the eccentric, intellectually brilliant hero-detective that was to become the model for later detective heroes such as Arthur Conan Doyle's Sherlock Holmes and Agatha Christie's Poirot. It also establishes some of the key conventions of this genre and illustrates points of cross-over between detective fiction and the Gothic: a gruesome crime is committed in baffling circumstances (two women are violently murdered in a locked apartment); the police initially suspect the wrong man; the detective must carefully interpret a succession of seemingly incongruous details in order to arrive at an ingenious solution to the crime – it was committed not by a man, but by an orang-utan. Two later stories develop further key motifs of the genre. In 'The Purloined Letter' (1845), the solution to a crime lies in the recovery of a stolen document and Dupin's success depends here upon his ability not only to interpret facts, but to understand the psychology of the perpetrator; the detective must identify with the criminal and thus, in a sense, 'double' the criminal, as Holmes in Conan Doyle's later narrative comes to double Moriarty (and, in a more overtly Gothic context, the vampire hunter Van Helsing 'doubles' Count Dracula). This tale moves away from the graphic violence of 'The Murders in the Rue Morgue' and substitutes for it the elaborate mind-games between detective and criminal that came to characterise later detective fiction, especially in its more Gothic manifestations (see Thomas Harris's 1988 *The Silence of the Lambs* and its film adaptation). In 'The Mystery of Marie Roget' (1850), meanwhile, Poe narrates the tale using textual fragments – newspaper clips in this instance – a narrative technique frequently employed by Gothic novelists from Mary Shelley to Bram Stoker.

The writer credited with the development of detective writing in England is Wilkie Collins, whose association with Gothicism through his sensation fiction of the late 1850s and 1860s has already been discussed. In 1868, Collins published a dark, psychologically complex mystery novel which T. S. Eliot claimed to be 'the first and greatest of English detective novels':[13] *The Moonstone* (1868). Like many sensation fictions and most Gothic novels of the period, the text is written from multiple narrative perspectives which enable the reader to piece together the plot and the mysteries it unfolds much in the manner of an amateur detective. Like other Gothic fictions, moreover, the novel symbolises the violence and psychopathology not only of certain human beings, but of the wider culture which they inhabit. The novel begins in 1799 with the theft by John

Herncastle, an officer of the British army, of a sacred Hindu diamond, the moonstone. This diamond had been set in a statue of the Hindu moon god and was guarded by three Brahmins; Herncastle killed the Brahmins and returned to England with the jewel. Herncastle is presented as a character with few redeeming features and his crime is related to a wider colonial context of violent occupation and exploitation of the east by the imperial powers.

The narrative of *The Moonstone* shifts forward to contemporary England. The jewel has been presented to the aristocratic Rachel Verinder by her suitor, Franklin Blake. Overnight it goes missing from her room and the famous detective, Sergeant Cuff, is engaged to solve the case. Brilliant as Cuff is, however, he does not succeed in finding the thief and in this respect the novel reveals another aspect of its strong generic relation to Victorian Gothicism. The man who unravels the mystery of the moonstone is a scientist, Ezra Jennings. The meticulous depiction of his extraordinary skill in the new Victorian science of forensic detection establishes a key convention of the detective novel, but Jennings is a deeply conflicted character whose commitment to science is combined with a visionary sensibility, an imaginative, Romantic and dream-like quality that estranges him in many ways from his contemporaries. Jennings's appearance likewise alienates him from respectable bourgeois society; he looks much older than his years, is exceptionally thin and tall, and his hair is half black, half white. He appears almost spectral and is regarded with suspicion by a culture that scapegoats and outcasts him. Jennings is also posited as a racially 'othered', colonial subject: he grew up in the colonies and is of mixed parentage. He is, additionally, an opium addict, and this novel was written in the aftermath of the colonial opium wars between Britain and China (1839–42). The British Empire profited immensely from the opium trade in the Far East and the backdrop to this was widespread addiction at home and in the colonies. The opium context ultimately provides the solution to the mystery of the moonstone. Jennings proves with considerable scientific rigour that Franklin – also an addict – stole the diamond whilst under the influence of the drug.

Science thus ambivalently combines with and contests a wider culture of pathology, exploitation and addiction. In this respect, *The Moonstone* anticipates later *fin de siècle* and modern Gothic fictions (discussed in the following chapter) that use Gothic motifs of hybridity, psychological trauma and excess in order to interrogate the unstable politics of an empire in decline

Nineteenth-century American Gothic

Along with British Romanticism, the Gothic took root in America early in the nineteenth century where it developed into a distinct form suited to the articulation and interrogation of nationally specific tensions and anxieties. America during this period was in the process of forming for itself a national identity apart from Europe; out of this process a certain myth of origin and identity emerged that stressed America's unique commitment to reason, commerce and liberty.[14] Underlying this idealisation of America as a self-made, entrepreneurial, free society, however, were deep conflicts pertaining to religious expression, class and race. These conflicts are evident in the psychologically complex Gothic narratives of Charles Brockden Brown, Nathaniel Hawthorne and Edgar Allan Poe. Brown's *Wieland* (1798) is based on the 1781 case of a farmer who, after hearing 'divine voices', murdered his wife and children. Brown's novel is narrated by Clara Wieland, the sister of Theodore Wieland who murders his own wife and children under apparently divine influence and then commits suicide. Brown adds a significant, highly Gothic detail to the plot, however; a traveller named Francis Carwin infiltrates the Wieland household and carries out various acts of deception using his talent as a ventriloquist, though he adamantly denies being the 'voice' behind the murderous command to Wieland. Whilst the text thus resists straightforward religious interpretation in terms of the actual demonic possession of Theodore, it is clear that Theodore's intense religious fundamentalism makes him deeply vulnerable to suggestion – even to the verge of madness – once the equivocal stranger appears in the family: Theodore is, in a sense, 'possessed'. The text thus plays out tensions in the complex religious life of the new republic; Wieland's father migrated to America from Germany in order to be able to pursue freely the same idiosyncratic, fundamentalist beliefs that make the younger Wieland so tragically susceptible to what might well have been simply the malicious machinations of a stranger. The pursuit of religious freedom in the new world thus turns into a drama of murder and self-destruction that ends with the surviving members of the Wieland family escaping back to the old world, to Europe.

Nathaniel Hawthorne's *The Scarlet Letter* (1850) depicts the paranoia and persecutions that characterise an early Puritan community in Massachusetts. The protagonist, Hester Prynne, is made a scapegoat by this community on account of her adultery and the birth of her illegitimate daughter, Pearl. Hester is made to wear a scarlet letter 'A' to symbolise her sin: the extent of her psychological victimisation by this community is reminiscent of early English, highly political Gothic novels such as William Godwin's *Caleb Williams*. The text, however, manipulates the symbolism of the scarlet letter so dexterously and ambivalently that it seems to slip away from its original signification – it could, ultimately, mean 'Angel'.[15] Hester's name also signifies warmth and nurturance, and it is made clear that Hester possesses these qualities in far greater abundance than the men and women who terrorise her and her daughter. Hawthorne's text exposes the gap between appearance and reality in this society, as well as the hypocrisy and paranoia that characterise the 'respectable' Puritan ancestors of Hawthorne's contemporary America.

The writer most closely associated with the rise of American Gothic in this century is Edgar Allan Poe, who was heavily influenced by the British Romantic poets (his 1845 poem *The Raven*, for instance, evokes strongly the Gothic Romantic writings of John Keats). Poe is best known for his Gothic short stories and his work did much to develop and popularise the short story as a form especially suited in many ways to the narration of Gothic tales. Poe's fiction also renegotiates, in an American mid-nineteenth-century context, many of the themes of early British Gothicism and, crucially, he domesticates these themes; his narratives in many ways suggest the pathology of middle- and upper-class social and family life at this historical moment. 'The Fall of the House of Usher' (1839) is perhaps the exemplary text in this regard and, like many Gothic narratives of this period in Britain and America, it seems to anticipate psychoanalytic accounts of the subconscious that emerged some half a century later. Indeed, an edition of Poe's work was published in 1933 with an introduction by Sigmund Freud. 'The Fall of the House of Usher' begins with the narrator's arrival at the large family house of his boyhood friend, Roderick Usher, a man who is clearly suffering from a variety of neurotic disorders. The house is a typical Gothic space: gloomy, isolated and crumbling, it is reminiscent of the Gothic castles of late eighteenth-century Gothic romance, with the added twist that Roderick believes the house to possess a malevolent consciousness of its own. Roderick, says the narrator, 'is enchained by certain superstitious impressions in regard to the dwelling' that, combined with some 'constitutional and family evil' virtually incapacitates him.[16]

The text thus anticipates later Gothic narratives (Henry James's 1898 *The Turn of the Screw*, for instance) in which a house is not so much haunted as itself haunting its inhabitants. The house, moreover, is the embodiment of the fading power of the Usher dynasty, and its malevolent influence over Roderick suggests the destructive hold of the past over the last remaining heirs of the family. The expression the 'house of Usher' refers not only to the family mansion, but to the Usher dynasty which from the outset is portrayed as a corrupted, dysfunctional, dying entity. Roderick and his twin sister, Madeline, are both suffering from strange illnesses that the narrator intimates might be attributed to the intermarriage of the family; the aristocratic practice of marrying within the family in order to preserve land and status is thus posited as one cause of the paranoia and unrest that is played out literally and symbolically within the 'house of Usher'.

Poe uses the Gothic motif of the double here to represent the protagonist's derangement; Roderick's psyche is deeply and destructively divided, and this finds symbolic expression in various ways. Roderick is in a sense 'doubled' by the house itself which becomes, in critic Edward Davidson's words, 'the symbolic embodiment of this individual'.[17] He is 'doubled' also by his twin with whom he shares 'sympathies of a scarcely intelligible nature'. There is a hint of perversity here, possibly incest or at least an extraordinary subconscious connection that seems to turn the two of them into one monstrous, conflicted figure.[18] Madeline can be seen to represent symbolically a part of Roderick's psyche that he has cut off from himself and that he ultimately attempts to destroy, and the symbolism of Madeline's grotesque live burial is key here. Roderick announces that Madeline is dead and enlists the narrator's help in burying her in a deep vault that is located directly beneath Roderick's bedroom. The tense, dislocated narration of this dreadful event gives Poe's tale the quality of 'an exemplary case study in classic Freudian pathography'.[19] Following the burial, Roderick's behaviour becomes increasingly disordered until he reveals that his sister was not in fact dead when she was buried; she eventually escapes and her 'enshrouded figure' – emaciated and covered in blood – appears during a violent storm. In her dramatic return from the dead (and the scene here bears all the hallmarks of Gothic 'terror' writing that Poe inherited from Ann Radcliffe), Madeline symbolises what psychoanalytic theory would later term 'the return of the repressed': Roderick's gesture of self-denial and repression fails and he is confronted with the aspect of his own disordered self that he had sought to disavow. Madeline's final death agony claims Roderick's life too; she embraces him violently and the two fall to the ground dead. At this moment, the building itself begins to crumble and collapse; the narrator flees for his life and turns back only once to see 'the walls of the mansion come crashing down ... and the deep, dank tarn close sullenly and silently over the fragments of the House of Usher'. The literal and figurative 'fall of the house of Usher' is complete and even the narrator admits that he has been 'infected' by it. The composed rationality of the narrator (and by implication that of the culture he represents) is severely compromised by events that cannot be isolated and explained as a unique consequence of one family's neuroses: these events symbolise the cultural inheritance of the narrator – and the contemporary American reader.

Extended Commentary: Stevenson, *The Strange Case of Dr Jekyll and Mr Hyde* (1886)

This analysis considers a novel of the early *fin de siècle* that has, like *Frankenstein* and *Dracula*, become an iconic Gothic text since its publication in 1886: Robert Louis Stevenson's *The Strange Case of Dr Jekyll and Mr Hyde*. This text brings into focus a number of key points pertaining to the development of and transformations within Gothicism during the Victorian period, many of which have been considered already in this chapter. The novel can be read as a complex psychological study of the 'split self'. Like Poe's Roderick Usher, Jekyll has an aspect of his personality that he seeks to conceal and repress, though in this instance the doctor finds a means to allow the repressed 'other' to emerge. In addition, the narrative domesticates Gothic terror and, through the grotesque transformation of a seemingly ordinary, respectable man, functions to interiorise monstrosity. As Andrew Smith observes, 'one of the most telling characteristics of the Gothic from the 1790s to the 1890s concerns the progressive internalisation of "evil"'.[20] This is indeed one of the most significant motifs of Victorian Gothic on both sides of the Atlantic. In most of the texts that have been considered in this chapter, there is a sense in which the monster lives within the protagonist; the threat of evil does not emanate from 'externally manifested sources of danger', as Smith puts it,[21] but from within the body and mind of individuals in recognisable, contemporary social situations. This Gothic turn inwards (reflecting, amongst other things, the increasing Victorian secularisation of 'evil' through discourses of psychology and anthropology) finds possibly its consummate contemporary expression in Stevenson's novel.

Like other Gothic fictions of the period, *The Strange Case of Dr Jekyll and Mr Hyde* is narrated from multiple viewpoints. The first portion of the tale is related in the third person from the narrative perspective of a lawyer named Utterson. Utterson fulfils a narrative function similar to that of Brontë's Lockwood in *Wuthering Heights*; these sensible men of law provide a stable focus for the narration of increasingly extraordinary events, whilst their rationality and ordinariness at the same time render the events yet more peculiar and terrifying. In this first part, the characters of Hyde and Jekyll are introduced and there are various suggestions that the two are connected. A friend of Utterson, Enfield, is presented with a cheque from Hyde in the name of Jekyll, for example, and Enfield assumes that Jekyll is being blackmailed by Hyde. The section ends with the death of another friend of Utterson and Jekyll, Dr Lanyon. The death appears to be connected in some way with the mystery surrounding Jekyll and Hyde, and Utterson acquires two documents written by Lanyon and Jekyll that he is instructed not to open unless Jekyll either dies or disappears. The second and third parts of the narrative consist of these two documents, read by Utterson after Jekyll has indeed disappeared. Lanyon's document is a first-person account of his discovery of Jekyll's secret; the final narrative is Jekyll's own 'statement of case'. He describes his discovery of a chemical formula that enables him to metamorphose into his monstrous double, Hyde. Hyde is described throughout as a brutish, atavistic being with a disturbing simian appearance who appears to be entirely at the mercy of his increasingly violent and, finally, murderous passions. As Jekyll's experiments with his double identity become more frequent, he is increasingly unable to control them; the novel ends with Jekyll apparently on the verge of transforming permanently into Hyde. A most uncanny feature of this mode of narration is that the 'I' of the narrative – Jekyll – speaks of his impending death as if the final transformation into Hyde is a kind of suicide or murder, and he speculates about the fate of Hyde as if this creature were quite a separate entity from himself. There is no direct narration from Hyde in the text and thus Hyde is 'othered' or, to play on the implications of his name, hidden from the reader.

There are, as the wealth of critical material on this text demonstrates, a number of possible readings of this complex narrative. A point of access into the text is to consider its most striking and innovative Gothic aspect – the monstrous 'doubling' of Jekyll by Hyde. The Gothic motif of doubling appears to work in this novel so as to project the inner, monstrous aspect of Jekyll outward in the form of a creature that simultaneously is and is not Jekyll. The immense physical and psychological differences between Hyde and Jekyll signify a distance between the two of them and it would be overly reductive to read the 'monster' simply as a version of Jekyll that has had to be kept hidden and that finally finds release through the chemical formula. The twenty-first-century discourse of pop psychology and self-help might assert that Hyde is the 'real' Jekyll, and that the doctor is simply posing as a proper English gentleman to conceal the fact that the monster is his 'authentic' self. Stevenson's narrative is more sophisticated than this, however; it queries not only the authenticity of the respectable, professional, middle-class Jekyll, but the stability *per se* of the sort of subjectivity that Jekyll represents. The persona of Jekyll is just that – a persona, a provisional 'self' constructed through an observance of certain contemporary social conventions. The opening narrative, told from the perspective of Utterson and involving several members of the professional classes of London, emphasises the importance to these men of social ritual and convention. There appears to be an emptiness to these rituals, however, that is suggested especially by the description of Utterson's relationship with his friend Enfield. The two go walking every Sunday and 'put the greatest store by these excursions', but they say nothing to each other and seem utterly bored by each other's company. None of the characters in fact has close friendships and the prevailing ethos of the society depicted here is perhaps summed up by Mr Utterson's motto: 'I let my brother go to the devil in his own way.'[22]

Andrew Smith observes that the novel 'can easily be caricatured as merely being about the warring factions within Dr Jekyll'.[23] The above analysis suggests that this is, indeed, a simplistic misreading of a text that is critically engaged with its social and political milieu. Through its representations of transformation and otherness, the text expresses deep anxieties in late Victorian culture pertaining to differences of class, race and the existential status of the 'human'. The animalistic appearance and savage behaviour of Hyde, for example, reflects the emergence in the 1870s of the Darwinian theory of evolution that posits an association between the human and the animal that was disconcerting to middle-class Victorian sensibilities. Darwin asserted in *The Descent of Man*:

> [Man is] descended from a hairy, tailed quadruped …
> probably descended from an ancient marsupial animal, and
> this through a long series of diversified forms, from some
> amphibian-like creature, and this again from some fish-like
> animal.[24]

Seen within this context, Hyde can be understood in evolutionary terms as a throw-back to an earlier stage in the development of the species; in Utterson's words, 'the man seems hardly human! Something troglodytic, shall we say?' (p. 16). Jekyll's increasingly chaotic and uncontrollable transformations into Hyde suggest the contemporary fear that man might indeed regress to a more primitive state under the influence of certain social, cultural and scientific forces. This fear of species degeneration was implicated in, and in many ways the product of, a colonial imperialist ideology that regarded the white race as superior and that opposed any form of racial miscegenation precisely on the grounds that it would lead to a degeneration of the species. Jekyll's transformations can thus be read as a form of miscegenation that turns the 'civilised', middle-class, white Jekyll into the darker skinned, 'savage' Hyde. At the same time, however, the text arguably cuts against a racist ideology that it appears initially, in its depiction of Hyde especially, to uphold. This is because the novel comes to question profoundly the notion of a stable human identity constructed through categories of racial and (as is discusssed below) class differences. The terms civilised and savage as applied to Jekyll and Hyde were placed in inverted commas in the preceding text. This is to signal that the integrity of these terms cannot be take for granted in Stevenson's novel; the ostensibly 'civilised' person of Jekyll slips with increasing ease into the ostensibly 'savage' person of Hyde and the line between 'civilisation' and 'savagery' as mutually opposed categories becomes impossible to maintain. The subversive suggestion, of course, is that Jekyll always was Hyde – the chemical transformations simply realise an aspect of Jekyll's (and his white, bourgeois culture's) own highly contingent 'self'.

Another way to read the unstable dichotomy here between Jekyll and his other is in terms of class differences and what they would have signified, potentially, to a middle-class reader in the 1880s. Certain areas of Victorian London (notably the East End) were notorious for criminal and quasi-legal activities: prostitution, gambling, alcohol and opium consumption, and so on. These deprived areas were largely the province of the working classes who had little choice but to live and work within them, but they were also frequented by many middle- and upper-class men (and some women) who sought to engage in the sort of transactions strictly forbidden within mainstream society. For Jekyll, Hyde becomes a means to explore with apparent impunity the dangerous pleasures of this other world. Again, the ease with which the identity of Jekyll slides into that of Hyde suggests a precariously unstable ideological and geographical distinction between respectable bourgeois society and the working-class criminal underworld. Symbolically, this other world infiltrates and takes over middle-class social space as Hyde takes over the doctor.

Elaine Showalter's influential reading of 'otherness' in Jekyll and Hyde, meanwhile, places the novel within the context of Victorian attitudes towards male homosexuality, which was made an imprisonable criminal offence in 1885.[25] The social world inhabited by Jekyll is entirely male; all the characters are bachelors and women figure only as domestic servants. Showalter's argument is that the social bonding of this close male grouping demands the repudiation of any suggestion of homoeroticism, even though the text repeatedly reproduces certain key cultural codings that would have been taken to allude to homosexuality in the 1880s: thus, Hyde's 'pleasures' are accompanied by 'morbid shame'; there is deemed to be 'something unspeakable' about Hyde who evokes in men both disgust and fascination (Utterson becomes mentally 'enslaved' by Hyde and dreams of him appearing at Jekyll's bedside). Hyde represents another demonised Victorian other according to this analysis and Jekyll's transformation is a symbolic working out of the consequences of sexual repression and persecution at the *fin de siècle*.

Notes

1   See, for example, David Punter, *The Literature of Terror* (London: Longman, 1996) and Andrew Smith, *Gothic Literature* (Edinburgh: Edinburgh University Press, 2007).

2   Sandra M. Gilbert and Susan Gubar, *The Madwoman in the Attic: The Woman Writer and the Nineteenth-century Literary Imagination* (New Haven, CT: Yale University Press, 1979), p. 249.

3   See Christopher Frayling, *Vampyres: Lord Byron to Count Dracula* (London: Faber & Faber, 1992).

4   John Polidori, *The Vampyre*, in Anne Williams, *Three Vampyre Tales* (New York: Houghton Mifflin, 2003).

5   James Twitchell, *The Living Dead: A Study of the Vampire in Romantic Literature* (Lexington, MA: Duke University Press, 1981), p. 118.

6   Emily Brontë, *Wuthering Heights* (London: Penguin, 2003), p. 36.

7   This led Eric Solomon to argue that Heathcliff might be Mr Earnshaw's illegitimate son: see 'The Incest Theme in *Wuthering Heights*', *Nineteenth-century Fiction*, 14:1 (1959), pp. 80–3.

8   Quoted in Patrick Bratlinger, *The Reading Lesson: The Threat of Mass Literacy in Nineteenth-century British Fiction* (Bloomington: Indiana University Press, 1988), p. 151.

9   Wilkie Collins, *The Woman in White* (London: Penguin, 1985), p. 33.

10   Alison Milbank, *Daughters of the House: Modes of Gothic in Victorian Fiction* (London: St Martin's Press, 1992), pp. 25–53. See also Tamar Heller, *Dead Secrets: Wilkie Collins and the Female Gothic* (New Haven, CT: Yale University Press, 1992).

11   See Smith, *Gothic Literature*.

12   Charles Rzepka, *Detective Fiction* (Cambridge: Polity Press, 2005), p. 10.

13   Ibid., p. 101.

14   See Allan Lloyd-Smith, 'Nineteenth-century American Gothic', in David Punter (ed.), *A Companion to the Gothic* (Oxford: Blackwell, 2000), pp. 109–21.

15   See Eric Savoy, 'The Rise of American Gothic', in Jerrold E. Hogle (ed.), *The Cambridge Companion to Gothic Fiction* (Cambridge: Cambridge University Press, 2002), p. 179.

16   Edgar Allan Poe, 'The Fall of the House of Usher', in *The Fall of the House of Usher and Other Writings* (London: Penguin, 2003), pp. 95–6.

17   Edward Davidson, *Poe: A Critical Study* (London: Belknap Press, 1957), p. 79.

18   Scott Brewster, 'Gothic and the Madness of Interpretation', in Punter (ed.), *A Companion to the Gothic*, p. 286.

19   Ibid., p. 285.

20   Smith, *Gothic Literature*, p. 87.

21   Ibid.

22   Robert Louis Stevenson, *The Strange Case of Dr Jekyll and Mr Hyde* (London: Penguin, 2003), p. 5.

23   Smith, *Gothic Literature*, p. 100.

24   Charles Darwin, *The Descent of Man* (London: Wordsworth Classics, 1998), p. 311.

25   Elaine Showalter, *Sexual Anarchy: Gender and Culture at the Fin de Siècle* (London: Viking, 1990).

From the *Fin de Siècle* to Modern Gothic: Stoker, Wells, M. R. James and Lovecraft

This chapter considers developments in Gothic fiction in the period from the 1880s and 1990s (the Victorian *fin de siècle*) to the Second World War. Whilst the decades of the *fin de siècle* produced some of the most iconic Gothic texts in the tradition[*] the years associated with the emergence of literary Modernism (from the early 1900s to the 1930s) have often not been considered to be especially fruitful in terms of literary Gothicism. Part of the reason for this undoubtedly has to do with the literary and cultural status of Modernism; associated with a 'high' literary aesthetic, Modernism tended to define itself, and later to be defined by critics against 'low' forms of popular fiction such as Gothic, the detective novel and so on. In this respect it is possible to identify a conceptual and historical connection between a Modernist antipathy towards Gothicism and the Romantic hostility towards 'low' culture discussed in Part Three: 'Romantic-era Gothic'. The Romantic and Modernist movements were both motivated to differentiate themselves from modes of writing perceived to be formulaic, sensationalistic and lacking intellectual seriousness. The prevailing critical view until recently supported this disassociation of Modernism from Gothicism; before the beginning

---

[*]   Stevenson's *The Strange Case of Dr Jekyll and Mr Hyde*, discussed in the previous chapter, is an early *fin de siècle* work and Stoker's *Dracula* and Wilde's *The Picture of Dorian Gray* were published during this period and are both discussed here.

of the twenty-first century, critics did not tend to emphasise any points of cross-over between the two and the Gothic was not deemed to have much of a literary presence in English and American culture between 1900 and the Second World War. It is perhaps telling, therefore, that an area in which the Gothic was identified as having a presence and, indeed, a substantial influence, was in relation to certain genres of European and American cinema (German expressionism in the 1920s, and horror film in the 1930s, for example): before film had acquired sufficient intellectual authority to figure in academic discourse, cinema could safely be acknowledged to have incorporated 'low-brow' Gothicism.

Two critical studies from the first decade of the twenty-first century have sought to remedy previous oversights in this regard: John Riquelme's *Gothic and Modernism* (2008) and Andrew Smith's and Jeff Wallace's *Gothic Modernisms* (2001).[1] These studies identify a distinct Gothic strain within the Modernist movement (the vampiric imagery in T. S. Eliot's *The Waste Land*, for example) and illustrate the extent to which the Modernist emphasis upon individual and cultural alienation and disorder drew implicitly upon key Gothic tropes, themes and motifs. Writers of the Modernist period who are not widely considered practitioners of the Gothic, moreover, often used its narrative strategies overtly to articulate the alienation, dislocation and, indeed, the monstrousness of Western modernity. Rudyard Kipling, for example, used the ghost story format to narrate the brutality of the British colonial project as early as 1890 in 'The Mark of the Beast' (see Part Four: 'Nation and Empire'). The influence also ran the other way; the empty, alienated voices that narrate many of M. R. James's and H. P. Lovecraft's horror stories in the early to mid-twentieth century suggest a distinct Modernist strain within Gothicism in this period.

This chapter considers the movement from late nineteenth-century to Modern Gothic and foregrounds those aspects of *fin de siècle* and early twentieth-century fictions that express and interrogate specifically modern concerns. Whilst these texts may embody distinct elements of earlier Victorian Gothicism, they are read here predominantly as responding to a rapidly shifting political and cultural landscape and as gesturing towards the tensions and anxieties of mid-twentieth-century Europe and America, especially in the aftermath of two world worlds and the advent of the nuclear age.

Gothic in the 1890s: Disease and Degeneration

The extended commentary at the end of the previous chapter considered the extent to which the representation of Hyde in Stevenson's 1886 novel was influenced by contemporary theories of species degeneration. In 1896 the anxieties occasioned by certain interpretations of Darwin's account of evolution reached their highest pitch with the publication of Max Nordau's *Degeneration*, the language and tone of which is distinctly Gothic; Nordau warns that the whole of civilisation is under threat from nameless forces of destruction that 'wrap all objects in a mysterious dimness, in which all certainty is destroyed and any guess seems plausible … The day is over, the night draws on.'[2] Other discourses in this period (Cesar Lombroso's theory of criminal anthropology, for example) emphasise the perceived inherent criminality or deviance of certain types of individual, or even the susceptibility of all individuals to degeneration under certain conditions. These pseudo-scientific theories were invariably refracted through Victorian ideologies of class and race according to which certain social and racial groups were considered to have a much greater tendency towards degeneration than others; Gothic narratives often articulate these ideologies, featuring villainous protagonists who are meant to display their 'degeneration' to the reader by means of physical characteristics related to their class or race.

Oscar Wilde's *The Picture of Dorian Gray* (1891) resembles Robert Louis Stevenson's *The Strange Case of Dr Jekyll and Mr Hyde* in projecting outwards the symptoms of its protagonist's degeneration; in one of the most famous instances of Gothic 'doubling', Dorian remains young and beautiful whilst his portrait not only ages, but becomes hideously deformed as Dorian's behaviour becomes more uncontrolled and violent. The capacity for an individual to degenerate under the influence of forbidden desires that cannot, nevertheless, be denied is darkly alluded to in the novel by Sir Henry who articulates a version of what would soon become Freud's theory of repression: 'Resist [temptation]', he tells Dorian, 'and your soul grows sick with longing for the things it has forbidden to itself, with desire for what its monstrous laws have made monstrous and unlawful.'[3] Henry's point is that civilisation renders certain desires 'monstrous' and creates conditions which induce pathology in individuals who seek at all costs to repel those desires; a significant subtext here, as with Stevenson's novel, is the criminalisation of homosexuality – a 'monstrous law' that psychologically cripples homosexual men. The text cuts against its implicit interrogation of these 'monstrous laws', however, by depicting Dorian as unable to resist any temptation; he becomes the embodiment of moral deformity. The narrative derived its horror from contemporary fears concerning the instability of the self, its susceptibility to internal, irrational and amoral forces, and its capacity for total dissolution under their influence, all demonstrated by its anti-hero Dorian.

A vivid and more violent expression of the horror of degeneration and dissolution in this period is Arthur Machen's *The Great God Pan* (1894), a text that is rather neglected today in spite of its popularity in the mid-1890s. The text articulates and symbolises a range of nineteenth-century, and specifically *fin de siècle*, concerns: the power of science in the hands of amoral men; the fading influence of the Christian religion; and the capacity for violence that appeared to reside within humanity beneath the thin veneer of civilisation. A scientist in the mould of Victor Frankenstein carries out an experiment on the brain of a young woman which has bizarre occult results: she becomes able to commune with spirits. This ability destroys her reason and health, and she dies shortly after giving birth to a daughter who is intimated to be the offspring of the god Pan. The child initiates a series of violent suicides amongst professional men of the West End by apparently conjuring up spirits and engaging in 'nameless infamies' with them. The text also cleverly manipulates the reader's anxieties about violent crime in London by setting the killings in 1888 – the year of the 'Ripper' murders in Whitechapel. The 'Ripper' scenario is reversed as the woman's apparently demonic sexuality violently destroys the respectable West End men who might well have been the clients of the victims of the Ripper. The text does not make it clear, however, whether the supernatural interventions are real or imagined and this tension between haunting and hallucination, madness and monstrosity is evident in later works by Henry James, M. R. James and H. P. Lovecraft.

Modernity and Monstrosity

The fictions for which H. G. Wells is most famous were written during the 1890s, yet their thematic and stylistic concerns anticipate powerfully the conflicts, anxieties and literary movements of the later modern period. Wells produced two influential novellas which were implicated in contemporary debates concerning the origin and ultimate fate of the human species, and the growing ability of science to manipulate and transform matter. At the same time, they have a dark, apocalyptic quality that makes them appear decidedly modern: they are *The Time Machine* (1895) and *The Island of Dr Moreau* (1896). Before considering Wells's innovative engagements with *fin de siècle* concerns, it is necessary to examine the generic status of these narratives. They have been classified as amongst the first examples of science fiction and Wells was indeed conscious of creating a new genre of literature along these lines. This begs the question as to whether either of these works can rightly be termed 'Gothic'. Several critics have identified a close generic relation between science fiction and Gothicism,[4] and Wells himself was alive to the origin of his new form of fiction in the Gothic narratives of the previous century. He observed, 'It occurred to me that instead of the usual interview with the devil or a magician, an ingenious use of scientific patter might with advantage be substituted.'[5] The diabolical villain who persecutes innocents in earlier modes of Gothic becomes in science fiction the scientist who persecutes life itself and who is often located in the sort of gloomy, isolated Gothic space that easily becomes the external embodiment of his paranoia. *Frankenstein* is the clear prototype here and many critics have described Shelley's novel as the first work of science fiction, with the novels of H. G. Wells following its example some eighty years later.

The Time Machine was one of the first fictions to consider the possibility of time travel and to use representations of future human life to explore contemporary concerns (as science fiction has tended to do ever since). The novel, innovatively for the period, posits time as a fourth dimension through which it might be possible to travel as through the three dimensions of space. The protagonist constructs a time machine and journeys many millions of years into the future. He finds himself inhabiting a civilisation apparently populated by a peaceful, beautiful, egalitarian race known as the Eloi. The civilisation is characterised by a childlike playfulness and innocence, and an absence of any real physical or intellectual exertion; the protagonist – asserting his own strong Victorian work ethic – considers the race charming, but indolent and primitive. Speculating along the lines of Darwinian theory, he concludes that evolution has worked upon humanity to eliminate any need for strife and competition and, therefore, any further form of social and intellectual progress. Thus, although the community appears idyllic, it is presented by the time traveller as primitive and rather decadent – it constitutes (again by Victorian standards) a regression from a higher state of civilisation in spite of its apparent tranquillity and equality. It therefore stands, one could argue, as a warning to idealists in Wells's time who conceived of human development in terms of the gradual elimination of risk and hard work. The text expresses the concern that what was conceived as scientific and social 'progress' might in fact tend towards the opposite – towards languor, stasis and ultimately degeneration.

However, the protagonist slowly discovers that the Eloi civilisation is not the safe, tranquil idyll it initially appears. The Eloi are preyed upon by a carnivorous, subterranean race called Morlocks; dark skinned, muscular and brutally violent, the Morlocks are the antithesis of the Eloi and the time traveller again projects on to these people a Darwinian account of their existence. Abandoning his original scientific appraisal of the world of the Eloi, he concludes that the division between Eloi and Morlock is a remnant of the class divide between nineteenth-century capitalists and labourers. These classes have evolved – or devolved – into two varieties of human as distinct as to almost constitute two species. Although the protagonist does not state as much directly, the assumption is that the capitalist class became so corrupted by their increasing wealth and privilege that they ultimately lost the capacity to manage their society effectively; the increasing brutalisation of the labourers, conversely, transformed them into a race of savages who now hunt and kill the Eloi for food. The economic and social milieu of late nineteenth-century England is thus stripped down to expose its latent tendency towards violent degeneracy, and the organisation of space in the novel (the upper/lower worlds of the Eloi/Morlocks) symbolises the increasingly stark division of Victorian public space into the comfortable, well-ordered bourgeois areas of residence and commerce, and the overcrowded urban slums of the working class. Thus the novel may be read, in the words of critic W. Warren Wagar, as 'a parable of class struggle'.[6]

The novel ends with the protagonist journeying yet further through time, and the narration of his travels presents an apocalyptic account of the end of life on earth presented in terms that powerfully evoke late Victorian discourses of degeneration and anticipate the dystopian visions of the mid-to-late twentieth century. Max Nordau's account of a 'dark night' populated by formless, monstrous shapes becomes a reality in Wells's fiction as the narrator witnesses the demise not only of human civilisation, but of the earth itself. The sun grows dimmer; the earth becomes a freezing, dark, near lifeless environment. The narrator is petrified by the sight of this alien landscape that was once humanity's home and comments plaintively on the removal of all signs of human existence:

> All the sounds of man, the bleating of sheep, the cries of birds, the hum of insects, the stir that makes the background of our lives – all that was over. A horror of this great darkness came upon me ... a deadly nausea seized me.[7]

He is finally stirred to action by the sight of a monstrous form that seems to be devoid of the capacity for wilful action; it is simply a sickening blob of matter that 'hops fitfully about'. Wells's depiction of this dreadful thing – living matter in its most incomprehensible, apparently purposeless mode – provided a significant precedent for the horror fiction of H. P. Lovecraft some forty years later and his broader vision of apocalypse influenced fiction and film considerably in later years. Moreover, the narrative is replete with Gothic imagery. The protagonist is in a state of abject terror as the vision of life's dissolution unfolds before him. Earth is gloomy, 'crawling with foul, slow-stirring monsters', hung over with 'a sense of appalling desolation': earth has become a Gothic space.

Wells returned to the themes of degeneration and apocalypse the following year in *The Island of Dr Moreau*. The novel is narrated by a well-to-do English gentleman named Edward Prendick who, like the frame narrator Wells uses in *The Time Machine* (and similar to Brontë's Lockwood and Collins's Hartright in earlier fictions), acts as a recognisable point of reference for the reader. Prendick is shipwrecked in the Far East and rescued by a ship carrying a cargo of live animals to Moreau's island. Moreau is a disgraced vivisectionist forced to leave England who has transformed the island into a grotesque dystopia populated by the mutant results of his experiments, including a community of hybrid 'beast-men' controlled by Moreau. He reveals to Prendick that his ambition is to create a fully-formed human out of an animal; to replicate, in other words, the Darwinian process of evolution. Moreau's attempts at human generation, however, result only in *de*generation;

he laments that 'the stubborn beast flesh grows, day by day, back again'. Moreau's dystopia is evocative of Max Nordau's description of Western civilisation succumbing to chaos and disintegration as 'forms lose their outlines, and are dissolved in floating mist'. Against this chaotic dissolution of boundaries, Prendick seeks to re-assert the stable values and carefully delineated categories of his native England, but significantly Prendick finds himself 'degenerating' under the influence of the beast-men. As in earlier Gothic narratives of the 1880s and 1890s, there is shown to be no clear demarcation between the 'civilised' and the 'savage'; even when Prendick does escape back to England, his sanity has been severely compromised and he can no longer fit into his respectable niche in upper-class society. The sailors who transport him back to Europe think he is mad when he tells his story and he acknowledges that he seems to have been infected by some of the 'wildness' of the islanders. Moreover, he is 'haunted' on his return by the possibility that the men and women around him are themselves 'beast people', or at least have the capacity to become such very easily; they appear to him as 'animals half wrought into the outward image of human souls, and that they would presently begin to revert'. This final, evocative passage brings into sharp focus contemporary fears concerning the imminence of humanity's degeneration into sub-humanity:

When I lived in London the horror was well-nigh insupportable. I could not get away from men: their voices came through windows; locked doors were flimsy safeguards. I would go out into the streets to fight with my delusion, and prowling women would mew after me; furtive, craving men glance jealously at me; weary, pale workers go coughing by me with tired eyes and eager paces, like wounded deer dripping blood; old people, bent and dull, pass murmuring to themselves; and, all unheeding, a ragged tail of gibing children. Then I would turn aside into some chapel, – and even there, such was my disturbance, it seemed that the preacher gibbered 'Big Thinks,' even as the Ape-man had done; or into some library, and there the intent faces over the books seemed but patient creatures waiting for prey. Particularly nauseous were the blank, expressionless faces of people in trains and omnibuses; they seemed no more my fellow-creatures than dead bodies would be, so that I did not dare to travel unless I was assured of being alone. And even it seemed that I too was not a reasonable creature, but only an animal tormented with some strange disorder in its brain which sent it to wander alone, like a sheep stricken with gid.[8]

For Prendick, something beast-like already resides within these modern men and women; his descriptions of them are resolutely animalistic and, however much he tries to convince himself that these are 'perfectly reasonable creatures, full of *human* desires [my emphasis]', he cannot escape the appalling conclusion that they have regressed already, or that they always were in some sense degenerate. Note also here how the signifiers of civilised modernity – the 'trains and omnibuses' – are implicated in this discourse of degeneration; commuters are 'blank, expressionless … they seemed no more my fellow-creatures than dead bodies would be'. The beginning of this chapter considered the relation between Gothicism and Modernism; this passage from Wells's text is highly evocative of T. S. Eliot's description of London in one of the foremost texts of Modernism, *The Waste Land*: 'A crowd flowed over London Bridge, so many/ I had not thought death had undone so many'.

Cosmic Horror

An American writer contemporaneous with the Modernist movement and also associated with the rise of science fiction and new forms of Gothic literature is H. P. Lovecraft who used the term 'cosmic horror' to describe a profound experience of dread in the face of a vast, apparently meaningless universe. As he readily admitted, Lovecraft was deeply indebted to the style of Gothic short story developed in the mid-nineteenth century by Edgar Allan Poe (see the previous chapter) and many of Lovecraft's narratives share the disorienting, ambiguous quality of Poe's tales. Lovecraft was concerned to develop his own Gothic aesthetic, however, and in his essay 'The Supernatural Horror in Literature' (first published in 1927) he established the key components of a style that was to have a considerable influence over horror fiction especially in America. Interestingly, this essay is evocative of Ann Radcliffe's essay 'On the Supernatural in Poetry' published a century earlier. This fact is worthy of comment since Radcliffe's aesthetic turned upon what she described as the effect of 'terror'. Terror literature depends upon the evocation of obscurity and ambiguity (the very qualities that characterised much of Poe's writings), whereas horror was, at the time that Radcliffe was writing, associated with a more graphic depiction of violence and the supernatural. Lovecraft echoes Radcliffe's analysis of the terror of the unknown, observing, 'The oldest and strongest emotion of mankind is fear, and the oldest and strongest kind of fear is fear of the unknown.'[9] What Lovecraft designates as 'horror' literature – narratives that evoke this fear of the unknown in various forms (not necessarily supernatural) – thus bears many of the hallmarks of Radcliffean terror: the evocation of 'certain phantasmal shapes' and an 'atmosphere of breathless and unexplainable dread', for instance. It is fair to say, then, that Lovecraft's work marks a break away from the earlier distinction between two modes of Gothic: the Radcliffean division dissolves into a single designation – horror.

Lovecraft's aesthetic of horror was also crucially informed by a world-view that he shared with key writers and philosophers associated with Modernism. The sense of alienation and futility that was increasingly seen to characterise the human condition from the *fin de siècle* onwards was powerfully articulated by Lovecraft in a letter of 1927 in which he asserts that all his fiction is 'based on the fundamental premise that common human laws and interests and emotions have no validity or significance in the wider cosmos-at-large'.[10] This notion of the indifference of the cosmos to humanity is the logical consequence of modern developments in science that stressed the material origins of mankind in impersonal evolutionary forces, and the vastness of a universe governed apparently by chance.* Lovecraft's perception of humanity's irrelevance to the universe, and mankind's despair at this realisation, led him to develop a Gothic literature of 'cosmic horror'. The object of dread in his narratives is invariably an object or process that embodies or symbolises the purposelessness of life in a chaotic, indifferent universe. Whereas in earlier Gothic fiction the central mystery often tended to provoke a misunderstanding that was ultimately rectified, Lovecraft's work more often reveals the maddening impossibility of any understanding of the mystery that confronts the protagonist. In the short story 'Dagon' (1919), the narrator encounters a landscape strongly reminiscent of H. G. Wells's depiction of future earth in *The Time Machine*:

> The region was putrid with the carcasses of decaying fish, and other less describable things which I saw protruding from the nasty mud of the unending plain. Perhaps I should not hope to convey in mere words the unutterable hideousness that can dwell in absolute silence and barren immensity.[11]

The difference between this environment and that represented in Wells's novella is that Lovecraft's putrid region is positioned as contemporaneous with the civilised America of the protagonist. The monsters that emerge in these landscapes, moreover, are often associated not with the future, but with the past; they appear to represent an earlier stage in the evolution of life on earth and also to be associated with earlier cultures that are experienced as profoundly alien and threatening by the narrators of Lovecraft's tales. From this, it might be supposed that these fictions ultimately re-assert the necessity of human progress in conformity with a certain late

---

* Lovecraft was familiar with, and deeply disquieted by, Einstein's theory of relativity, for example.

nineteenth-century colonial ideology; whilst these putrid landscapes and their monsters might continue to exist in uncultivated pockets of the globe, they will be superseded by the forward march of human progress. This notion of progress – of a meaningful human civilisation in opposition to primeval chaos – is precisely what these tales of 'cosmic horror' repudiate, however; in accordance with their author's philosophy, civilisation is posited as no more than a contingent configuration of primeval slime that is destined ultimately to dissolve back into it.

The most influential expression of this apocalyptic vision occurs in the short story 'The Call of Cthulhu'. This tale has acquired cult status since its publication in 1928, generating numerous imitations across various media, including computer role-playing games. The tale follows the typical trajectory of a Lovecraft horror story; a narrator is confronted with a mystery that seems to defy any rational explanation and his investigation of it results in a horrific confrontation with a malign monster or cosmic force that challenges, and often destroys, his reason. The story begins with the narrator recounting the death of his great uncle which seems to be in some way connected with a statue of a grotesque, many-tentacled monster. The narrator learns through various sources that the statue is associated with an occult religion on a remote island which centres on the worship of the monster, known as Cthulhu. According to this cult, Cthulhu has been sleeping for generations and his awakening will signify apocalypse – Cthulhu will devour the earth. The main body of the text is recounted through the reading by the narrator of a manuscript left by a Dutch explorer named Gustaf Johansen. Johansen and his crew encounter the Cthulhu cult, and eventually the monster itself, on a voyage of exploration to the island. The island itself is a disturbing Gothic space, 'non-euclidean, and loathsomely redolent of spheres and dimensions apart from ours'. The monster emerges from a 'monstrously carven portal ... a phantasy of prismatic disorder [in which] all the rules of matter and perspective seemed upset' (p. 166). The 'Thing' is the embodiment of Lovecraftian 'cosmic horror', so dreadful that 'there is no language for such abysms of shrieking and immemorial lunacy, such eldritch [strange] contradictions of all matter, force and cosmic order'. Having read Johansen's account, the narrator is left on the brink of madness no longer able remotely to sustain the ordered, scientific world-view that he had entertained at the outset, a view that prompted his investigations secure in the knowledge that whatever was out there was capable of rational explanation.

To end this discussion of monstrosity and horror in Gothic fictions of the early to mid-twentieth century, it is worth returning briefly to the legacy of H. G. Wells. In 1938, the year after Lovecraft's death, the actor and broadcaster Orson Welles produced a radio adaptation of Wells's *The War of the Worlds* (1898). The radio play used a technique that will be familiar to twenty-first-century readers, though it was much less familiar to the population of New York in 1938: the broadcast presented itself as an authentic news report of an alien landing. It began ostensibly with a music programme that was interrupted by a 'news flash' detailing strange events north of New York. Thousands of New Yorkers took the fictitious news report for real; there was mass panic and a significant proportion of the city's population began to flee their homes. On the eve of the Second World War, and at the end of the Great Depression of the 1930s, it seemed plausible to these New Yorkers that the horrors depicted by Wells might well be playing themselves out in close proximity to their city. The incident is a dramatic illustration of the ability of the Gothic to articulate the monstrous aspects of twentieth-century modernity.

Haunting and Hallucination

The last chapter discussed the extent to which Gothic from the early nineteenth century onwards began to 'interiorise' and 'domesticate' evil. By the end of that century, a key facet of Gothicism as it moved towards modernity and postmodernity was its increasing evocation of disturbed psychological states and the association of these states with the weird, the uncanny and the supernatural. This to some extent reflected the growing scientific and popular interest in the workings of the mind, and such interest in psychology intersected significantly with contemporary discourses of degeneration: human vulnerability to psychological as well as physical deterioration contributed significantly to *fin de siècle* anxieties concerning the regressive tendencies of the individual and the species. Theories of madness, moreover, had a deeply gendered dimension with women considered, by virtue of their biology, to be far more susceptible than men to mental illness, particularly the condition referred to as 'hysteria'.* The doctor who did a great deal to popularise – or, as Elaine Showalter argues, actually to invent – this nervous condition was Jean-Martin Charcot. Charcot was not only a successful doctor, but something of a showman; he staged extravagant exhibitions of his patients and their symptoms which had a distinctly Gothic quality about them. Showalter contends that Charcot 'used techniques that suggested the diabolism of the witch hunt, such as searching for hysterical "stigmata"'.[12] The notion that hysterical women were somehow 'possessed' became a common feature of certain Gothic narratives in this period. The murderous female in Machen's *The Great God Pan*, for example, could be interpreted as presenting 'hysterical stigmata' and the susceptibility of women in Stoker's *Dracula* to vampiric influence is implicitly associated with their tendency towards mental instability (see the extended commentary below).

Gothic fictions thus began to establish a relationship between haunting and hallucination in this period, suggesting that terrors represented as apparently supernatural in origin could be the result of the disordered imagination of the protagonist. A key text here is Henry James's *The Turn of the Screw* (1898) in which it is extremely difficult to interpret the source of weird events mediated through the consciousness of the female protagonist. James's governess is employed to care for two young children in a country manor that appears to be the scene of a grotesque haunting that centres on the

---

* A term derived from the Greek word *hystera*, meaning 'womb'.

boy and girl in her care. The protagonist has visions of the ghosts of the former governess and her lover, the brutish and violent Quint. She becomes increasingly convinced that these ghosts are exerting a diabolical influence over the children, but the narrative continually questions the reliability of the governess's grasp of reality. Indeed, it has been common to read the novel's 'supernatural' elements as a 'projection of her sexual hysteria in the form of stereotypes deeply embedded in the mind of the culture'.[13] These 'stereotypes' arose out of the *fin de siècle* discourse of degeneration; Quint's appearance, for the late nineteenth-century reader, is that of a 'degenerate' physical and mental type (like Stevenson's Hyde) and the governess projects on to Quint her repressed, implicitly degenerate sexual feelings. She thus becomes, as Stanley Renner puts it, 'a virtual Victorian cliché of sexual ambivalence'.[14]

It is not necessarily through women that the Gothic reveals its increasing psychologisation of terror, however. In the fiction of M. R. James, episodes of haunting frequently possess an ambivalent psychological dimension that casts some doubt upon the sanity of highly educated, middle-class men. James has sometimes been relegated almost to a footnote in the development of Gothic fiction; his 'bland tones' and unsubtle regurgitation of 'Gothic stereotypes', moreover, have been seen to subtract from his ghost stories any convincing psychological element.[15] It is nevertheless possible to see in James's work a complex evocation not only of individual mental disorder, but of a wider cultural malaise that relates James to literary Modernism. His protagonists are usually scholarly men who encounter an artefact that turns out to be in some way 'haunted'. James was an enthusiastic antiquarian and he entitled his first two collections of short fictions 'Antiquarian Ghost Stories'. These narratives describe the return of a past atrocity, or superstition, through the antiquarian object in which the protagonists have a scholarly, rational, historical interest. The academic objectivity of the narrators is invariably shattered, however, by the intrusion into their comfortable college enclave of objects which materialise the horrors of the past in the ostensibly civilised present of Edwardian England. The 'bland tones' of James's fiction are crucial to this Gothic psychologisation of terror; the apparent emotional vacuity of the protagonists can be read as a symptom of deep psychological repression that eventually manifests itself through hauntings that symbolise a traumatic, Freudian return of repressed, irrational drives.

The protagonist of James's most famous tale, 'Oh Whistle, and I'll Come to You, My Lad' (1904), is one Professor Parkins who is 'young, neat and precise in speech'. He is represented initially as utterly devoid of imagination and he speaks in such a highly mannered, almost stilted style that he almost seems to be a parody of an emotionless, intellectual Victorian gentleman. Like many of James's protagonists, he has no meaningful family or social life and at the beginning of the narrative he is about to set off alone on a golfing holiday. He is persuaded by a colleague to visit a Templar monument where he finds a metal object which intrigues him. Rather tellingly, he pockets the object concluding that it must be 'of some slight value'; his viewpoint is that of the commodity hunter and his small-scale desecration of the monument here is suggestive of the Gothic theme of a cursed object recklessly appropriated by naive colonial explorers.* Parkins's appropriation of the object signals an immediate shift in the tone of the narrative and in his emotional state; stylistic blandness is replaced with an effective, psychologically nuanced Gothicism:

> Bleak and solemn was the view on which he took a last look before starting homeward. A faint yellow light in the west showed the links, on which a few figures moving towards the club-house were still visible, the squat martello tower, the lights of Aldsey village, the pale ribbon of sands intersected at intervals by black wooden groynes, the dim and murmuring sea. The wind was bitter from the north, but was at his back

---

* Such an idea first appeared in Gothic fiction as early as 1869 in Louisa May Alcott's short story 'Lost in a Pyramid, or the Mummy's Curse'.

when he set out for the Globe. He quickly rattled and clashed through the shingle and gained the sand, upon which, but for the groynes which had to be got over every few yards, the going was both good and quiet. One last look behind, to measure the distance he had made since leaving the ruined Templars' church, showed him a prospect of company on his walk, in the shape of a rather indistinct personage, who seemed to be making great efforts to catch up with him, but made little, if any, progress. I mean that there was an appearance of running about his movements, but that the distance between him and Parkins did not seem materially to lessen ... 'What should I do now,' he thought, 'if I looked back and caught sight of a black figure sharply defined against the yellow sky, and saw that it had horns and wings? I wonder whether I should stand or run for it.'[16]

In spite of Parkins's stern dismissal of ghosts in the opening conversation with his colleague, he is now prepared to entertain the prospect that he might be pursued by some sort of demonic fiend. When he returns to his lodgings, he discovers that the metal tube taken from the monument is a whistle, and he sounds a few notes. The whistle appears to conjure up a ghost that Parkins encounters in his room at the end of the narrative, but what is interesting is the extent to which Parkins's disturbed psychological state can be read as the cause of this manifestation. As soon as he blows the whistle, he closes his eyes and has a disturbing vision that suggests his earlier encounter with the figure on the shore. There is a reference to his 'overworked brain [and] excessive smoking' which conflicts with the ultra-rationality of the protagonist at the beginning of the tale. When the 'ghost' finally appears it has 'a face of crumpled linen' (p. 76), and when another guest arrives to investigate the commotion he finds only Parkins collapsed on the floor next to a pile of bed clothes. The narrator asserts that Parkins 'was somehow cleared of the ready suspicion of delirium tremens' (p. 76) which clearly conveys the possibility that this episode was a hallucination. An apparent haunting thus occasions an interrogation of the sanity of this respectable, ostensibly rational man, and of the propriety and sanity of the culture he embodies.

Extended Commentary: Stoker, *Dracula* (1897)

Like Mary Shelley's *Frankenstein*, *Dracula* has become an iconic Gothic fiction that has generated a popular contemporary mythology of considerable cultural influence. The vampire is probably the most ubiquitous figure in Gothic film and fiction, and frequently acts as a lightning rod for the specific cultural anxieties of the moment. Bram Stoker's text did not initiate the vampire legend in Gothic literature, however; there was considerable interest in vampirism from the late eighteenth century onwards and vampire literature originated in a recognisably modern form during the Romantic period. Indeed, John Polidori's *The Vampyre* (1819) is frequently cited as the first vampire narrative to establish the conventions of this mode of Gothicism; for the critic Christopher Frayling, 'it is probably *the* most influential horror story of all time [and] the first story to fuse the disparate elements of vampirism into a coherent literary genre'.[17]

However, Stoker's novel achieves a combination of elements of vampirism that were firmly established in the popular imagination by 1897 with aspects of modernity that lend to the tale a new dimension altogether. Stoker's text is in various ways implicated in contemporary debates concerning the status of science, the decline of religion, the nature and peculiar vulnerabilities of the human psyche, the position of women and the relationship of the British to other cultural and racial groups. Like other Gothic fictions of the *fin de siècle*, the novel's complex and often conflicted engagements with its social milieu serves to interrogate, or even to render monstrous, the cultural and scientific developments that were coming to characterise Western modernity at the close of the nineteenth century. This is evident in the text's treatment of science, madness, sexuality, religion, class relations and racial 'otherness' as mediated through the figure of the Count and his victims' responses to him.

Dracula's Transylvanian origin is of considerable interest with regard to the wider political context of this novel. Contrary to common belief, as critic Stephen Arata points out, Stoker's location of his vampire in this region of Eastern Europe did not reflect an already established association of vampirism with Transylvania.[18] Dracula's castle was initially to be situated in Styria, the region in which Le Fanu's *Carmilla* had been set twenty years earlier (see Part Four: 'Gothic Bodies'). The shift of location can be understood in terms of the fraught colonial backdrop to Stoker's novel; Transylvania was a region beset by racial strife and the source of considerable anxiety for the British government in the 1880s and 1890s. Dracula himself alludes to this turbulent history in his remark to Jonathan Harker that, 'there is hardly a foot of soil in all this region that has not been enriched by the blood of men, patriots or invaders'.[19] The reference to blood enriching the soil of Dracula's native land anticipates the Count's infiltration of English society and his 'enrichment' by the blood of his victims; Dracula becomes an embodiment of this blood-soaked region, a member of a 'conquering race' whose move to England vividly articulates contemporary concerns regarding what Arata describes as 'reverse colonization' and the decline of Empire.[20]

The elevated class status of Dracula also resonates with the political concerns of the moment. The Count in many ways conforms to earlier Gothic representations of decadent aristocrats whose reliance on inherited wealth allowed them to exert a leaden, one might indeed say vampiric, influence upon a society which perceived socially useful capital (as opposed to wealth tied to land) as the creation of the entrepreneurial bourgeoisie. The Count's aristocratic privilege, in the form of his family's wealth and the cultural superiority associated with his nobility, allows him to infiltrate English society in spite of the strangeness, even ferocity, of his appearance. Moreover, the Count preys especially upon young middle-class women in a manner that symbolically evokes cultural anxieties concerning the sexual exploitation of this group of women by libertine aristocrats, and the inability of middle-class men to defend them. Mina Harker in particular – and she is the exemplary middle-class woman of virtue in the text – suffers an attack by Dracula that is represented in overtly sexual terms:

> Kneeling on the near edge of the bed facing outwards was the white clad figure of his [Jonathan's] wife. By her side stood a tall, thin man clad in black. His face was turned away from us, but the instant we saw we all recognised the Count – in every way, even to the scar on his forehead. With his left hand he held both Mrs Harker's hands, keeping them away with her arms at full tensions; his right arm gripped her by the back of the neck, forcing her face down on his bosom. Her white nightdress was smeared with blood, and a thin stream trickled down the man's bare breast which was shown by his torn-open dress. (p. 247)

The scene is hardly subtle. It is figured symbolically as an act of rape with the signifier of brutalised innocence and virginity (the white robe stained with blood) adding to the horror of the moment. Mina's husband, the middle-class solicitor Jonathan, is present, but utterly immobilised – 'as though in a stupor' – and significantly Mina's rescue depends on the intervention of another European aristocrat, Van Helsing. The episode thus symbolically enacts and reflects unease relating to the impotence of middle-class men before the prowess of the aristocratic male: rapacious and damnable in the case of the Count; heroic and redemptive in the case of Van Helsing.

Female identity and sexuality are deeply problematised in *Dracula*, as the above passage intimates. There is throughout a focus on the quasi-sexual threat which the Count poses to women and the vulnerability of Mina, and especially her friend Lucy Westenra; this threat signals the perceived weakness of women and their need of protection from men. The text engages with contemporary discourses around gender and the position of women which often centre on the late nineteenth-century figure of the 'New Woman'.[*] Mina is the closest to a New Woman figure in the narrative and in many respects she is positively represented; she collaborates with Van Helsing's team in combating Dracula and at times, like Marian Halcombe in Wilkie Collins's *The Woman in White*, she appears more rational and self-possessed than her male associates. Nevertheless, Mina does not stray too far from the stereotype of ideal Victorian femininity and her status as such is essential to the redemptive ending of the novel: Mina's son, 'will some day know what a brave and gallant woman his mother is [and] how some men so loved her, that they did dare much for her sake' (p. 327). Mina, then, is the sort of woman who inspires men to heroism and the novel's closure thus sets the whole narrative of struggle against the vampire in the context of domestic harmony restored. Lucy, on the other hand, is a woman whose psychological and, implicitly, sexual instability threatens to undermine this domestic order. As Lucy falls increasingly under the vampire's influence, she displays many of the characteristics associated with female sexual hysteria as theorised by Jean-Martin Charcot (see the discussion above). Charcot is mentioned in the text by the psychiatrist Dr Seward and Stoker was a great admirer of Charcot's work; his depiction of Lucy under the hypnotic influence of Dracula has many points in common with Charcot's showcasing of hypnotised women at his Parisian surgery. Lucy easily falls into degeneracy and, having become a vampire, her perversity and violence far exceed that of Dracula himself. There are strong parallels here with other Gothic fictions of the period; in *The Island of Dr Moreau*, for example, it is the female hybrids created by Moreau that are the most degenerate and threatening. The trope of the degenerate female reflects the common cultural understanding that women were closer than men to irrationality and animality, and therefore more likely to regress to subhuman states. The response to Lucy's

---

[*] This was a term applied to women who sought independence and education and who campaigned for female emancipation; there was considerable conservative hostility towards the New Woman movement and *Dracula* reflects, at the very least, ambivalence towards it.

degeneration by Van Helsing's team is unequivocal and exceptionally violent; she is murdered with a stake through the heart administered by her fiancé, Arthur, and the scene, like that involving Dracula and Mina cited above, is overtly sexual:

> The Thing in the coffin writhed; and a hideous, blood-curdling scream came from the opened red lips. The body shook and quivered and twisted in wild contortions; the sharp white teeth champed together till the lips were cut, and the mouth was smeared with a crimson foam. But Arthur never faltered. He looked like a figure of Thor as his untrembling arm rose and fell, driving deeper and deeper the mercy-bearing stake, whilst the blood from the pierced heart welled and spurted up around it. His face was set and high duty seemed to shine through it; the sight of it gave us courage, so that our voices seemed to ring through the little vault. (p. 192)

The passage evokes the standard of masculine heroism that is asserted in the final paragraph of the novel; this violent, phallic exorcism of female vampirism re-establishes male potency, opening the way for the final defeat of Dracula and the restoration of proper middle-class domesticity.

The relationship of Dr Seward to his patient, Renfield, is also significant in terms of the novel's treatment of madness. Seward makes a case-study in madness out of Renfield and becomes obsessed with cataloguing the minutiae of his patient's bizarre behaviour. There is a doubling of Renfield in Seward, who admits to his own melancholic, obsessive tendencies: the more he observes Renfield the more he seems drawn towards Renfield's compulsions. This Gothic doubling suggests that Seward is to some extent infected by the madness of Renfield and, since Renfield's madness is increasingly a manifestation of Dracula's influence over him, Seward himself comes indirectly under the hypnotic sway of the Count. Seward is, moreover, a character closely associated with discourses of science and modernity that are themselves rendered suspect through their inability to explain or control the vampiric threat. Seward uses a phonograph to dictate his notes, a modern touch; he is familiar with the latest developments in psychiatry and is the character least disposed to believe in any supernatural explanation of events. Like the male characters stupefied before vampiric power, however, Seward's scientific methodologies are incompetent to deal effectively with the madness afflicting first Renfield (and indirectly Seward himself) and then Lucy. It is Van Helsing who convinces the other men after Lucy's death that this threat is immune to the interventions of modern science; the defeat of Dracula must be achieved through the evocation of religious ritual. It is telling that the exorcism of the undead Lucy – the most brutal, ritualistic moment in the text – is narrated in the diary of Dr Seward: through this ultra-modern man of science, the text simultaneously implicates modernity in, and reveals its utter impotence in the face of, the threat of vampirism.

Notes

1   John Riquelme, *Gothic and Modernism* (Baltimore, MD: Johns Hopkins University Press, 2008); Andrew Smith and Jeff Wallace (eds), *Gothic Modernisms* (London: Palgrave, 2001).

2   Quoted by Glennis Byron, 'Gothic in the 1890s', in David Punter (ed.), *A Companion to the Gothic* (Oxford: Blackwell, 2000), p. 132.

3   Oscar Wilde, *The Picture of Dorian Gray* (New York and London: Norton, 1988), pp. 185–6.

4   David Ketterer, *New Worlds for Old: The Apocalyptic Imagination, Science Fiction and American Literature* (London: Doubleday, 1974); Patrick Bratlinger, 'The Gothic Origin of Science Fiction', *The Novel: A Forum*, 14:1 (1980), pp. 30–43.

5   Bratlinger, 'The Gothic Origin of Science Fiction', p. 32.

6   W. Warren Wagar, *H. G. Wells: Traversing Time* (Middletown, CT: Wesleyan University Press, 2004), p. 49.

7   H. G. Wells, *The Time Machine* (London: Signet Classics, 2009), p. 99.

8   H. G. Wells, *The Island of Dr Moreau* (New York: Barnes & Noble, 2004), p. 132.

9   H. P. Lovecraft, 'The Supernatural Horror in Literature', in Clive
     Bloom (ed.), *Gothic Horror: A Guide for Students and Readers* (London:
     Palgrave, 2007), p. 104.

10   H. P. Lovecraft, *The Call of Cthulhu and Other Weird Stories* (London:
     Penguin, 2002), p. xvi.

11   Lovecraft, 'Dagon', in *The Call of Cthulhu and Other Weird Stories*,
     p. 2.

12   Elaine Showalter, *Hysteries: Hysterical Epidemics and Modern Culture*
     (New York: Columbia University Press, 1997), p. 32.

13   Stanley Renner, 'Sexual Hysteria, Physiognomical Bogeymen, and the
     "Ghosts" in *The Turn of the Screw*', *Nineteenth-century Literature*, 43:2
     (1998), p. 176.

14   Ibid., p. 177.

15   David Punter, *The Literature of Terror*, vol. 2, *The Modern Gothic*
     (London: Longman, 1996), pp. 68, 89.

16   M. R. James, *Casting the Runes and Other Ghost Stories* (Oxford: Oxford
     University Press, 1999), p. 63.

17   Christopher Frayling, *Vampyres: Lord Byron to Count Dracula* (London:
     Faber & Faber, 1991), p. 108.

18   Stephen Arata, *Fictions of Loss in the Victorian Fin de Siècle: Identity and
     Empire* (Cambridge: Cambridge University Press, 1996), p. 113.

19   Bram Stoker, *Dracula* (New York and London: Norton, 1996), p. 34.

20   Arata, *Fictions of Loss in the Victorian Fin de Siècle*, p. 107.

Twentieth-century American Gothic: Faulkner, King, Rice and Brite

Part Three: 'Nineteenth-century Gothic' discussed the development of American Gothic in the 1800s through the work of Charles Brockden Brown, Nathaniel Hawthorne and Edgar Allan Poe. American Gothic was indebted generically to Romantic-era Gothicism in Britain, but it acquired a distinct style and voice during the 1800s in response to its specific literary, cultural and political contexts. This chapter considers the forms taken by, the contexts of and the influences upon American Gothic from the mid-twentieth century to the present day. A fair amount of literary and historical terrain is covered here, but what unites the various sections within this study is the extent to which American Gothic – from Faulkner's 'Southern Gothic' to the horror fiction of Poppy Z. Brite and Stephen King – reflects key historical contexts and conflicts that have shaped, and that continue to shape, the country's political and cultural landscape.

Southern Gothic

The designation 'Southern Gothic' has been applied to a particular, highly influential sub-genre of American literature located in the American South that uses the tropes, motifs and conventions of the

Gothic in order to narrate personal and social traumas that often turn upon events related to the region's turbulent political history, notably (though not exclusively) the legacy of slavery and the American Civil War. As critic Leslie Fiedler put it, 'the essential sociological theme of the American tale of terror ... is slavery and black revenge'.[1] Southern Gothic has its origins in the plantations of the South in the nineteenth century, though it expanded thematically to become associated with the work of some of the foremost dramatists and novelists of the mid-twentieth century – Tennessee Williams, Truman Capote, William Faulkner, Flannery O'Connor – many of whom consciously evoked Gothicism as central to their style and purpose.[*] Tennessee Williams's last play is a tragicomic story of madness and sexual dysfunction entitled *A House Not Meant to Stand: A Gothic Comedy* which Williams described as a 'Southern Gothic spook sonata'.[2] Most of Williams's earlier plays do not evoke the supernatural at all, but their focus on the macabre, paranoid, violent and destructive dimension to family life, and especially sexual relations between men and women, lends a Gothic quality to these works in terms of theme, style and tone: see especially *Cat on a Hot Tin Roof* and *A Streetcar Named Desire*.

The work of Mary Flannery O'Connor likewise tended to eschew conventional representations of the supernatural, but her preoccupation with the grotesque – with disfigurement, estrangement and bizarre distortions of reality – is typical of the Southern Gothic style. O'Connor was especially productive in the genre of the Gothic short story, and many of her tales carry an atmosphere of violence and emotional emptiness that seems often to verge on nihilism. In the story 'A View of the Woods' (1955), for example, a man and his nine-year-old granddaughter live a lonely life together in a state of violent, bitter conflict. The narrative ends shockingly with the grandfather smashing the girl's head against a rock and killing her, before dying himself of a heart attack. In spite of the pessimism of many of her Gothic stories, however, O'Connor

---

[*] A more recent instance of a Gothic negotiation of the legacy of slavery in the USA is Toni Morrison's *Beloved* (1987), discussed in Part Four: 'Nation and Empire'.

was a deeply religious writer who used the Gothic to represent the clash of good and evil, and the reality of sin, that for her characterised the human condition. As Lauren Goodlad observes, 'O'Connor conjures Gothic visions that foremost are symptoms of psychological, psychic and spiritual stress'.[3]

The novelist often credited with originating this sub-genre is William Faulkner in whose work the conflicted racial politics of the South feature prominently. Racial politics, moreover, are frequently refracted through disturbances in families that reverberate and intensify over generations; as in Poe's work (see especially 'The Fall of the House of Usher' discussed in Part Three: 'Nineteenth-century Gothic') there is a vivid sense of the past haunting the present, of earlier misdemeanours returning to curse the family line. Faulkner's exploration of individual, familial and wider societal dysfunction began with a series of novels based in a fictional region of Mississippi named Yoknapatawpha County, the most influential being *Absalom, Absalom!* (1936).[*] Like many Gothic fictions, this novel turns upon the revelation of a family secret that has disastrous consequences as its effects proliferate and poison later generations. The novel narrates from various perspectives the traumatic history of the Sutpen family. Henry Sutpen meets a charming young college student named Charles Bon who visits the family home during a Christmas vacation. Charles falls in love with Henry's sister, Judith, but Henry learns from his father, Thomas, that Charles is in fact his half-brother – the son of Thomas's first marriage. Thomas ended this marriage when he learned that his wife was of mixed race. Henry responds with horror not so much to the fact that his sister might be about to embark on an incestuous marriage, but to the revelation that Charles has black blood; he murders Charles on the day of the wedding. The cycle of violence resumes some forty years later when another illegitimate child of Thomas Sutpen – his daughter by a slave woman – burns down the plantation killing herself and Henry.

The violent, perverse history of the Sutpen family is figured as

---

[*] Others include *The Sound and the Fury* (1929) and *Light in August* (1932).

representing, in microcosm, the history of the South. One of the narrators, Quentin Compson, makes this association clear when he is asked by his Harvard room-mate to describe Yoknapatawpha County: Quentin's response is to narrate the Sutpen story. The novel thus situates the South in opposition to a northern, intellectual, implicitly more civilised milieu within which the Sutpen family history becomes a horrifying, exoticised tale of the 'other'. This opposition, however, is complicated by the novel's final gesture: Quentin's room-mate, Shreve, asks him, 'Why do you hate the south?'[4] Shreve interprets Quentin's response to his question – the narration of this violent family drama – as evidence that Quentin is deeply uneasy about his origin in a region that, by the narration of this tale, he seems willing to stereotype as irredeemably brutalised by its own history. This loaded question subverts a reductive reading of the Sutpen history in terms of a single, stereotypical representation of the American 'deep South'; it suggests that the tragedy that unfolds does not necessarily emanate from an essentially 'southern' milieu, but from a deeper national malaise that is projected on to the South as the nation's internal other.

In the short story 'A Rose for Emily' (1930), Faulkner explores from a slightly different angle the community he depicts in the novels. The narrative's central themes are deterioration (mental and physical) and isolation explored through the fate of the Grierson family in Jefferson, Yoknapatawpha County. The family home – formerly a grand plantation manor house – is falling into total dilapidation and is occupied by the last surviving member of the family, Emily. The physical deterioration of the house and the physical and mental deterioration of Emily symbolise the declining grandeur of the southern states and the instability generated by a period of rapid change in the early to mid-twentieth century. Emily is in a sense, like her home, a relic from quite a different era; as an unmarried woman unable to forge an identity for herself outside of marriage because of the older, more conservative generation to which she belongs, she becomes increasingly isolated and unhinged. The narrative proceeds by way of the subtle suggestion and nuanced description that characterises terror writing and that contributes powerfully to the atmosphere of putrefaction that thickens as the story progresses. It is divided into five sections, the first of which describes Emily's death and funeral. The following sections move back in time to recount disturbing episodes in the increasingly reclusive woman's life as recalled by the townsfolk. Following her father's death, his corpse is kept in the house by Emily who refuses to admit that he has died until the putrid smell prompts an investigation. Later, Emily (apparently deserted by the man she was supposed to marry) takes up with a local construction worker named Homer Barron. When Barron disappears, the community assumes that he too has abandoned Emily and she becomes a complete recluse. After her death, however, the townsfolk discover in a locked room the decayed corpse of the man and, by its side, a single grey strand of hair; the implication is that Emily has been sleeping by the side of the corpse.

Thus, although Faulkner avoids evocations of the supernatural or the overtly fantastical, the narrative generates a distinctly Gothic effect through its depiction of extreme psychological states that are associated symbolically with the decaying social structures of a past that figuratively haunts small-town southern America. The mode of delivery of the tale also creates a narrative ambiguity typical of Gothic fiction. The first-person narrator is anonymous and ungendered; no indication is given as to his/her relation either to Emily or the town of Jefferson. The narrator might be read as the collective voice of the town; perhaps more accurately, though, s/he might be interpreted as the collective voice of a nation simultaneously fascinated and horrified by what the South has come to represent, which is, as Margie Burns contends, 'an ideological other for the nation as a whole'.[5]

The American Vampire

In a 1999 article on 'Vampire Gothic', the critic Teresa A. Goddu observes that 'Vampires seem to be on the rise, at least in my part of the world.'[6] Goddu describes the discovery of a teenage vampire cult across three states in the heart of the southern Bible Belt (Louisiana, Kentucky and Florida) and the consequent media outcry: these young men and women were apparently engaging in role-playing games that included drinking each other's blood and sacrificing small animals. Media reports of the cult's increasingly violent activities cast the teenage vampires as 'a threatening image of family values gone awry – the child as soulless killer, as home-grown horror'. The perversion of family values and the consequent violent disruption of often religious, culturally homogenous small-town American communities (a central concern of Southern Gothic narratives in the mid-twentieth century) becomes a key theme of American Gothic in the later twentieth century; as Goddu observes, Gothic becomes 'the repository of cultural anxieties' and in particular it can be seen to symbolise and negotiate these anxieties through a resurrection, as it were, of 'the rootless cosmopolitan vampire of the nineteenth century'.[7]

Following the publication of his first novel, *Carrie*, in 1974, Stephen King became one of the most prolific and globally successful writers of Gothic fiction. His second novel, *Salem's Lot* (1975), is one of the first works of later American Gothic to engage directly with the literary legend created by Bram Stoker in 1897. In a 1999 afterword to the novel (reprinted in 2004), King makes clear the profound influence of Stoker's *Dracula* upon his early writing career, describing how '*Dracula* was the first fully satisfying adult novel I ever read and I suppose it is no surprise that it marked me so early and so indelibly'.[8] *Salem's Lot* follows closely the conventions and tropes of Stoker's novel, but transfers the vampire from nineteenth-century Europe to a small, modern community in the American state of Maine: Jerusalem's Lot. The protagonist of the novel is a professional writer named Ben Mears who returns to Salem's Lot (as the town is locally known) some years after the death of his wife in order to write a book about the town and, in a sense, to exorcise his personal demons in so doing. At the centre of the novel is a typical Gothic space – a foreboding, abandoned mansion called Marsten House – which is the former residence of a violent mobster named Hubert Marsten who in 1939 hanged himself after shooting his wife. This event appears to have had a defining influence over the community and over the personal history of Mears who has never been able to shake free the memory of a childhood incident, recalled early on in the narrative, which sets the tone for the rest of the novel. Mears as a young boy was dared by local boys to break into the house and return with some object from it. He does so, but goes further than the boys' challenge in venturing up to the bathroom where Marsten committed suicide. When he opens the bathroom door, he sees the body of Marsten swinging from the roof beam. In typical Gothic style, King leaves open the possibility that this was merely a hallucination whilst giving enough physical detail for the reader reasonably to suppose that the event might have happened: 'Hubie['s] ... face wasn't black at all. It was green. The eyes were puffed shut. His hands were livid ... ghastly. And then he opened his eyes' (p. 55). Mears recounts the incident to his girlfriend, Susan, an arch-sceptic whose role (like that of narrators such as Lockwood in *Wuthering Heights*) is to anchor the narrative in a rational objectivity that is nevertheless increasingly undermined as events unfold. Susan is unsettled by the story, but responds, 'You don't really think you saw Hubert Marsten, do you, Ben?' (p. 55). Ben's reply is an attempt to interpret his experience in a manner that hovers between rational scepticism ('probably I hallucinated the whole thing') and a kind of quasi-scientific explanation of the supernatural in terms of trapped emotional energy. He concedes that there may be 'some truth in the idea that houses absorb the emotions that are spent in them,' that they hold 'a kind of ... dry charge. Perhaps the right personality, that of an imaginative boy, for instance, could act as a catalyst on that dry charge, and cause it to produce an active manifestation of ... of something', but is quick to add, 'I'm not talking about ghosts precisely. I'm talking about a kind of psychic television in three dimension. Perhaps even something alive. A monster, if you like' (p. 55).

This passage exemplifies the terror mode of Gothic writing; King ratchets up the suspense, hinting at the presence of the supernatural ('an active manifestation of ... of something') whilst still leaving room for a natural (if unorthodox) explanation of the event. As the narrative progresses, however, the presence of the supernatural becomes impossible to repudiate as a rising number of unexplained disappearances and deaths are eventually discovered to be the work of a vampire, Kurt Barlow, who has migrated from Austria via England to purchase the Marsten house. A key theme in this novel, as in Stoker's, is the inability of modern, rational schemes of thought to account for and effectively deal with the threat posed by monsters that have their origin in a pre-modern Europe that insisted upon the supernatural reality of good and evil. This theme is developed in *Salem's Lot* through the characters' increasing immersion in the rituals and symbols of the Catholic Church. A critical figure here is the town's Catholic priest, Father Callahan, a rather insipid representative of his faith who is torn between his commitment to the ancient beliefs of Catholicism and a modern world which insists upon psychological and societal interpretations of evil; he is 'neither a new priest nor an old one; he found himself cast in the role of a traditionalist who can no longer even trust his basic postulates' (p. 219). Father Callahan's crisis of faith is symptomatic of the ambivalent cultural retreat from religion initiated in the late 1800s; to combat his spiritual malaise, he seeks a genuine spiritual challenge, an unequivocal old-style 'battle against EVIL' (p. 219), and to some extent the vampire threat restores Callahan's sense of mission by offering him precisely that. However, Callahan's faith fails him at a crucial moment; confronted by Barlow, the power of his crucifix diminishes as he momentarily doubts his own priestly power. In a mockery of Catholic communion, Callahan is then forced to drink Barlow's blood and, whilst the experience does not kill him, it certainly damns him: as he desperately tries to enter his church in the hope of doing penance, the door handle burns his hand and he flees Salem, literally and figuratively a marked man.

The text still insists upon the potency of religious symbolism in repelling the vampire, however, and, paradoxically, the characters who are less committed to Catholicism are able to wield these symbols most effectively, perhaps because they are less encumbered by the intellectual and spiritual conflicts that assail Father Callahan. Significantly, the young Mark Petrie (one of the only survivors of the vampire attack on Salem along with Ben Mears) converts to Catholicism and with Mears eventually 'purifies' the town by setting fire to it (p. 597). *Salem's Lot* thus unambiguously conforms to, even as it modernises and re-situates, the conventions of the nineteenth-century vampire Gothic.

Since the 1970s, vampirism has become an increasingly dominant theme in American Gothic to the extent that, in the first decade of the twenty-first century, the figure of the vampire is almost ubiquitous in Gothic fiction, film and television drama (the global success of Stephenie Meyer's *Twilight* saga in fiction and film is evidence of the current hold of the vampire over the popular imagination). After *Salem's Lot*, the vampire narrative developed in new directions largely under the influence of Anne Rice whose series *The Vampire Chronicles* began in 1976 with *Interview with the Vampire*. Whereas King's novel, with certain variations, is firmly in the mould of Stoker's *Dracula*, Rice's work departs from this tradition radically in her representation of the vampire and her contextualisation of vampirism. First, there is in Rice's work a tendency to portray the vampire as victim, and in this respect her vampire narratives reflect a postmodern trend towards the humanisation of the Gothic monster. As Fred Botting observes, monstrous figures in late twentieth-century Gothic become 'sites of identification, sympathy and self-recognition'[9] and in Rice's *Interview with the Vampire* this 'identification' works principally through the representation of the vampire Louis.

The novel begins with Louis keen to tell his story to a young reporter who records Louis's narrative and who is clearly in awe of his interviewee; thus, Louis is cast somewhat in the role of a misunderstood contemporary celebrity relating his traumatic life story to a journalist in order to provoke identification and sympathy in the reader. The story of Louis's initial transformation into a vampire and his struggle to adapt to his condition is indeed traumatic; Louis at first cannot accept his new identity and refuses to renounce his humanity, signified most potently by his decision to drink the blood of animals instead of humans. Even as Louis abandons his initial squeamishness in this regard, moreover, the text at no point portrays either the protagonist or any of the other vampires as objectively evil. Even Lestat and the child-vampire Claudia – the most bloodthirsty and amoral of Rice's characters – are ultimately portrayed so as to engage a degree of sympathy and identification. Claudia – whose tragedy is that she is frozen ambivalently between girlhood and adulthood – yearns for a mother as if she were a child, and for a lover as if she were a woman. Lestat ends the novel as a tortured, dishevelled and reclusive outcast following his murder of Claudia. Seen from the perspective of Louis – who throughout the narrative has shifted between revering and loathing his mentor – Lestat emerges as a creature to be pitied rather than feared and reviled. In discussing contemporary American vampire Gothic, Punter and Byron make the following point with regard to this type of characterisation of the vampire:

> In nineteenth-century vampire fiction, the representation of the vampire as monstrous, evil and other serves to guarantee the existence of good, reinforcing the formally dichotomized structures of belief ... Vampire fiction of the later twentieth century becomes increasingly sceptical about such categories [and] the oppositions between good and evil are increasingly problematised.[10]

In *Interview with the Vampire*, this point is eloquently if disconcertingly expressed by Armand (a powerful European vampire who is the oldest of his kind) who denies the existence of God and of any supernatural force of Evil that the vampire is supposed somehow to embody. This conceptualisation of vampirism in terms of the dualism of good and evil had formed the basis of Louis's understanding of his vampire identity up to this point; deprived of it, Louis sinks into existential despair: 'Then it began to sink in. It was as I had always feared, and it was as lonely, it was as totally without hope.'[11] The hopelessness of the vampire's situation is reinforced by Armand's explanation of why he is the oldest surviving vampire; it is not that vampires did not exist before Armand, but that vampires have a tendency ultimately to kill themselves through deliberate exposure to daylight. Armand describes the existential horror of the vampire whose 'immortality becomes a penitential sentence in a madhouse of figures and forms that are hopelessly unintelligible and without value' (p. 306). Armand's notion of the vampire as a creature driven to suicide by the weight of a meaningless existence resonates strongly with twentieth-century conceptualisations of an alienated humanity in a period without the stable religious and cultural norms of previous centuries, and again it shifts the status of the vampire from monster to victim.

The text's departure from the conventions of earlier vampire Gothic also entails an explicit repudiation of aspects of old vampire folklore. Louis informs his interviewer that crucifixes, garlic and even stakes through the heart have no impact whatsoever on vampires. There is indeed very little that does adversely influence the new American vampire and it is telling that, unlike earlier narratives, Rice's novel does not follow the plot trajectory of vampire killers seeking victory over demonic adversaries: her vampires are virtually invincible and what tends to destroy them is not the utilisation of religious ritual by heroic vampire slayers, but the vampires' own existential despair. Moreover, the text opens up a gap between 'New World' (American) and 'Old World' (Eastern European) vampires that again reinforces the novel's distance from earlier examples of the genre. Louis, Lestat and Claudia encounter and are attacked by 'Old World' vampires in Eastern Europe; these creatures appear as little more than zombies, apparently devoid of any will or intelligence, with 'their wagging bovine heads, their haggard shoulders, their rotted, ragged clothing' (p. 212). Such a distinction might be read as encoding an American perception of itself as a new and vibrant space that has transcended the decaying old world out of which it originated, but this would be a simplification of the way this text, and modern Vampire Gothic generally, treats such oppositional categories. The fate of Lestat is a case in point here; by the end of the novel he has more in common with the 'haggard' creatures of old Europe than with the sophisticated, urbane vampires of the new America. The novel opens up spaces of difference only to complicate them and to subvert binary oppositions between old and new, good and evil, victim and villain, and so on.

Poppy Z. Brite's first novel, *Lost Souls* (1992), offers further variations on the major conventions, tropes and motifs of vampire fiction. Like Rice, Brite presents the reader with vampires often capable of evoking sympathy and identification. The ironically named Christian in *Lost Souls* is a vampire at odds with his identity who kills because he has to, because 'the drinking of a life left him a little less alone than he had been before'.[12] The novel's title also gives an ironic twist to earlier conventions of vampire fiction: it carries multiple meanings, referring not only (and in fact not even primarily) to the 'lost souls' of vampires, but to a rock band of that name fronted by the novel's human protagonists, Steve and Ghost. It can also be read as referring more widely to the 'lost' generation to which Steve and Ghost belong, a generation of young people which Brite presents as having no place of belonging in a consumerist, homogenised and censorious culture. These rootless youngsters haunt (Ghost's name is, like Christian's, significant in terms of the novel's thematic and symbolic structure) underground bars and clubs in which they become vulnerable to vampires less scrupulous and considerably more predatory than Christian.

Brite's most notable subversion of the conventions of vampire Gothic, however, is the repudiation in *Lost Souls* of the standard mythology surrounding the genesis of the vampire. The vampires in Brite's novel have never been human; they are not transformed through the traditional rite of biting and blood-sucking, but are members of an entirely separate race who are born out of sexual relations between a vampire and a human. In Brite, therefore, the metaphorical treatment of sexuality encountered in much vampire fiction from the nineteenth century onwards (consider the sexualised encounters between women and Count Dracula in Stoker's novel, for instance) becomes more literal: a woman impregnated by a vampire will inevitably die in childbirth, as is the fate of two women in the novel – Jessy and Ann – who fall under the powerful sexual spell of the text's lead vampire, Zillah. The association between sex, violence and death is made much more explicit in *Lost Souls*, a gesture that can be read as reflecting and negotiating complex contemporary anxieties concerning sex, disease, youth and the family in the aftermath of the 1960s cultural revolution and the AIDS epidemic of the 1980s. Teresa Goddu analyses the extent to which late twentieth-century American vampire fiction taps into these anxieties, especially in the Bible Belt states of the South (and Louisiana is the setting for *Lost Souls*). Zillah is an androgynous, promiscuous vampire who tours the southern states with his acolytes Molochai and Twig in search of victims. Like Louis and Lestat in Rice's novel, Zillah is highly mobile, sophisticated and cosmopolitan, but he is also far more predatory in an explicitly sexual way. He is, in a sense, a tourist trading in sex and death and the following observation by Goddu brings into sharp focus the moral anxieties that underlie the characterisation of Zillah:

> The conjunction of morality and monstrosity in the Bible Belt vampire is evident in a public service advertisement at the Nashville International Airport ... Visible immediately after passing through the metal detectors, the image of a bat flying through an open window with a full moon in the background warns the traveller: Beware of Fly-By-Night Relationships. AIDS. See the Light.[13]

Lost Souls is not a morally conservative fiction, however; the victims of Zillah, Molochai and Twig are not promiscuous, amoral teens who are represented as somehow deserving their fate. As suggested above, they are, on the contrary, vulnerable young people who are invariably the victims of a culture presented as alienating, amoral and violent. Both of the women who fall victim to Zillah, for example, are victims of sexual abuse: Jessy from her father and Ann from her boyfriend, Steve, who rapes her. Other victims are runaways, or young people desperately seeking intimacy and belonging. The teenagers who frequent the Goth clubs which are often the vampires' stalking ground are portrayed as innocents, as 'lost souls' who are frequently referred to poignantly as 'children'. In terms of the novel's treatment of the alienation and vulnerability of these 'children', a symmetry emerges between vampire and human. The vampire son of Zillah and Jessy is aptly named 'Nothing'; he has no sense of his own identity and, like Louis in *Interview with the Vampire*, is unable to define himself productively as either 'human' or 'vampire'. When he discovers his vampire nature he is initially exhilarated at finding a 'family' in Zillah, Twig and Molochai, but this turns quickly to desperation as he recoils at the brutality that seems to him to characterise the vampire's existence. Like Louis, he is a humanised vampire, a 'site of identification' for the reader, and his sense of despair at his meaningless existence is radically foregrounded every time he is asked his name and has to reply: 'I'm Nothing'.

American Horror

Horror fiction[*] has become one of the most enduringly popular sub-genres of Gothic fiction since the Second World War, especially

---

[*] Horror Gothic arose alongside 'terror' writing in the late eighteenth century. 'Horror' was distinguished by an explicit emphasis on violence and shocking, brutal supernatural interventions; 'terror' relied more on subtle suggestion and evocation of suspense – see Part Three: 'Romantic-era Gothic'. The distinction blurred in the twentieth century; Stephen King's novels, for example, contain elements of horror and terror (e.g., the explicit violence and nuanced evocations of dread present simultaneously in *The Shining*).

in America, and horror fiction in its twentieth-century form can be classified as a predominantly American variety of Gothicism: the majority of its practitioners from H. P. Lovecraft to Poppy Z. Brite have been American writers responding to specifically American social and cultural contexts. Indeed, critics have frequently attributed the genre's success not only to its explicit sex, violence and supernaturalism (which have undoubtedly enhanced its appeal to a lucrative market of increasingly prosperous teenagers), but also to its capacity to capture and reflect back to its readers the most pressing and unsettling social and political concerns of the moment. Thus, novels such as Jack Finney's *The Body Snatchers* (1955) and Ira Levin's *The Stepford Wives* (1972), both made into successful films, represent the paranoia and insecurity of a rapidly changing America in the Cold War era; in both instances, humans are replaced by alien doubles which infiltrate previously peaceful, mainstream American communities. Representations of kidnap, killings and invasion evoke contemporary fears centring on the USSR as a perceived aggressor throughout the Cold War years, but they suggest also a paranoia regarding potential US government surveillance of its own citizens in this period. As Mark Jancovitch observes, 'there was a deep-seated anxiety [in the 1950s] that America was becoming an increasingly homogenous, conformist and totalitarian society'.[14]

Stephen King's horror fiction has a broad thematic range and often it brings into sharp focus the cultural and political anxieties of late modernity, anxieties concerning the family, childhood, shifting gender relations and increasing levels of violence and societal dysfunction. Apparently peaceful, civilised communities explode into violence; the perpetrators often emerge from within these communities, giving expression to pent-up conflicts and tensions that King represents as lying always just beneath the surface of American family life. King's first novel, *Carrie*, utilises the Gothic motif of the possessed child in order to explore the alienation and violence that often characterise relations between parents and children, and between children and each other. King's novel subverts the idealised version of family and childhood promoted by mainstream culture with increasing intensity since the Second World War, especially through advertising and the Hollywood film industry. Carrie is a lonely teenager bullied by her peers and abused by her mother. Carrie's persecution by her schoolmates reaches a symbolically significant climax when she is ridiculed in the school showers for starting her period. However, at this moment in her adolescent development Carrie discovers that she has telekinetic powers which she begins to use to take revenge on her mother and schoolmates. King's association of the onset of menstruation with the development of destructive occult powers has led some critics to argue that the novel expresses a fear of, or at least an anxiety towards, the female body and female sexuality. Gail E. Burns and Melinda Kanner, for example, observe:

> Stephen King's work reveals that the powerful reproduction/ sexuality/death dialectic is present in all his work and provides the symbolic matrix in which all girls and women are embedded. Menstruation, mothering, and female sexual desire function as bad omens, prescient clues that something will soon be badly awry.[15]

Whilst this is a credible interpretation, it is possible to consider what happens to Carrie not in terms of the novel's misogyny, but with attention to the cultural taboos pertaining to female sexuality and especially menstruation that persisted to some degree in the 1970s in spite of the sexual revolution and the rise of the women's liberation movement. From this perspective, the novel might be read as expressing the point that the female body and menstruation are still perceived in negative terms by the repressed, dysfunctional society that terrorises Carrie, a society that is duly punished when Carrie's psychic powers symbolically give back to it everything that it has already projected onto her: her awkward, adolescent, female body becomes 'demonic'.

If the depiction of the female body as a site of demonic possession is a common theme in horror fiction (see also Ira Levin's 1967 *Rosemary's Baby* and William Blatty's 1971 *The Exorcist*, for example), one finds also within the genre frequent representations of violent and alienated masculinity. The depiction of the male serial killer has become especially prevalent over recent decades – a response in part to the growing public horror of and fascination with actual serial killers who tend to achieve a degree of notoriety and celebrity within contemporary culture. There has been an increasing trend, moreover, to narrate serial killing from the perspective of the murderer and to posit the killer as a 'logical and inevitable product'[16] of violent and alienating social forces; he emerges out of mainstream society as a manifestation – albeit an extreme manifestation – of that society's prevailing ethos. A vivid contemporary example of this phenomenon from American popular culture is the popular drama series *Dexter* (first screened in 2006). The protagonist of this drama works for the Miami police as a forensic scientist who examines blood patterns at murder scenes. The twist is that Dexter himself is a serial killer, albeit an unusual murderer who conforms strictly to a certain moral code of killing: he murders only other killers. Dexter is no heroic vigilante, however; he is a self-confessed 'monster' incapable of forging meaningful connections with others.[*]

The serial killer in earlier instances of this genre often has self-aggrandising fantasies; he is individualistic, often sexually voracious, acquisitive and greedy for power and, as such, his basic motivation is in tune with a sexualised culture that promotes acquisitiveness, individualism and ambition. The perverse symmetry between the serial killer and the society from which he emerges is vividly represented in Bret Easton Ellis's *American Psycho* (1991).[17] The protagonist, Patrick Bateman, is an ambitious Wall Street trader devoted with equal enthusiasm to three causes:

---

[*] The *Dexter* series also employs to great effect the Gothic trope of the 'double' which is discussed further in Part Four: 'Gothic Bodies'. Dexter personifies his own compulsion to kill, referring to it as the 'dark passenger'.

consumerism, sex and killing. The novel's detailed depiction of the murders of Bateman's female victims, narrated with chilling detachment, gave rise to widespread accusations of misogyny against the author in the early 1990s, in response to which Ellis claimed that his novel was meant to be a work of satirical social criticism and not a reflection of his own antipathy towards women.[18]

The charge of misogyny has nevertheless been a common critical response to horror fiction in spite of the self-professed motivations of authors such as Ellis. As Joseph Grixti points out, it is perhaps difficult to respond otherwise to a genre in which 'images of liberated women being sexually violated by pathologically violent men' proliferate.[19] Moreover, horror fiction has traditionally been dominated by men both as writers and consumers of the genre. A notable exception is Poppy Z. Brite. In 1997, Brite published *Exquisite Corpse*, a novel that in many respects exceeds in explicitness the sexual violence represented in *American Psycho*. Indeed, Brite's UK publisher Penguin refused to take on the book citing as its reason the disturbing quality of an intense first-person narration that seemed to establish a possible emotional identification between reader and killer. This perhaps supports Botting's point that serial killer fiction does appear rather disconcertingly to present the murderer as a traumatic 'site of identification' for the reader.[20]

The novel begins with serial killer Andrew Compton inducing in himself a death-like coma so convincing that he is certified dead; he thereby manages to escape from prison in England and move to New Orleans. Compton is thus figuratively represented as a kind of vampire, a monster uncannily resurrected from the dead who is able easily to infiltrate new territories. In New Orleans, he begins to prey on young gay men along with his accomplice and lover, Jay. The fact that the text places scenes of murder, necrophilia and cannibalism in the specific context of gay sexual relationships might render it tempting to read the text as a conservative response to the moral panics of the 1980s and 1990s concerning homosexuality and especially AIDS: Compton might be compared to the vampiric sexual tourist warned against in the Nashville public advertisement discussed above – an even more deadly version of the homophobic stereotype of the dangerous, promiscuous gay male. Compton does indeed contract HIV and responds with the sinister observation that 'this virus in your blood makes people afraid of you. Anytime someone is afraid of you, you can use it to your own advantage.'[21] A number of points undercut this interpretation, however. Just as Stephen King's *Carrie* can be read not as a manifestation of King's own misogyny, but of society's persistent demonisation of the female body, so *Exquisite Corpse* may be interpreted as an interrogation of homophobic anxieties that produce out of the popular imagination monsters such as Andrew Compton: Compton becomes according to this interpretation the symbolic embodiment not of Brite's homophobia, but of society's worst fear – a gay serial killer. Moreover, the novel is not concerned exclusively, or arguably even primarily, with the murderous activities of Compton and his accomplice. Like Brite's 1993 novel *Drawing Blood* (in which the relationship between two young men, Zach and Trevor, enables both of them to overcome the trauma of past abuse), *Exquisite Corpse* narrates a painful love story between two gay men – Tran and Luke. The novel is in part narrated by these characters both of whom have been deeply damaged and alienated by a hostile culture that renders them vulnerable to male predators like Compton and Jay. (Tran is thrown out by his parents, for example, as soon as they discover his sexual orientation.) Brite's novels invariably validate the emotional experiences of gay men such as Tran and Luke (and Trevor and Zach in *Drawing Blood*) and articulate the challenges posed to non-heterosexual orientation in cultures that remain largely patriarchal and homophobic; furthermore, they do so subversively from within a mainstream genre ordinarily renowned for its staunch commitment to a masculine, heterosexual paradigm.

Extended Commentary: King, *The Shining* (1977)

The Shining reflects many of the key cultural concerns of twentieth-century American Gothic fiction: family dysfunction, alienated masculinity and, especially, the malevolent influence of fathers over sons. Moreover, the novel employs many tropes and symbols associated with older Gothic fictions; indeed, the extended quotation from Edgar Allan Poe that prefaces the text places it firmly within a tradition of Gothic fiction that goes back to the mid-nineteenth century. It has points in common also with English Gothic fictions of the eighteenth and nineteenth centuries: the Overlook Hotel is a modern version of the ancient Gothic castle that harbours devastating secrets; it is haunted by ghosts that are a manifestation of its violent history; and it becomes the scene of a grotesque family drama that replays the violence of the past. The plot follows the trajectory of Gothic narratives that work to realise repressed conflicts and traumas that are implicit from the outset in the psyche of the protagonist and the perverse dynamics of his or her family life. The novel begins with a tense exchange between Jack Torrance and the manager of the Overlook Hotel as Jack reluctantly accepts the job of caretaker. Jack's anger, carefully concealed from his prospective employer, is immediately evident as the text delivers Jack's thoughts in italics as a running commentary on the conversation: '*officious little prick, officious little prick – couldn't you at least spare the sales talk?*'[22] The first chapter hints at the violence to follow, suggesting that Jack's simmering anger during this encounter might well erupt violently in the confines of the Overlook Hotel. The previous caretaker, Grady, murdered his wife and daughters, a tragedy the manager attributes to a case of cabin fever and 'too much cheap whiskey'. The possibility of a repeat of this tragedy is then intimated by Jack's admission that he is a recovering alcoholic and his surprisingly detailed knowledge of the psychological effects of cabin fever. Although Jack is keen to distance himself from the former caretaker (he is an educated graduate who hasn't had 'so much as a glass of beer in the last fourteen months'), he is able to imagine almost too easily the pressures that might have driven Grady to murder: the boredom, the drinking, the slow build-up of emotional stress, until, finally, 'Boom, boom, boom' (p. 10).

Jack is thus established from the outset as a vulnerable man who is likely to be susceptible to the adverse effects of extended isolation. The portion of the narrative that precedes the move to the Overlook functions further to establish Jack's flaws and vulnerability and to anticipate the violence that is later to engulf the family. This is achieved primarily through the character of Jack's five-year-old son, Danny. Danny has a psychic gift referred to as 'Shining'; so does his mother, Wendy (though to a much lesser extent), and the Overlook's cook, Halloran, who is posited early on as Danny's protector – his surrogate father, as it were. This group comes to form an alternative 'family' united by the Shining, a gift that Jack does not share and that therefore further alienates him from his wife and his son. Jack is, and is painfully aware of being, an ineffectual father who seems to exist on the margins of his own family; more problematically, he is a violent parent who appears compelled to repeat the cycle of abuse perpetuated by his own father. Jack was (amongst other things) beaten by his father for stuttering and he threatens the same violence against Danny; significantly, Danny's sudden instance of stammering is occasioned by a premonition – a waking nightmare – of the violence that is to unfold in the Overlook. His parents find him almost in a trance and his stuttering response to their attempts to bring him round begets an explosive reaction from Jack, who screams at his son. Danny dissolves into tears, provoking Jack's remorseful response: 'Oh honey, I'm sorry. I'm sorry, doc' (p. 137). Danny's premonitions in the early chapters of the novel are often mediated through his imaginary friend, Tony, who appears to be, as Punter and Byron contend, a 'kind of double' of Danny *Anthony* Torrance.[23] Tony is an ambivalent figure who is not entirely benign; he is greeted by Danny as an 'old friend' who nevertheless inspires a 'prick of fear, as if he had come with some darkness hidden behind his back' (p. 34). He embodies a psychic force that torments Danny with visions he cannot decipher and which are intimately related to the family conflicts which terrorise him. His visions often seem to be triggered by moments of trauma; after fretting about another burst of temper from his father, for instance, Danny is transported by Tony to a dark room with a mirror across which is scrawled the word 'Redrum'. This word becomes a signifier (unintelligible to Danny, who can barely read, but not to the reader who understands that it spells 'murder' backwards) of the violent forces to be unleashed in the Overlook Hotel and of the violence that already characterises the relationship between Danny and Jack. The vision of the mirror gives way to an image of Danny 'crouched in a dark hallway' with a shape advancing on him shouting, '*Come and take your medicine! Take it like a man!*' (p. 36).

The phrase, 'Take your medicine! Take it like a man!' is a sinister Torrance family mantra used by Jack's father against him and by Jack against Danny. Danny's psychic power can thus be interpreted not only as a means of anticipating future events (important though this is in terms of the text's narrative trajectory and the generation of horror and suspense), but also as a means whereby Danny represents to himself a dysfunctional family dynamic that, as a child, he cannot rationally comprehend.

As the family relocate to the Overlook, the potential for violence increases and is symbolically figured through the representation of the hotel as the Torrances view it for the first time. The hotel is an archetypal Gothic space evoking the castles and haunted houses of earlier Gothic fiction. King uses the landscape of the Colorado Mountains to enhance the sense of dread associated with the hotel in a manner evocative of Ann Radcliffe's and Mary Shelley's use of the sublime to maximise the effect of terror in the late eighteenth and early nineteenth centuries. On their way to the hotel, the family stop at a viewpoint to catch their first glimpse of it and the sublime, mountainous landscape disorientates, terrifies and nauseates Wendy momentarily; a few paragraphs later it is associated with the threat of violence that Danny has been anticipating since the move to the Overlook was proposed: 'Whatever Redrum was, it was here' (p. 69).

The supernatural violence that is unleashed against the Torrance family in the Overlook Hotel is closely related to the emotional deterioration of Jack as his situation begins increasingly to conform to the precedent set by the former caretaker, Grady. Jack begins to drink again and to dwell upon his various failures as an aspiring writer; he increasingly displays those symptoms of cabin fever that he described so fluently in the opening chapter. As Joseph Grixti observes, 'the ghosts of the hotel make their appearances at those moments when Jack's repressed instincts make themselves felt'[24] and, indeed, the novel offers some scope for interpreting the hotel's ghosts as psychic projections of Jack's psychological conflicts, especially his growing hostility towards his son. As Grixti again points out, 'it is at those moments when his irrational "irritation and even real anger" towards his son comes to the fore that the ghostly appearances make themselves seen and felt'.[25] Like the hotel's temperamental boiler which is in constant danger of overheating, Jack's emotional temperature, as it were, seems to determine the level of supernatural activity present in the hotel. The psychological reading of the supernatural is problematised, however, by the narrative's seeming insistence upon the physical reality of the various hauntings experienced by the Torrance family. Significant in this respect is what happens in the malevolent centre of the Overlook: room 217. Danny has been warned against entering this room and has already obliquely envisaged what it might contain in one of his earlier visions. When he does eventually enter, he sees what appears to be the long-dead corpse of a woman in the bath. Danny has been encouraged by the cook Halloran to believe that the 'ghosts' of the hotel cannot harm him; they are simply 'like pictures in a book … close your eyes and they'll be gone' (p. 240). Danny thus convinces himself that this is a hallucination only to find the hands of the woman closing around his neck. The fact that Danny is later found by his parents with clearly visible marks around his throat reinforces the reality of the event, though it has to be said that even here there is some room for doubt. Wendy assumes that Jack has injured Danny, a reasonable assumption given that Jack in the past has broken Danny's arm in a fit of rage and appears to be becoming increasingly unhinged in the hotel. It is possible that Danny's experience in room 217 is an imagined reaction to a trauma inflicted on him by his father. The novel thus comes to resemble Henry James's *The Turn of the Screw* and some of M. R. James's short stories (see the previous chapter) in its ambiguous treatment of the line between the supernatural and the psychological.

Finally, *The Shining* shares with several of King's other novels a concern with wider political and cultural issues that are negotiated through representations of Gothic space, individual psychological trauma and the supernatural. In the Overlook's basement, Jack discovers a pile of documents relating to the history of the hotel including a scrapbook of newspaper cuttings. From this it emerges that the hotel has throughout its past been mired in scandals involving sex, drugs, gangsterism, murder and suicide that appear to have reached into the high echelons of American political life. The Overlook's ghosts might thus be read as a manifestation of what King posits as the seamy underside of American culture. In the following passage, rich in Gothic literary allusion, Jack finds a dinner invitation dated 1945 and imagines the high-society party hosted by the hotel's most notorious owner, Horace Derwent. His erratic thoughts evoke the quotation which prefaces the novel and which is taken from Poe's allegorical fiction 'The Masque of the Red Death': Jack envisages, 'The masks coming off and ... (*the Red Death held sway over all!*) He frowned. What left field had that come out of?' (p. 170). Poe's story describes the outbreak of a plague called 'Red Death' in a country ruled by a frivolous and corrupt prince. Without any thought for his subjects, he shuts up his castle to keep the plague out and throws an extravagant masked ball. The plague nevertheless infiltrates the castle in the form of a mysterious guest who wears a death-mask and a funeral shroud. Jack's 'left field' evocation of this classic Gothic tale thus serves to set his tragedy within the wider context of the Overlook's history, a history which the text presents as a microcosm of the history of twentieth-century America.

Notes

1   Leslie Fiedler, *Love and Death in the American Novel* (New York: Stein & Day, 1966), p. 414.

2   Tennessee Williams, *A House Not Meant to Stand* (New York: New Directions, 2009), p. 2.

3   Lauren Goodlad, *Goth: Undead Subculture* (Lexington, KY: Duke University Press, 2007), p. 196.

4   William Faulkner, *Absalom, Absalom!* (New York: Vintage, 1990), p. 303.

5   Margie Burns, 'A Good Rose Is Hard to Find: Southern Gothic as Signs of Social Dislocation in Faulkner and O'Connor', in David B. Browning and Suzanne Bazargan, *Image and Ideology in Modern/Postmodern Discourse* (Albany: State University of New York Press, 1991), p. 106.

6   Teresa A. Goddu, 'Vampire Gothic', *American Literary History*, 11 (1999), p. 125.

7   Ibid., p. 126.

8   Stephen King, *Salem's Lot* (London: Hodder & Stoughton, 2004), p. 747.

9   Fred Botting, 'After Gothic: Consumption, Machines and Black Holes', in Jerrold E. Hogle (ed.), *The Cambridge Companion to Gothic Fiction* (Cambridge: Cambridge University Press, 2002), p. 286.

10 David Punter and Glennis Byron, *The Gothic* (Oxford: Blackwell, 2004), p. 270.

11 Anne Rice, *Interview with the Vampire* (London: Time Warner, 2003), p. 257.

12 Poppy Z. Brite, *Lost Souls* (London: Penguin, 2010), p. 68.

13 Goddu, 'Vampire Gothic', p. 125.

14 Mark Jancovich, *Rational Fears: American Horror in the 1950s* (Manchester: Manchester University Press, 1996), p. 22.

15   Gail E. Burns and Melinda Kanner, 'Women, Danger and Death: The Perversion of the Female Principle in Stephen King's Fiction', in Diane Christine Raymond (ed.), *Sexual Politics and Popular Culture* (London: Popular Press, 1990), p. 159.

16   Punter and Byron, *The Gothic*, p. 206.

17   Bret Easton Ellis, *American Psycho* (New York: Vintage, 1991).

18   Julian Murphet, *Bret Easton Ellis' American Psycho: A Reader's Guide* (London: Continuum, 2002).

19   Joseph Grixti, *Terrors of Uncertainty: The Cultural Contexts of Horror Fiction* (London: Routledge, 1989), p. 23.

20   Botting, 'After Gothic', p. 286.

21   Poppy Z. Brite, *Exquisite Corpse* (New York: Touchstone, 1996), p. 103.

22   Stephen King, *The Shining* (London: Hodder & Stoughton, 1978), p. 3.

23   Punter and Byron, *The Gothic*, p. 248.

24   Grixti, *Terrors of Uncertainty*, p. 71.

25   Ibid.

British Gothic in the Late Twentieth Century: Carter, Ballard, Mantel and Waters

In the late twentieth century, British Gothic assumed increasingly diverse forms to the extent that its generic affinity with the fictions that originated literary Gothicism in the late eighteenth and early nineteenth centuries (those of Walpole, Radcliffe, Lewis, Mary Shelley and so on) can appear somewhat remote. Nevertheless, albeit within different social and cultural contexts, British Gothic continues to explore experiences of profound dislocation, persecution and confinement and to do so through evocations of the uncanny and the weird, loathing and repugnance that often occur within familiar, domestic locations. There is, for instance, a line of influence from the 'domesticated' Gothic of the Victorian period (see Part Three: 'Nineteenth-century Gothic') to the fictions of Angela Carter, Iain Banks, Hilary Mantel and Sarah Waters in which familial and domestic relations emerge as disturbingly dysfunctional. Indeed, contemporary British Gothic is frequently characterised by its insistence upon the extent to which perversity, strangeness and violence occupy and in a sense define the 'safe' space of mainstream British society and culture. This is true also of varieties of American Gothic fiction in the postwar period, much of which functions to render grotesque, and to estrange the reader from a white, middle-class milieu that emerges as profoundly disturbed. Evocations of the supernatural in American horror fiction, for example, often serve to manifest repressed tensions that return to haunt and even destroy individuals, families and communities (see the previous chapter).

Whilst this is true of British Gothic fictions of the same period, it is noticeable that such fictions tend to eschew the extreme manifestations of supernatural horror that often characterise its American equivalent. One mode of contemporary British Gothic tends to represent more psychologically interiorised forms of dread (often set within specifically British locations – the middle-class suburban family, the deprived inner city, the English village and country house) than those associated with supernatural horror fiction. Another (associated especially with the work of J. G. Ballard since the 1960s) explores societal dysfunction through the creation of weird dystopias that closely reproduce, even as they distort, the contemporary British urban landscape.

New Literatures of Terror

Part Three: 'Eighteenth-century Gothic' discusses the distinction between 'terror' and 'horror' as two modes of literary Gothicism that emerged in the 1790s through the work of Ann Radcliffe and Matthew Lewis. The distinction has been evoked elsewhere.[*] To some degree, the separation between these styles of Gothic closed during the course of the twentieth century with the term 'horror' often used as a generic term for Gothic fictions irrespective of their style. To some extent, this reflects market pressures that require publishers to use a term that is readily understood by the public, and no doubt 'horror' serves this purpose perhaps more than 'Gothic'. Moreover, the distinction itself has always been relatively fluid, with writers often employing both techniques in the same fiction.[†] However, the distinction still carries weight in the

---

[*] See the preceding chapter's discussion of American horror fiction, for example.

[†] An example is Stephen King whose work frequently builds up suspense and uncertainty as a prelude to explicit depictions of violent supernatural events.

discussion of fictions that do situate themselves firmly within the terror mode of Gothic and this is especially true of certain contemporary British novel that draw on the style, tone and psychological intensity of terror writing in the late eighteenth and nineteenth centuries.

Susan Hill has written several novels and novellas that evoke the conventions and style of nineteenth- and early twentieth-century Gothic. *The Man in the Picture* (2007), for example, employs the Gothic trope of the 'cursed' painting.* Hill is best known, however, for *The Woman in Black* (1983), which was adapted successfully for the theatre.† *The Woman in Black* is set in the late nineteenth century and through the first-person narrator (a slightly pompous, highly proper Victorian gentleman named Arthur Kipps) it reproduces the narrative voice of a certain form of mid- to late Victorian Gothic. Arthur's initially detached, slightly didactic tone resembles that of Collins's Walter Hartright, or Brontë's Lockwood. He is a solicitor, a man of reason (as he constantly points out), and his increasing susceptibility to moments of profound fear and emotional disorientation enhances the slow build-up of suspense and dread as the narrative progresses. The use of narrators such as Kipps contributes significantly to the production of terror in this type of Gothic fiction; Kipps struggles, and eventually fails, to assert his rational world-view ('I do not believe in ghosts' is one of his most frequent claims) in the face of increasingly weird and threatening occurrences. As is often the case in terror fiction, it is more the emotional crisis of the protagonist that generates narrative momentum than explicitly detailed supernatural interventions. Indeed, it is a generic marker of terror fiction that it eschews explicitness in its treatment of trauma, violence and the supernatural.

---

* See Oscar Wilde's *The Picture of Dorian Gray* (1891) and M. R James's short story 'The Mezzotint' (1904).

† The novella's title evokes Wilkie Collins's *The Woman in White*, discussed in Part Three: 'Nineteenth-century Gothic'. The close generic association between sensation fiction and the Gothic, and Collins's debt to the instigator of terror writing, Ann Radcliffe, is also discussed in that chapter.

The plot of the text also closely follows the conventions of nineteenth-century Gothic fictions in which old family secrets return literally or figuratively to haunt the present generation (and the novel's title, of course, will alert the reader familiar with Collins's text to the possibility that this secret might turn upon the identity of a wronged woman). Hill establishes both the distance and the continuities between past and present through the use of a frame narrative, again a staple of the genre. Kipps is initially presented as married to his second wife with several stepchildren (though seemingly none of his own) and about to enjoy a family Christmas. There are already intimations that Kipps suffers from the effect of a past trauma ('I was prone to occasional nervous illnesses and conditions, as a result of the experiences I will come to relate')[1] and when the children begin to tell ghost stories, and urge him to join in, he runs out of the room almost hysterical. He is prompted, however, to write down the events that have so traumatised him in the hope that this might alleviate his distress. A distinctly modern theme thus emerges: the notion of confessional writing as a form of therapy.

The narrative then shifts back several decades to Kipps as a young solicitor engaged to tie up the estate of the deceased Alice Drablow. At the woman's funeral, Kipps catches his first glimpse of the woman in black and again the text reveals a more modern treatment of its subject: the appearance of the figure is in no sense ghostly. She seems to have flesh and bones – to be a genuinely material presence – and her wasted state makes her appear almost as one of the living dead, as a zombie of contemporary horror film one might say. Kipps is able to describe her clearly even after the most cursory glance:

> She was suffering from some terrible wasting disease, for not only was she extremely pale, even more than a contrast with the blackness of her garments could account for, but the skin and, it seemed, only the thinnest layer of flesh was tautly stretched and strained across her bones, so that it gleamed with a curious blue-white sheen, and her eyes seemed sunken back into her head. (p. 49)

When Kipps visits Mrs Drablow's former home, Eel Marsh, he sees the woman again and once more she appears to be a thoroughly real, material presence albeit one that exudes such 'evil and hatred and loathing' that Kipps is thoroughly disconcerted: '[I had] never known myself gripped by such dread and horror and apprehension of evil. It was as though I had become paralysed' (p. 66). When he goes through Mrs Drablow's papers he discovers that the sister of Alice Drablow, Jennet Humfrye, was forced to give up her illegitimate child to Alice for adoption. She remained passionately attached to her son, however, and developed the wasting disease from which she eventually died after his drowning in an accident for which she blamed his mother. Her vengeful ghost has become associated in the village with unexplained child deaths ever since and, indeed, Kipps's narrative ends with his own child's death following his final sighting of the woman in black, years after his departure from Eel Marsh house.

The Woman in Black may be read as part of a wider literary development: the contemporary reworking of the nineteenth-century Gothic in British fiction. As the title indicates, it is acutely aware of the literary traditions that are being appropriated and at one point it comments ironically on these appropriations. Kipps observes as he receives the Drablow brief from his employer:

> The business was beginning to sound like something from a Victorian novel, with a reclusive old woman having hidden a lot of ancient documents somewhere in the depths of her cluttered house. I was scarcely taking Mr Bentley seriously. (p. 31)

This observation suggests a certain cynicism on the part of Kipps towards his new brief and the conventions of Victorian Gothic that he faintly disparages here; nevertheless, Kipps becomes irrevocably traumatised by a working out of precisely those conventions. His observation in the context of the narrative as a whole could be taken as a commentary on the continuing efficacy of the literature of terror.

The contemporary writer most associated with appropriations of the conventions of Victorian fiction is Sarah Waters whose early work is set in the late nineteenth century and who uses the narrative devices of the Victorian novel to explore issues pertaining to Victorian – but also of continuing relevance to contemporary – British society.* *The Little Stranger* (2009) is set in 1948, however, and uses a first-person male narrator to generate a psychologically complex narrative of terror. The text foregrounds the social and political contexts of Britain in the late 1940s and uses Gothic motifs and tropes (an apparently rational narrator, the return of past trauma in the form of ambiguous 'hauntings', a dysfunctional and paranoid family) to negotiate and symbolise the social tensions of that period. The narrator is Faraday, a doctor from a working-class background who is aware of his conflicted and precarious social position. In spite of his professional status, he lacks the financial cushion of a wealthy family background and worries that the establishment of the NHS under the postwar Attlee government might severely curtail his income. Faraday has a family connection – and increasingly a powerful emotional connection – with the aristocratic Ayres family who have occupied the village manor house, Hundreds Hall, for generations. His mother was a servant at the house and an incident that Faraday recalls early in the novel hints at his ambivalent relationship to the family. Faraday remembers his mother taking him into the manor during a village fête held in its grounds. He was overawed by the grandeur of the hall's interior and broke off a piece of the elaborate plasterwork to take away as a souvenir. This minor act of violence against Hundreds Hall anticipates Faraday's conflicted response to the family when he later becomes their doctor. Though the novel never makes this point explicit, it strongly suggests a degree of hostility on Faraday's part towards the Ayres family based on class antagonism. Faraday recalls how his mother had to scrimp to afford

---

* These include lesbianism and the repression of homosexuality in *Fingersmith* (2002) and *Tipping the Velvet* (1998), and the confinement, repression and rebellion of women in *Affinity* (1999).

his education and how overwork probably contributed to her death. As a man who lacks the connections and easy social manners of his higher-class acquaintances, Faraday remarks: 'I'm a nobody. People don't even see me half the time.'[2] He insinuates himself into the Ayres inner circle and the traumatic events that unfold can be read as the consequence of Faraday's machinations, or as the outward projection of Faraday's repressed anger towards the family and what it represents.

The house appears to be haunted by the ghost of the family's daughter, Susan, who died of diphtheria aged seven. The novel follows the conventions of terror Gothic, however, in leaving the cause of the weird occurrences at Hundreds Hall open to interpretation. The precarious position of the family, occasioned by the declining power of their class in postwar Britain (they are forced, for instance, to sell off large portions of the grounds for the building of council housing), induces a siege mentality in the family. The eldest son, Roderick,[*] laments that 'they'd like nothing better than to hang us all from the mainbrace; they're just waiting for Attlee to give them the word' concluding, '[o]rdinary people hate our sort now, don't you see?' (p. 58). Roderick becomes the focus of events that seem to beg a supernatural explanation: objects move about his room, strange marks appear on the walls and a fire ignites spontaneously. Roderick is convinced that the house itself hates and wishes to destroy him. His insecurities are deemed to have generated delusions, however, and Faraday convinces the family that Roderick should be committed to an asylum. His motives appear to be purely professional – at least, this is how he narrates them – but his increasingly obsessive interest in the fate of Hundreds Hall and his romantic involvement with Caroline Ayres, a woman he has declared to be sexually unattractive, suggests that Faraday might well have designs on the house that he will not make explicit, or that he cannot even admit to himself. Mrs Ayres is the next victim of what could be interpreted as psychosis, as genuine

---

[*] The name is a reference to Edgar Allan Poe's protagonist in 'The Fall of the House of Usher' (1839).

supernatural activity, or as the manipulative manoeuvres (albeit possibly subconscious) of Faraday; she becomes convinced that her dead daughter is haunting the house, is tormented by seemingly inexplicable noises and voices, and eventually hangs herself. Finally, Caroline is found dead having broken off her engagement to Faraday and announced her intention to sell the house. In a twist that again suggests Faraday's responsibility for the 'haunting' of Hundreds Hall, he narrates how he dreamed of being in the house on the night of Caroline's death, and at the inquest the maid recalls hearing Caroline investigate a noise in the corridor and exclaim, 'You!'(p. 482). Given the almost complete social isolation of the family at this point, and the fact that Faraday has a key to the house, it is difficult to see who this visitor could be apart from Faraday, unless it is the ghost of Susan. The ambiguity subtly implicates the working-class Faraday in the gradual annihilation of an aristocratic family already in the process of 'collapsing like a pack of cards' (p. 27) under the pressure of seismic shifts in the social and political structure of postwar Britain.

Terror and Trauma

Hilary Mantel's *Beyond Black* (2005) does not attempt to capture the style and tone of an earlier mode of the Gothic. It is set in 1990s Britain and uses a disjointed, ambiguous third-person narrative to recount the past and present traumas of a psychic, Alison, and her assistant, Collette. The novel taps into and articulates late twentieth-century anxieties concerning abuse and the dehumanising tendencies of postmodern British culture. The broken, staccato phrases of the opening paragraph create a dark, violent Gothic tone in which images of modernity and suburban domesticity are starkly subverted:

> Travelling: the dank oily days after Christmas. The motorway, its wastes looping London: the margin's scrub-grass flaring

orange in the lights, and the leaves of the poisoned shrubs striped yellow-green like a cantaloupe melon. Four o' clock. Teatime in Enfield, night falling on Potter's Bar.[3]

This is one of the new landscapes of British Gothic fiction, a dirty wasteland populated by 'scapegoats, scarred with bottle and burn marks' (p. 1); it bears a marked resemblance to J. G. Ballard's city dystopias discussed in the following section. This novel nevertheless has points in common with earlier Gothic fictions and especially those located within the tradition of terror writing. A key motif of terror fiction is that a mystery surrounds the identity of a protagonist who is persecuted, often to the point of madness, by forces that appear unassailable. Where the supernatural is present, it is usually related to a traumatic, violent past. Violence is rarely explicitly represented in terror writing, however,[*] and the exact nature of the protagonist's predicament may be rendered obscure throughout most of the narrative; the effect of terror is generated through the oblique manner in which scenes of trauma are related. In Mantel's novel, Alison has no idea who her father is and constantly speculates that he might be one of her mother's criminal, abusive associates. Her psychic abilities, which manifest the supernatural throughout the text, are related in various ways to this history of family dysfunction and violence, the full extent of which is carefully obscured from the reader because its details have been firmly repressed by the protagonist. Alison is terrorised by flitting images of childhood abuse – of 'greasy faces looking down on her' (p. 116) and hands lifting her out of bed. Her memories have the quality of a grotesque theatre of shadows and when asked by Collette to recall her past, Alison can only wander from one half-remembered incident to another in a state of anxious disorientation.

---

[*] As discussed above, some texts work to combine the psychological subtlety of 'terror' with the more explicitly gruesome aspects of the 'horror' mode of Gothic. The distinction is by no means fixed and absolute. Edgar Allan Poe's 'The Black Cat' (1843), discussed in Part Four: 'Gothic Bodies', is an early example of the combination of these styles.

Her abject predicament as she attempts to negotiate her own history resembles that of a Radcliffean heroine trying to find a meaningful reference point in her castle-prison: Alison's past becomes a kind of Gothic space populated by half-glimpsed spectres and unnamed atrocities.

In so far as Alison's past acquires any manifestation beyond her pained, inarticulate recollections, it takes the morbid shape of the ghost of Morris, an associate of the group that abused Alison who appears whilst she is still a child to act as her 'spirit guide'. Like Hill's ghost in *The Woman in Black*, Morris has a fleshy human form that does not appear remotely spectral. The only thing that differentiates him from the rest of humanity is the fact that only Alison can see him. Indeed, Morris's physicality takes the form of a gross, venal materiality supplemented by his obscene vocabulary. He first appears in the text like a pervert about to expose himself: 'He was on the floor, half sitting, half slumped against the wall: his stumpy legs were spread out, and his fingers playing with his fly buttons' (p. 5). As Alison's 'spirit guide' he is no benign gateway to the afterlife, but a predatory, abusive spirit who keeps Alison under his control with violent, often sexual threats. When she first encounters him at the school gates, the episode has the disturbing quality of a paedophilic abduction:

> Morris lurched away from the wall and came limping towards her. He ignored the traffic, and a van must have missed him by inches. He could limp very fast; he seemed to scurry like some violent crab, and when he reached her he fastened his crab-like arm into her arm above the elbow. She flinched and twisted in his grasp, but he held her firmly. Get off me, she was crying, you horrible pervert, but then, as so often, she realised that words were coming out of her mouth but no one could hear them. (p. 126)

These past experiences and the control that Morris continues to exert over Alison efface her sense of identity. The only reality that Alison can construct for herself is the stylish, composed persona that emerges when she is on stage during a psychic performance, but even here there is a sense in which Alison's spiritual power serves only as another means whereby she can be abused. Morris is always in the wings, muttering threats or exposing himself; there is the constant fear that other malevolent spirits might assail her; and even her audience can be fractious, demanding and unforgiving: 'The public had paid its money and it wants results' (p. 1). The supernatural in *Beyond Black*, therefore, is not simply a means to generate Gothic terror: because the protagonist is psychic, her mind itself becomes a site of haunting to which all manner of malevolent spirits have access. For Alison, there is no possibility of closing off this influence and the novel's title can thus be interpreted as suggesting the dire existential predicament of a traumatised subject for whom there is little possibility of what contemporary psychologists have come to refer to as 'closure'.

Postmodern Dystopias: Cities and Suburbs

From the 1960s onwards, the novels and short stories of J. G. Ballard (beginning with his early works of science fiction) have represented various post-apocalyptic scenarios many of which are set in the very near future or in versions of the present in which contemporary urban landscapes are distorted into monstrous, violent Gothic spaces. Punter and Byron point out that the Gothic element in Ballard's work lies decidedly in its capacity to depict 'the terrifying labyrinths of a world where there is little except persecution'.[4]

Two early short stories reveal Ballard's interest in the alienating effects of the modern, urban experience. 'Concentration City' (1957) depicts a terrifyingly vast, grossly over-populated city that exists thousands of years into the future. The protagonist, Franz, drives for weeks through this city seeking an escape only to find himself back where he started. 'Billenium' (1961) depicts a similar urban dystopia, though one that is set closer to the present. A vast bureaucracy exists to control the diminishing space available for human occupation with individuals allocated tiny cubicles often situated, rather comically, in marginal, transitional spaces inappropriately set aside for dwellings: the central character, for instance, lives half way up a staircase.

In later novels, representations of the urban landscape and its capacity to terrorise humanity become much darker and more violent. The novel *Concrete Island* (1974) reflects a typical concern of Ballard (appearing first in *Crash* in 1973): the motor car as a symbol of modern technology's increasing ability to transform human subjectivity. The protagonist, Robert Maitland, is travelling along a motorway in outer London when a tyre bursts and he crashes on to a traffic island. His comfortable, professional existence is suddenly closed down by this violent mini-apocalypse: 'The sequence of violent events only micro-seconds in duration had opened and closed behind him like a vent of hell.'[5] The island becomes a bizarre Gothic space, piled up with debris and 'home' to two intimidating, damaged individuals: the neurotic Jane and the brain-damaged ex-acrobat, Proctor. As traffic speeds by, Maitland becomes part of a dysfunctional community with each person struggling for power over the others; he becomes increasingly paranoid and violently domineering displaying a 'will to survive, to dominate the island and harness its resources' (p. 47). Moreover, Maitland eventually abandons any attempt to escape from the island. This is understandable in one sense since motorists cannot see him from the road and their speed makes it difficult for him to negotiate his way across the potentially lethal rush of traffic. On the other hand, Maitland is presented with opportunities to seek help and he fails to do so. Instead, he adapts to his new environment and dispenses with any abilities 'irrelevant to the task of coming to terms with the island' (p. 126). The capacity to adapt readily to rapidly changing circumstances – to be mobile and mutable – is a key survival skill within fluid contemporary cultures, but here it works against Maitland. He proves so adept at conforming to this new reality that he precludes the possibility of his escape from it. Thus, the structure and function of this hyper-modern setting and those conditions of modernity that render human subjectivity so susceptible to rapid transformation leave Maitland stranded in an alternative reality located within and constructed out of the contemporary urban landscape.

Ballard's *High Rise* (1975) and *Millennium People* (2003) can both be described as examples of what Peter Brigg calls 'urban disaster' fiction.[6] The earlier novel takes its name from a forty-storey block of luxury apartments housing upper middle-class professionals who turn against each other and abandon their comfortable, civilised city lives. The novel is disconcertingly realistic in its depiction of a horrifyingly easy transition from tenants' irritated reactions to the ordinary inconveniences of urban living, to slightly more aggressive displays of anger, to extraordinary explosions of violence. High-functioning, ostensibly civilised individuals quickly transform into savage players in power struggles that eventually reduce the entire block to chaos. The novel exemplifies Ballard's technique in depicting with a high degree of realism an aspect of contemporary society that is entirely familiar to the reader, but which is distorted just sufficiently to shift it from banal regularity to monstrous abnormality. The novel begins with precisely this sort of Ballardian negotiation between the familiar and the perverse: the protagonist, Dr Laing, observes that 'everything had returned to normal' whilst he is preparing to eat an Alsatian dog.[7]

The setting of *Millennium People* is a 'gated community' called Chelsea Marina, a location that embodies in its fences, gates and high-tech security the anxieties of middle-class professionals who seek to isolate and protect themselves from crime; ironically, the enclosed community becomes a site of increasingly traumatic violence. The text posits this violence as the inevitable outcome of a landscape that generates delusion and disillusion. It is a place of simulation, a fake city that attempts to replicate the famous streets and landmarks of London. Its abject reality, however, belies the utopia marketed by the developers and estate agents:

So this is Chelsea Marina. It feels more like ...
Fulham? It is Fulham. 'Chelsea Marina' is an estate agent's
con. Affordable housing for all those middle managers and
civil servants just scraping by.
And the marina?
The size of a toilet bowl and smells like it.[8]

The population's growing alienation turns to rebellion under the
direction of a former paediatrician, Richard Gould. Gould's
professional association with children makes his rapid
transformation into a terrorist fanatic all the more unsettling; he
embarks on an increasingly sophisticated and ambitious terror
campaign against the various organs of the British establishment –
murdering a television presenter, planting a bomb at Heathrow
airport and attempting to assassinate a government minister. The
narrator, Richard Markham (whose wife is killed in the Heathrow
bombing), becomes obsessed with Gould's attempted revolution
which he comes to perceive as an almost heroic attempt to
challenge the inauthenticity that defines contemporary modernity
and that is reflected not only in the faked 'London' of Chelsea
Marina, but in the faked 'London' of London itself. Walking along
the Thames, Markham points out 'two fakes' in the landscape: the
'replica of Shakespeare's Globe and an old power station made over
into a middle class disco, Tate Modern' (p. 180). In his discussion
of the novel Sebastian Groes refers to this as 'dislocated
signification';[*] Groes points out that Shakespeare's Globe, for
example, is 'a reconstruction of the original theatre not even built
at its original location'.[9] Amidst this meaningless proliferation of
signs, Gould's desperate campaign acquires a certain dignity for
Markham: 'In his despairing and psychopathic way, Richard
Gould's motives were honourable ... He believed that the most
pointless acts could challenge the universe at its own game'
(p. 292). Like the 'monsters' of horror fiction discussed in the

---

[*] Dislocated signification is the reproduction of signs that no longer have any
meaningful reference point.

previous chapter, Gould becomes a 'site of identification' for Richard Markham; the narrator comes to recognise in his namesake the victim of a monstrous culture of dissimulation.

Growing Pains: Gender and Adolescence

Traumatised adolescence and its location within dysfunctional family units is a recurrent theme in contemporary British Gothic, and it can be interpreted as a response to volatile debates concerning shifting family structures, the legal and cultural status of the child, and the changing social roles of men and women. Gothic fictions since the 1970s have explored in diverse ways issues of child abandonment and abuse, delinquency, the fluidity of gender identity and the often painful transition from childhood to sexual maturity in a culture that can appear simultaneously to demonise and idealise the child. Angela Carter's *The Magic Toyshop*, discussed in the extended commentary below, is an example of the use of the Gothic in this context, and Carter's collection of short stories, *The Bloody Chamber* (1979), reworks fairy tale and folk tale narratives in order to interrogate the myths and symbols that function within patriarchy to initiate girls into a highly problematised, conflicted womanhood (see Part Four: 'Female Gothic').

Ian McEwan's *The Cement Garden* (1978) is a short, tense fiction that narrates from the perspective of the teenage Jack the surreal disintegration of his family following the death of both parents. The family is presented at the outset as under the repressive influence of an obsessive, bullying father who is both feared and (secretly) ridiculed by his older children, Jack, Sue and Julie. His compulsive, controlling personality is symbolised by the regimented, sterile back garden of the novel's title: it is comprised of an elaborate rockery with virtually no flora ('he did not like bushes or ivy or roses. He would have nothing that tangled')[10] and bizarre narrow, twisting paths and flights of steps that lead from one garden feature to another. A revealing detail in terms of the psychological dynamic of this family is that the children can walk in the garden only if they follow these elaborate routes; when the father sees his youngest son, Tom, 'walking straight up the side of the rockery using the path like a short flight of stairs', he roars out of the window, 'walk up it properly' (p. 14).

The novel, like much Gothic fiction, places Oedipal conflict at the centre of the family dynamic. Jack's father is in poor health and Jack is poised to take his place as male head of the family. Indeed, there is a sense in which Jack does symbolically murder his father. He agrees to help lay cement in the garden, but sneaks off to masturbate; whilst his father is dying of a heart attack caused by over-exertion, Jack is having his first orgasm in the bathroom. The head of the family is removed precisely as the eldest son achieves sexual maturity.

When the children's mother dies some months later, they are terrified at the prospect of being taken into care and resolve not to tell anyone: in a truly Gothic twist, they bury their mother in the cellar in a trunk which they fill with the left-over cement. The fact that the children manage to live for a considerable time with no one querying their welfare or the whereabouts of their mother signifies not only the breakdown of family structures, but the radical failure of late twentieth-century bureaucratic systems that are meant to protect children. Their lives become increasingly chaotic within a house that is the modern suburban equivalent of a Gothic castle: '[The] house was old and large. It was built to look like a castle, with thick walls, squat windows and crenellations above the front door' (p. 23). The second part of the novel, moreover, narrates a disturbing level of adolescent sexual and emotional dysfunction: Jack becomes violent and self-alienated; the young Tom regresses to babyhood and his sisters begin to dress him as a baby girl; the relationship between Jack and Julie becomes increasingly incestuous and the novel ends with the two of them discovered having sex by Julie's boyfriend. Jack and Julie come to occupy the roles of father and mother in a perverse twist of the 'normal' structure of the nuclear family.

Similarly, Iain Banks's *The Wasp Factory* (1984) is a compelling Gothic exploration of issues pertaining to gender identity and the symbolic structures that support subjectivities conventionally based upon a clear demarcation between 'masculine' and 'feminine'. As Freud observed, 'When you meet a human being, the first distinction you make is "male or female" and you are accustomed to make the distinction with unhesitating certainty.'[11] Feminist theory in the late twentieth century, however, has considerably undermined the notion that sex is biologically determined and that it is possible to make 'unhesitating' judgements about the nature of sexed identity. Simone de Beauvoir observed that one 'becomes' a woman, one is not irrevocably born into womanhood.[12] More recently, Judith Butler has argued that gender is a matter of what she calls 'performance'; it is a fiction generated through the absorption and performance of culturally defined behaviours deemed appropriate for, and considered to define, the supposedly fixed, oppositional categories of 'male' and 'female'.[13] Banks's novel represents the fluidity of gender identity as it came to be understood in the late twentieth century and interrogates deeply embedded cultural assumptions concerning gendered behaviours previously assumed to be innate.

The narrator of the novel is Frank, a seventeen year old who emerges in the novel's opening chapters as little short of a psychopath. He has established a mini-kingdom for himself in and around the house he shares with his father. The house is separated from a rural Scottish community by a narrow stretch of sea that affords Frank the isolation he needs to pursue his surreal, violent schemes. The novel often reads as a version of William Golding's *Lord of the Flies* (1954) with the difference that here there is only one protagonist who exists alongside, though in obvious alienation from, the surrounding adult community. Frank is a self-aggrandising adolescent obsessed with warfare, sacrifice and bizarre, seemingly meaningless rituals that revolve around marking territory and predicting the future. In the absence of human victims (though it emerges that Frank has in fact killed three other children, including his own brother), Frank wages war against the animals of the island and places the skulls of dead birds and rodents on what he calls 'sacrifice poles' that he erects in the sand dunes. The 'wasp factory' of the novel's title is an elaborate mechanism constructed by Frank to generate prophecies according to the manner in which the wasps caught in the machine die. In one of the most violent of Frank's excursions, he places home-made bombs in rabbit burrows and when the animals emerge, injured and terrified, he pours petrol over them and sets them alight. Moreover, he enjoys it; he posits himself as a war hero exhilarated by battle:

> I stood in the slanting sunlight, warm and yellow around me, the stench of burning flesh and grass on the wind, the smoke rising into the air from burrows and cadavers, grey and black, the sweet smell of leaking unburned petrol coming from the Flame-thrower where I'd left it, and I breathed deeply ... I felt *good*.[14]

At this point, according to cultural stereotypes of how adolescent boys are meant to behave, one might be tempted to say: so far, so typically male. Schoene-Harwood makes the pertinent point that Frank's behaviour can be interpreted according to 'the socially acceptable boundaries of what boys naturally tend to get up to'.[15] As Schoene-Harwood appreciates, however, there are certain features of Frank's behaviour, and his complex personal history, that complicate assumptions about what constitutes 'socially acceptable' male behaviour. If Frank's actions are taken to represent the adolescent boy in his natural state, then the inevitable conclusion is that adolescent masculinity – and by extension possibly masculinity *per se* – is psychopathic. Frank's violence extends to three young children that he murders using surreal means. He detonates an unexploded Second World War bomb in the face of his younger brother, Paul, by convincing him that it is a large bell that Paul should ring by hitting it with a stick. He puts a poisonous snake in the artificial leg of his childhood friend, Blyth. He contrives to get his cousin Esmeralda entangled in a huge kite that carries her away. After these killings, he shows no remorse and is in fact proud of his fake display of trauma after Esmeralda's disappearance that convinces his family he had nothing to do with it.

It is the notion that Frank's actions correspond to certain culturally valid expectations of masculinity, however, that the novel radically undermines. In typically Gothic fashion, the narrative offers clues about Frank's identity that are ultimately shown to be misleading. Frank reveals that he has some kind of genital deformity that means he has to sit down to urinate 'as though I was a bloody woman' (p. 17). Frank's understanding of the cause of his deformity is that as a small child he was badly bitten by the family dog, Old Saul, as a result of which he was castrated. This incident apparently coincided with the re-appearance of Frank's mother, Agnes, pregnant with another man's child. In a darkly comic twist, Frank's stepbrother Paul is born at the precise moment that his father is throttling Saul for castrating his son. The novel thus offers the reader a convincing psychological interpretation of Frank's hyper-masculine, violent behaviour: it is compensation for the loss of his penis. Frank's murder of Paul can be read as a subconscious act of revenge against the younger brother whose arrival coincides with this trauma. The sacrifice poles, meanwhile, can be interpreted as phallic totems, part of a complex network of symbols through which Frank attempts to rebuild a sense of masculine identity.

These interpretations, however, do not entirely displace the notion that sexed identity is innate and that Frank's extreme, compensatory behaviour is nevertheless a manifestation of a masculinity that defines his identity. Frank suggests as much:

> Both sexes can do one thing specially well; women can give birth and men can kill. We – I consider myself an honorary man – are the harder sex. We strike out, push through, thrust and take. The fact that it is only an analogue of all this sexual terminology that I am capable of does not discourage me. I can feel it in my bones, in my uncastrated genes. (p. 118)

And yet it is this assumption of biologically determined masculinity that *The Wasp Factory* ultimately refutes entirely by revealing that all the psychological interpretations of Frank's hyper-male violence offered by the narrative of his castration are misguided. The novel creates an account of adolescent dysfunction that is wholly convincing according to well-established cultural norms, only to reveal it as false: the novel in a sense sets the reader up to fail. In the final few pages it is revealed that Francis is in fact Frances; the narrator was born female and subjected to a hormonal sex-change experiment by her father who invented the fiction of castration to account for her lack of a penis. In the final chapter, Frances admits that she, too, had used the narrative of compensatory violence to justify her actions to herself: 'I – the unmanned – would out-man those around me' (p. 183). Deprived of this fiction of her identity, Frances is left without any cultural reference point through which to construct her sense of self, but this appears ultimately to be liberating: '*Now* the door shuts, and my journey begins' (p. 184). The revelation that gender identity is a cultural performance (a performance that Frances – as Frank -- happened to excel at, but which was never *more* than a performance) is posited, finally, as empowering.

Extended Commentary: Carter, *The Magic Toyshop* (1967)

Over the last thirty years, Angela Carter has been recognised as one of the most influential feminist novelists whose work initiated a new form of Gothicism that combines postmodern intertextuality with parody, the fantastical and fairy tale. *The Magic Toyshop* is a narrative of terror that uses contemporary literary strategies to explore issues pertaining to adolescence, family structures and, especially, the problematic status of girls and women within a patriarchal culture that objectifies and infantilises them.

Roland Barthes describes intertextuality as the process whereby texts become 'a multi-dimensional space in which a variety of writings, none of them original, blend and clash'.[16] For Barthes, all literature is to some degree intertextual; no work is ever entirely original, but is comprised of a 'tissue of quotations' taken from the wider culture, past and present. Postmodern writers such as Carter self-consciously deploy intertextuality as a strategy to reposition and rework older texts and (especially in Carter's case) myths and fairy tales. Intertextuality functions in *The Magic Toyshop* so as to position the protagonist, fifteen-year-old Melanie, as a female subject constructed through and to some extent in rebellion against patriarchal narratives that constitute ideal femininity as entailing obedience and sexual availability. At the beginning of the narrative, Melanie is represented as simultaneously exhilarated by and anxious about her developing body and the approach of sexual maturity. Melanie measures herself against her culture's prevailing notions of ideal womanhood and, in a series of richly evocative scenes, positions herself as the object of a hidden male gaze as she constructs her identity as 'woman' through various famous depictions of the female form:

> She posed in attitudes holding things. Pre-Raphaelite, she combed out her long, black hair to stream straight down from a centre parting and thoughtfully regarded herself as she held a tiger-lily from the garden under her chin. A la Toulouse Lautrec, she dragged her hair sluttishly across her face and sat down on a chair with her legs apart and a bowl of water and a towel at her feet. ...

> She was too thin for a Titian or a Renoir but she contrived a pale, smug Cranach Venus with a bit of net curtain wound round her head and the necklace of cultured pearls they gave her when she was confirmed. After she read *Lady Chatterley's Lover*, she secretly picked forget-me-nots and stuck them in her pubic hair.[17]

In so doing, Melanie projects herself into a future in which she imagines herself married to a man who resembles the hero of a typical romance fiction and her daydreams posit this future Melanie as the sexual object – albeit a romanticised object – of her husband: 'She gift-wrapped herself for a phantom bridegroom ... she could almost feel his breath on her cheek and his voice husking "darling".' Melanie is already assessing her young body from the perspective of this phantom male, and finding it wanting: 'In readiness for him ... she examined the swathed shape of her small, hard breasts. Their size disappointed her but she supposed they would do' (p. 2). This sequence of self-objectifying scenes culminates in a radically transgressive Gothic moment: whilst her parents are away in America, Melanie tries on her mother's wedding dress and, in the middle of the night, goes wandering in the garden imagining herself as a princess in a fairytale. The excitement, however, suddenly gives way to terror of the dark – a symbolic twist signifying that Melanie is still a child unprepared yet for the assumption of the role she is performing in her mother's gown. The garden becomes sinister and threatening – thoroughly Gothic – as Melanie races back to the house:

> Sobbing, she broke into a sudden run, stumbling over her skirts. Too much too soon. She had to get back to the front door and closed-in, cosy, indoors darkness and the smell of human beings. Branches, menacing, tore her hair and thrashed her face. The grass wove itself into ankle-turning traps for her feet. The garden turned against Melanie when she became afraid of it. (p. 18).

The door is locked, though, and (in an evocation of Eve and the apple in the garden of Eden) Melanie has to climb an apple tree to her bedroom window. In the process, the wedding dress is utterly mangled; Melanie's flirtation with adult female sexuality results in terror, injury and a symbolic loss of innocence signified by the torn and bloody dress. This theme of lost female innocence and punishment for transgression is pushed further when the next day news arrives of the death of Melanie's parents in a plane crash. In Melanie's imagination, the ruin of the wedding dress and her mother's death come together; she is 'the girl who killed her mother'.

Melanie's comfortable, middle-class childhood ends as she goes with her siblings, Victoria and John, to live in a toy shop in inner-city London owned by her maternal uncle, Philip Flowers. The novel's tone shifts markedly here. First of all, the Flowers family are 'othered' by Melanie in terms of their race and class; they are a working-class Irish family who seem to her to be simultaneously exotic and threatening. She nicknames them the 'red people' after their auburn hair; she sees them dancing to Irish music and is attracted by the strangeness and vitality of the scene, but at the same time repelled by what she regards as the squalor of their chaotic, unkempt house. It is the character of Melanie's cousin, Finn, who comes to embody for her a difference of identity that is compelling and unsettling, and it is Finn's maleness in particular that begins to unravel the romantic daydreams that she had entertained earlier. The phantom bridegroom of her imagination is replaced by the raw, sexual presence of Finn who audaciously appraises her as a 'fine grown girl for fifteen' (p. 45). Melanie becomes the object of a new male gaze and is forced to re-assess her sense of herself as 'woman' before this gaze.

The thematic significance of the male gaze is re-asserted later when Melanie finds a peep hole in her bedroom wall through which, she assumes, Finn has been spying on her. As Paulina Palmer points out, Carter uses this device to 'draw attention to the power exerted by the male gaze. The gaze is a practical means for men to impose control on women, as well as a symbol of male domination.'[18] Under the eye of Finn, Melanie is no longer able to script her own fantasies of seduction and sexual discovery using the idealised forms of feminine and masculine desire provided by patriarchal fairytale. This points to a key ideological function of fairytale: it 'bribes' women into obedience through narratives of romantic love that belie an oppressive, often violent reality. As Jean Wyatt contends, 'the violence of gendering is usually masked by the dynamic of love that produces it'.[19]

The house presided over by Uncle Philip is a grotesque fairytale world in which Melanie and her siblings, in Lorna Sage's analysis, exchange 'a world of common sense realism for one which works according to the laws of dreams, fairytales, folktales, myths and magic'.[20] Uncle Philip is a cross between an ogre in his castle and a malign magician. His wife, Margaret, was apparently struck dumb on her wedding day in a symbolic figuration of her total subservience to her husband. He makes and sells puppets, which are his obsession, and his family are drawn into his sphere of influence like puppets themselves. His relationship to Melanie is underscored by a threat of violence and malevolent sexual power that culminates in his staging of a perverse version of the myth of Leda and the swan. According to this myth, Leda is raped by the god Jove who assumes the form of a swan; it is one of a number of myths that narrate the sexual violation of women (Wyatt points out that 'Leda's is one of fifty rapes in Ovid's Metamorphosis alone')[21] and feminist critics have argued that these narratives serve ideologically to underpin a culture premised on the sexual domination of women by men. This mythology takes vivid shape in Philip's puppet theatre as he forces Melanie to act the part of Leda 'raped' by a puppet-swan operated by Finn. Melanie experiences the 'performance' as an actual assault; she is firstly alienated from her surroundings by a sense of powerlessness ('she felt herself not herself, wrenched from her own personality'), then completely terrified as the swan pins her to the ground, sinks its beak into her flesh and almost crushes her before leaving her with 'her dress [dragged] half off' (p. 167). As can happen with victims of sexual assault, Melanie's next humiliation is to have her account of the experience discredited: Philip accuses her of over-acting and 'cuffs her with the back of his hand'. Carter's intertextual appropriation of Ovid's myth of Leda thus serves here to play out a violence against women that is both theatrically fictive and dreadfully real: the patriarchal folklore slips into reality, constructing Melanie as actual and 'mythic' victim.

Melanie nevertheless to some extent rebels against her objectification and exploitation in Philip's household. When she discovers Finn's spy hole in her bedroom wall she uses it to spy on him, thus reversing the power dynamic of the gaze in patriarchal culture. Moreover, she establishes a relationship with Finn that increases in equality and mutual respect as the narrative progresses. After the Leda performance, Finn is so appalled by what Philip has done to Melanie that he takes the swan out and buries it. He emerges almost here as the hero of romance – the valiant protector of his virgin bride. This conventional narrative of seduction, which idealises woman only to secure her submission, no longer appears to have the power to construct Melanie's reality, however; she has moved beyond the daydreams of the opening chapter into a potentially more empowering reality with regard to Finn. It is symbolically significant that Finn's chivalrous act results in him catching a chill and seeking the protection of Melanie. He comes into her bedroom 'sick and sorry' and entirely lacking the power to dominate and disconcert Melanie that characterised their previous exchanges (p. 170). The moment entails a reversal of roles as Melanie holds him 'until his teeth stop chattering' and another of her romantic illusions drops away 'like a withered flower'; the image, of course, carries an important dual meaning given Finn's surname.

The text, however, does not allow for an unequivocal re-appraisal of Melanie's position within the structure of the patriarchal family in spite of its occasionally liberatory, role-reversing gestures. The ending of the novel is especially ambivalent; Philip embarks on a terrifyingly violent rampage having discovered Margaret in the arms of his brother, but perishes in a fire that consumes the toyshop. Melanie and Finn escape and the novel has already suggested that Melanie's fate is to marry her cousin. Some critics interpret this projection as irredeemably bleak, ensuring that 'Melanie's enclosure within patriarchal structures is thus complete'.[22] The novel's final sentence, though, does seem to hint at a future in which anything might be possible, especially as it harks back to the scene in the garden at the beginning of the novel in which it appeared that the future was not open, that Melanie's inevitable adult role was being rehearsed by her appropriation of her mother's wedding dress. The fire in the toyshop might be read as having dissolved all of the reference points of patriarchal culture as, 'at night, in the garden, they faced each other in a wild surmise' (p. 200).

Notes

1   Susan Hill, *The Woman in Black* (London: Hamish Hamilton, 1983), p. 11.
2   Sarah Waters, *The Little Stranger* (London: Virago, 2009), p. 39.
3   Hilary Mantel, *Beyond Black* (London: Fourth Estate, 2005), p. 1.
4   David Punter and Glennis Byron, *The Gothic* (Oxford: Blackwell, 2004), p. 82.
5   J. G. Ballard, *Concrete Island* (London: Vintage, 1994), p. 7.
6   Peter Brigg, *J. G. Ballard* (Rockville, MD: Wildsie Press, 1985), p. 67.
7   J. G. Ballard, *High Rise* (London: Jonathan Cape, 1975), p. 1.
8   J. G. Ballard, *Millennium People* (London: Flamingo, 2003), p. 51.
9   Sebastian Groes, 'From Shanghai to Shepperton: Crises of Representation in J. G. Ballard's London', in Jeannette Baxter (ed.), *J. G. Ballard* (London: Continuum, 2008), p. 91.
10   Ian McEwan, *The Cement Garden* (London: Vintage, 1978).
11   Sigmund Freud, *Femininity: New Introductory Lectures on Psychoanalysis* (Toronto: Hogarth Press, 1933), p. 47.
12   Simone de Beauvoir, *The Second Sex* (London: Penguin, 1984), p. 267.
13   See Judith Butler, *Gender Trouble: Feminism and the Subversion of Identity* (London: Routledge, 1990).
14   Iain Banks, *The Wasp Factory* (London: Macmillan, 1984), p. 36
15   Bertolt Schoene-Harwood, 'Dams Burst: Devolving Gender in Iain Banks's *The Wasp Factory*', *Ariel: A Review of International English Literature*, 30:1 (January 1999), p. 131.
16   Roland Barthes, 'The Death of the Author', in Stephen Heath (ed.), *Image-Music-Text* (New York: Hill & Wang, 1977), p. 146.
17   Angela Carter, *The Magic Toyshop* (London: Virago, 1981), pp. 1–2.
18   Paulina Palmer, 'From "Coded Manequin" to Bird Woman: Angela Carter's Magic Flight', in Sue Roe (ed.), *Women Reading Women's Writing* (Brighton: Harvester Press, 1987), p. 186.
19   Jean Wyatt, 'The Violence of Gendering: Castration Images in Angela Carter's *The Magic Toyshop*, *The Passion of New Eve* and "Peter and the Wolf"', in Alison Easton (ed.), *Angela Carter* (London: Macmillan, 2000), p. 67.
20   Lorna Sage, *Angela Carter* (Plymouth: Northcote House, 1994), p. 16.
21   Wyatt, 'The Violence of Gendering', p. 68.
22   Sara Mills, Lynne Pearce, Sue Spaull and Elaine Millard, *Feminist Readings/Feminists Reading* (London: Harvester Wheatsheaf, 1989), p. 138.

Part Four
Critical Theories and Debates

Narrative Instability and the Gothic Narrator

The French philosopher Maurice Blanchot (1907–2003) has argued that something rather unsettling occurs when words are committed to paper and texts are created: at the moment this happens, the idea that is to be communicated through the text comes to exist at one remove from the source of the idea in a person's intellect, memory or imagination. Texts therefore have the potential to introduce an element of uncertainty or even inauthenticity into processes of communication; because the author of a text is never (or rarely) present before the reader, the reader is confronted by a narrative that cannot be verified by means of first-hand knowledge of its origin. Thus, says Blanchot, writing is 'alien to all relationships of presence'.[1] The written word signifies the absence of a voice, of a speaking subject who can be identified as the origin of an utterance and interrogated if necessary, and thus textuality has often been regarded with some suspicion by philosophers within the Western intellectual tradition. Within this tradition, as the philosopher Jacques Derrida has observed in numerous contexts,[2] the spoken word has been associated with a greater degree of authenticity than written narratives precisely because speech emanates from a source that is present to the listener. Texts, on the other hand, are distanced from their source and once they begin to be copied and to circulate widely within a culture the possibility of error, or even of forgery, multiplies.

The narrative strategies of Gothic fiction bring into sharp focus the challenges and anxieties that Blanchot and Derrida associate with textuality. Indeed, because of the Gothic's tendency to manipulate its own alleged points of origin, and to cast doubt upon the authenticity of its narratives, it could be said that the Gothic is, more than any other form of literature, 'alien to all relationships of presence'. It is for this reason that David Punter contends that Gothic 'is the paradigm of all fiction, all textuality'.[3] Gothic tends to foreground what other forms of writing (the realist novel, for example) often seek to conceal: that its narratives are not necessarily trustworthy; that literary conventions bear a slippery relationship to the 'truths' they mean to communicate.

This chapter considers the various narrative strategies whereby the Gothic recounts its strange tales and, in the process, problematises its own narrative stability and reliability. The main focus here is upon eighteenth- and nineteenth-century Gothic fictions in which key conventions (the device of the 'lost' manuscript, prefaces, frame narratives, unreliable narrators and so on) begin to take shape. The final section, however, considers more recent appropriations of these conventions in postmodern Gothic novels in which the very status of a text as constituting any sort of reliable document (fictional or otherwise) overtly becomes the subject of the narrative. It can be argued that these often disorientating, ironic and multi-layered texts take to its inevitable conclusion the tendency within Gothic literature from the moment of its inception to disrupt the conditions of its own narrative production.

Narrating the Past

Early Gothic novels are frequently concerned with the narration of some kind of 'history'. They may be set in the Middle Ages, either in Britain or in southern Europe, and this strategy reflects to a large extent the eighteenth-century fascination with the medieval period as an age of 'Gothic' barbarism (when it was associated with southern

Catholic Europe) or 'Gothic' chivalry, freedom and vitality (when related to Britain and to a certain contemporary construction of 'Britishness').* Moreover, Gothic fictions sometimes made rather elaborate truth claims for the histories which they presented. Horace Walpole famously asserted in the preface to the first edition of *The Castle of Otranto* (1764) that the events narrated had some relationship to truth; these events were framed by this preface so as to constitute a 'history' of the medieval principality of Otranto revealed in a manuscript discovered in a library in the north of England. In the first Gothic fiction, therefore, one encounters two narrative strategies that were to become staples of the genre in later years: the use of a preface to make various claims for the narrative that follows (a device discussed more fully in the next section of this chapter), and the 'discovery' of an ancient manuscript the origin of which is somewhat obscure. Moreover, Walpole's preface reflects the extent to which the narration of the past in Gothic fiction invariably reflects contemporary cultural and political concerns.

The first edition of the novel was published on Christmas Day, 1764. Walpole was not cited as the author of the work; rather, its publication was attributed to the efforts of a fictitious 'editor', one William Marshall. It is Marshall who claims that he has found the manuscript in a library belonging to a Catholic family in the north of England. It is, interestingly, said to be written in 'the black letter', a term that describes the distinctive Germanic Gothic lettering associated with medieval documents.[4] The narrative is thus positioned as an authentic 'Gothic' artefact† relating the extraordinary misfortunes of Manfred, Prince of Otranto. The 'editor' points out that the fantastical events related in the manuscript are no doubt the

---

* See Part Two: 'A Cultural Overview' and Part Three: 'Eighteenth-century Gothic' for a discussion of the different connotations of the term 'Gothic' in the eighteenth century. On the one hand, 'Gothic' evoked the barbarism of medieval (even contemporary) Catholic countries; on the other, it alluded to the northern European, Germanic 'Gothic' tribes, regarded as the robust, libertarian forebears of the English.

† The same claim is made in respect of Ann Radcliffe's Gothic novel *Gaston de Blondeville* – see below.

product of a superstitious, medieval Catholic culture and he hardly expects that they can be believed by a sophisticated eighteenth-century English reader. Nevertheless, the origin of the text is surrounded with sufficient mystique in this preface (the origin itself is 'Gothicised', one might say) that the enlightened modern reader is given the opportunity to suspend disbelief, to indulge in that peculiar textual pleasure (a hallmark of Gothic fiction) of imagining that the fantastical might be true since, after all, the reader is dealing with Catholic Italy in the 'Christian dark ages' and not Protestant London in 1764. This preface therefore serves a significant cultural function: it distances the narrative from its readership, removing it from the domain of Enlightenment rationality, and it gives the reader permission to enjoy its extravagances. Moreover, the preface appeals to the reader's sound literary judgement; whilst this manuscript is the product of a crude, primitive culture, claims the editor, the style of it 'has nothing that flavours of barbarism' (p. 5). Here, then, is an author acutely aware of the cultural profile of his readership playing a clever game in the publication of this first edition: the novel-reading public is presented with a mysterious manuscript that the educated reader can admire intellectually on the level of style, whilst relishing emotionally the 'barbarism' of its content.

Although different in style and content to *The Castle of Otranto*,[*] Sophia Lee's *The Recess* (published in three volumes, 1783–5) is another text that calls into question the relation between fiction and history and that in various ways complicates its own status as 'fiction'. *The Recess* was a successful work in its time, running to seven editions in twenty years and being translated into five European languages. Although neglected for most of the twentieth century, the critic Montague Summers asserted in the 1930s that the novel 'is one of the landmarks of English literature' on account of its innovative structure and style.[5]

The Recess is set during the reign of Queen Elizabeth I and narrates the tragic lives of two fictional daughters of Mary Queen of Scots,

---

[*] See Part Three: 'Eighteenth-century Gothic' for a discussion of this novel's plot and overall narrative structure.

Matilda and Ellinor. In so doing (as the critic April Alliston observes), Lee draws on an older tradition of French romance, especially popular in the seventeenth century, whereby histories of noble families were reworked as fiction.[6] Lee adds a significant Gothic twist to this tradition of historical romance, however, through her use of the device of the discovered manuscript. In particular, she creates in relation to the manuscript an air of suspense and ambiguity (alluding to its secret origin which she is not at liberty to disclose, and to its dilapidated condition) that could be said to 'Gothicise' the material substance of the text itself, generating terror and mystery not only out of the events of the narrative, but out of the very form through which these events are recounted. In her 'Advertisement' to the first volume, she writes:

> NOT being permitted to publish the means which enriched me with the manuscript from whence the following tale is extracted, its simplicity alone can authenticate it. – I make no apology for altering the language to that of the present age, since the obsolete style of the author would be frequently unintelligible ... The depredations of time have left chasms in the story, which sometimes only heightens the pathos. An inviolable respect for truth would not permit me to attempt connecting these, even where they appeared faulty.[7]

This passage reveals a sophisticated understanding of the problematic relationship between textuality and history. Rather like a modern journalist reporting a sensitive story, Lee asserts that she is unable to reveal her source yet refers the reader to the straightforward 'simplicity' of the tale as a marker of its authenticity. She admits that she has updated its language for a modern readership, but denies making any attempt to fill in the gaps left in the crumbling manuscript by the 'depredations of time': note the direct assertion here of editorial integrity that forbids any addition to the text out of 'an inviolable respect for truth'. By this means, even the flaws and ambiguities in the text can be pointed to as evidence of authenticity;

they are signs that the text has suffered no alteration in content by an unscrupulous modern author. Lee thus creates a fiction of herself as the trustworthy editor of a reliable manuscript. Her strategy did not, nor was it probably intended to dupe the public (as Alliston points out, readers by the 1780s were sufficiently familiar with literary conventions of this kind not to take Lee's claims at face value), but it did allow Lee in this influential novel to assert the narrative power of a device that allows both author and reader to indulge in a fantasy of 'authentic' Gothic terror.

Sophia Lee was a significant influence on the best-selling Gothic novelist of the 1790s – Ann Radcliffe. Radcliffe's five most well-known novels feature, like Lee's *The Recess*, female protagonists terrorised by various regimes of authority, and the central motif of Lee's work (the confinement of women within secret Gothic spaces) is reproduced frequently by Radcliffe. However, it is a lesser-known work by Radcliffe, published posthumously in 1826, that constitutes the most complex and nuanced of her engagements with the fluid demarcations between past and present, history and fiction: *Gaston de Blondeville*.

This short Gothic romance differs in form and content from most of Radcliffe's work of the 1790s.[*] It is set in the time of Henry III and turns upon a mystery pertaining to Sir Gaston de Blondeville, a nobleman at Henry's court, who is accused of murder. Like *The Recess*, it uses the device of the discovered manuscript in order to mediate between past and present and to generate a mystery surrounding the very origin of the tale that is being narrated. Radcliffe's narration of the past is in many ways more complex than Lee's, however. The story of de Blondeville is contained within an ancient manuscript edited by an enthusiastic antiquarian named Willoughton whose discovery of the document whilst visiting

---

[*] It has most in common with Radcliffe's first novel, *The Castle of Athlin and Dunbayne*, in so far as it is set in medieval England rather than southern Europe. However, it is the only one of Radcliffe's fictions to feature an actual ghost; all her other works use the device of the 'explained supernatural' to attribute rational causes to apparently spectral apparitions (see Part Three: 'Eighteenth-century Gothic').

Warwick Castle with his friend, Simpson, frames the main narrative. The textual peculiarities of the document, its relationship to historical fact and Willoughton's struggle to render it comprehensible to a contemporary readership are thus embedded within the fiction itself, forming an important component of its narrative trajectory; the novel is as much concerned with issues of textual reproduction and historical authenticity as it is with the details of Gaston de Blondeville's life. Willoughton's acquisition of and response to the document also reflect a range of contemporary concerns relating to the value – both intellectual and economic – of literary and historical texts that purport to narrate the nation's past.

Willoughton and his friend are shown around Warwick Castle by a guide who alludes to certain ancient texts in his possession that were found, he alleges, beneath an old chapel ruined during Henry VIII's persecution of the monasteries. Through Willoughton, who insists on seeing all the documents, a number of contemporary economic, historical and literary issues are brought into focus. All the manuscripts are said to be 'printed in the black letter' (like *The Castle of Otranto* according to Walpole's first preface) and attention is drawn to their textual peculiarities. One of the works (the 'Trew Chronique' which Willoughton edits and publishes as the narrative of Gaston de Blondeville) is introduced by a preamble 'written almost in the form of a triangle'. Willoughton reproduces in his edition of the work this odd arrangement of the text: the Gothic script of the preamble does indeed taper down to form a visually striking black triangle. Willoughton admits that this is the only part of the text that he has preserved exactly as it appeared in the 'Trew Chronique' – in order, he says, to capture 'some of the quaintness of the original'[8] – and thus it becomes a marker of historical and textual authenticity, rather like the flaws left by the 'depredations of time' in Sophia Lee's *The Recess*.

For Willoughton, the history of this text is both illuminating and frustratingly obscure. It belongs, Willoughton is convinced, to a 'dark age' of superstition and downright mendacity on the part of monks eager to exploit a gullible population: its 'truth' is thus seriously open to question. At the same time, however, Willoughton acknowledges the historical and aesthetic importance of all of the texts in the guide's possession. Irrespective of their fabulous content and the possible motivations of their authors, the works are 'authentic' as historical and literary artefacts; they form part of a unique national heritage, a textual link between past and present. The most recent of the three texts is recognised by Willoughton to be 'one of the earliest books that came off the press in England' (p. 49). This text thus relates that 'dark age' (p. 57) of superstition to a modern publishing economy in which the printed word emerges as a commodity. Indeed, Willoughton's acquisition of the texts emphasises their problematic status as commodified artefacts within this modern economy. Willoughton negotiates the purchase of the works ignoring as he does so the advice of his companion Simpson to push the old man down to the lowest possible price. Willoughton refuses to make what for him would amount to a mercenary, dishonest deal. He pays the man according to his appraisal of the texts' historical and aesthetic value and, in so doing, he establishes his credentials as a man of taste and virtue. The economic value of this commodified text is subordinated to Willoughton's cultured judgements of 'authentic' aesthetic and historical worth. Radcliffe's text thus reproduces, through Willoughton's discovery of this fascinating artefact, complex contemporary conditions governing literary production, the very conditions that encouraged Gothic novelists to indulge in complicated forms of narrative game-playing with their readers. Radcliffe's novel does not attempt only to narrate the past, therefore, but it also purports to describe the conditions through which the past comes to be presented to the contemporary reader in Gothic fictions and elsewhere in late eighteenth-century culture.

Prefaces

A great many early Gothic fictions include prefaces by either the author or a fictitious 'editor' that make certain claims in relation to the main body of the text. These prefaces are often concerned to establish a certain authenticity or authority for the narrative. As discussed above, Walpole's first preface to *The Castle of Otranto* establishes a fictional 'history' for the tale that follows. Later prefaces are concerned less with questions of historical veracity than with issues of literary authority: they attempt to justify to the reader the author's motivations for publishing a work of Gothic fiction.* Such attempts at literary self-validation resume again with Walpole whose second preface to *The Castle of Otranto* (published to accompany a second edition of the novel in April 1765) radically repositions the text presented four months earlier as a 'black letter' manuscript discovered by William Marshall.

The first edition of *The Castle of Otranto* (1764) was enthusiastically received; it was declared 'a work of genius, evincing great dramatic powers' by the critic John Langhorne writing in the *Monthly Review* just a few weeks after the novel's appearance.[9] This positive critical reception prompted Walpole to publish another edition accompanied by a further preface. Here, Walpole admits his authorship and attempts at some length to justify his enterprise in quite specific literary and cultural terms. The second preface is an important document as regards not only the origins of Gothic fiction in the mid-eighteenth century, but wider debates concerning the generic status and literary merits of other forms of fiction, and the growing influence of Shakespeare over English national culture. Walpole posits *The Castle of Otranto* as a literary experiment aiming to marry two forms of fiction: the emerging eighteenth-century novel and the older romance. The novel is, for Walpole, a new form of narrative that eschews the fantastical excesses, the 'improbablities' of ancient romance; it is creditable in its ability to copy nature reliably, but in taking as their key artistic principle a 'strict adherence to common life', novelists have allowed 'the great resources of fancy [to be] damned up'.[10] Moreover, Walpole draws upon the growing cultural authority of Shakespeare to

---

* See Part Three: 'Eighteenth-century Gothic' and 'Romantic-era Gothic' for a discussion of the hostility that existed in this period towards Gothic fictions. This hostility helps explain why Gothic novelists were so keen to justify their writings to a literary establishment inclined to dismiss them as intellectually frivolous.

validate his experiment. Shakespeare is posited as the English genius whose literary innovations legitimise Walpole's project. Walpole commends the mixture of comedic and tragic elements, and of high and low social life in Shakespeare and explains how he modelled elements of *The Castle of Otranto* on this 'masterly pattern'. Walpole thus attempts to situate his modern Gothic romance within an emerging authoritative English literary tradition that was coming increasingly to define the cultural identity of the nation.

Two slightly later novels, both influential texts of the early Gothic period, also begin with prefaces that express and seek to resolve various anxieties concerning the literary and cultural status of Gothic fiction: William Godwin's *St Leon* (1799)[*] and Charles Maturin's *Melmoth the Wanderer* (1820).[†] *St Leon* narrates the story of Reginald St Leon, a French nobleman whose penchant for gambling threatens to bankrupt his family. He is offered by a mysterious stranger the 'philosopher's stone' that can guarantee immortality and unlimited wealth; these gifts destroy St Leon, however, who becomes (like Victor Frankenstein whose ambitions alienate him from humanity) an outcast from society. The preface of 1798 demonstrates a concern with questions of literary origin and authority; Godwin feels, like Walpole, the need to justify his Gothic project and he repeats the ambivalent claims of earlier Gothic fictions in suggesting that there might be a genuine historical source for the tale. Godwin also presents his novel as an intellectually serious work that deserves to be read not only by a reader seeking 'novelty' (and implicitly this reader is positioned as the typical consumer of Gothic fictions), but also by 'the severest judges' of literature.[11] To strengthen this sense of the fiction's intellectual gravity, Godwin acknowledges the literary influence of Shakespeare as a founding father who empowers the writer seeking to 'imagine [the] new' (p. xxxiii). This preface also implicitly invokes, in support of *St Leon*, the second preface of

---

[*] This novel influenced Godwin's daughter, Mary Shelley, in the writing of *Frankenstein* (1818).

[†] This novel influenced Edgar Allan Poe and Oscar Wilde in the later nineteenth century.

Walpole's *The Castle of Otranto*: the credible blending of human 'passions' with the marvels of old romance is given as a justification for the creation of a new form of literary Gothicism. Supporting this text, then, is a body of work (Shakespeare's, Walpole's) that Godwin cites in order to 'pardon the boldness and irregularity' of his unorthodox creation and even, he hopes, to have it ultimately 'rank among the classics of the language' (p. xxxiii).

Maturin's preface to *Melmoth the Wanderer* (the plot and structure of which are discussed further in the following section) is a revealing attempt by a Gothic novelist simultaneously to exploit and disavow its problematic literary context. Like William Godwin, Maturin the novelist must justify himself and his work before an imagined tribunal of good taste. In particular, he tries to distance his fiction firmly from the mass of disreputable Gothic romances which appear disconcertingly close, generically, to *Melmoth the Wanderer*. Interestingly, Maturin suggests that his text was censured in this regard even before publication. He describes reading a section of his draft to a friend who complained it contained 'too much attempt at the revivification of the horrors of Radcliffe-Romance, of the persecutions of convents and the terrors of the Inquisition'. Maturin defends his work on the grounds that his romance is not merely a narration of 'startling adventures', but an examination of 'the petty torments which constitutes the misery of life in general'.[12] He cites one of his own sermons (Maturin was an Anglican minister) as the origin of the idea behind the tale and he quotes from it in the preface. His preface justifies the fiction as a literary and theological meditation on the problem of evil and therefore as a legitimate creative enterprise for a clergyman to be engaged in.

Frame Narratives and Multiple Narrators

A frame narrative is a device whereby an author presents the reader with an initial, introductory scenario that leads into the main body of the text. For example, Emily Brontë's *Wuthering Heights* (1847, discussed in Part Three: 'Nineteenth-century Gothic') begins with the lawyer Lockwood describing in his diary his first meeting with Heathcliff, after which he asks the housekeeper Nelly Dean to recount to him the story of the house and its occupants. Frame narratives serve a variety of functions which are especially relevant to Gothic fictions. On the one hand, they can function to distance the contemporary reader from the weird events of the narrative, opening up a space for the reader to appreciate the fantastical without being drawn too closely to the superstitions and violence of a previous age or a different culture. As Gregory O'Dea observes, the frame narrative used in this way will 'distinguish our own experience in the world of real things from that represented in the framed narrative'.[13] For example, Radcliffe's *The Italian* (1797) begins with a group of English travellers visiting a church in Naples in 1764. When they spot a mysterious figure pacing around the church they enquire of the friar who the man is. The friar's response is to send to one of the group a manuscript which tells the history of the murderous monk, Schedoni. This frame aligns the reader with these sophisticated, contemporary English tourists and thus establishes the cultural position that the reader is to adopt in relation to the text.

On the other hand, a frame can work to undermine the credibility of the main body of the narrative. Henry James's *The Turn of the Screw* (1898) presents the reader with one of the most ambiguous and complex frame narratives of the nineteenth century. First of all, an anonymous narrator describes a visit, with several others, to the home of his friend Douglas. The group is listening to ghost stories when Douglas declares that he has a tale more frightening than any they have heard so far: it is contained in a letter written to him by his sister's former governess and it describes her experience as governess to two small children in an apparently haunted manor house. Before reading out the letter (written just before the governess's death) Douglas admits that he was in love with her. He also comments on the woman's youth and nervous disposition at the point when she took up the position in the manor house – a position that would have entailed 'really great loneliness', says Douglas. These details throw into question the governess's narrative and, indeed, the chief dilemma posed by this novel is whether the ghosts are real or a product of the young woman's nervous imagination. The critic Oscar Cargill points out that the writing of this letter to a man who has professed his love for the governess further complicates the reliability of her account: he argues that she may have written the narrative to convey why she could never have returned Douglas's love – she means to communicate to him the destructive instability of her personality.[14]

The use of frame narratives often overlaps in Gothic fiction with the deployment of multiple narrators whose accounts offer sometimes complementary, sometimes conflicting perspectives on the novel's events. Indeed, multiple narrations can function as multiple 'frames' within which many narratives are embedded one within the other. Two novels published almost contemporaneously serve as illuminating examples of this technique and its effects: *Frankenstein* (1818) and *Melmoth the Wanderer* (1820).

Frankenstein is narrated via three 'frames' each with its own first-person narrator. The explorer Captain Walton, en route to the North Pole, writes letters home to his sister, Mrs Saville. On the journey he meets Victor Frankenstein who tells Walton his story and embeds within it the story told to him by the monster. Walton transcribes these oral narratives and includes them in his letters. As Beth Newman observes, this is an unusual gesture that 'turns inside out' the narrative strategies deployed in Gothic fictions of the previous century. Instead of a written document found by an 'editor' who then presents it to the reader, Walton 'turns oral narratives into writing'.[15] This device again raises questions of the narrative's overall reliability since the reader encounters stories recited from memory by Victor (his own and the lengthy discourses of the monster) and then transcribed from memory by Walton. Here, then, is another Gothic fiction that appears deliberately to foreground the question of its own textual authenticity.

Maturin's *Melmoth the Wanderer* has a multi-frame narrative structure that is considerably more complex than that of *Frankenstein*, or indeed of any Gothic fiction of the nineteenth century. The novel begins in 1816 with John Melmoth (the first frame narrator) rushing to a dilapidated Irish manor house to be by the bedside of his dying uncle. The uncle entrusts to John an ancient document which he instructs his nephew to burn immediately; John does so, but only after reading the text. This fragmented, crumbling manuscript (which, to the frustration of John Melmoth, fades into incomprehensibility at key moments in the narrative) describes the persecution of an Englishman, Stanton, by a mysterious and seemingly diabolical figure known as Melmoth the Wanderer. Stanton encounters Melmoth first in Spain and then in England, where Melmoth predicts that Stanton will be incarcerated in an asylum. When this indeed occurs, Melmoth visits Stanton in his cell to tempt him with the prospect of freedom in return for a dreadful exchange, which the damaged manuscript prevents John (and, of course, Maturin's reader) from discovering.

The device of the discovered manuscript gives way to a multitude of narratives dealing obliquely with John's malevolent ancestor, the Wanderer. These narratives are mediated through a character named Monçada, a Spaniard whom John rescues from a shipwreck. Monçada describes his imprisonment within a Spanish monastery, his temptation by the Wanderer and his ultimate escape. He tells how he found himself within a subterranean apartment occupied by an 'awful figure with the appearance of a sorcerer' who offers Monçada protection if he will agree to act as his scribe in copying a manuscript which contains the histories of four skeletons kept in the cavern.[16] The manuscript is another decrepit, barely legible text. It contains a number of different narratives (more frames within frames) including a 'horrible secret' which Monçada is enjoined to 'hear and relate'. The secret concerns a noblewoman called Immalee who was seduced by and bore the child of the Wanderer. This is one of the chief points at which the novel foregrounds and problematises its own digressive and disorientating narrativity. It blurs the demarcation between narrative frames and different temporal and physical locations; in so doing, it establishes multiple parallels between readers and narrators that confuse the separation between the storyteller and the listener/reader, between the producer and the consumer of narratives. Monçada's position parallels that of Melmoth; both uncover in mysterious circumstances scarcely legible manuscripts which they read/recite with dread and fascination. The reader's position, moreover, doubles that of both narrators who are at various points readers of weird tales that comprise the disjointed structure of the novel. These narrative wanderings can be read as a textual metaphor for the wanderings of John's demonic ancestor: the text and Melmoth the Wanderer constantly transgress the borders between the 'inside' and 'outside' of multiple scenes of narration, just as Melmoth is narrated as moving supernaturally through space and time. By this means, the novel foregrounds its own peculiar narrativity until, ultimately, the opposition between the 'outside' of John Melmoth's originary narrative (the main frame, as it were) and the 'inner' narratives enclosed by this frame collapses: the Wanderer actually appears in John Melmoth's chamber just as Monçada is promising to relate further and more dreadful tales about him. The demonic excess represented by the Wanderer is thus projected outwards through narrative progressions away from John Melmoth, only to return as the text turns in on itself, abolishing the textual and physical distance between the Wanderer and his descendant. The critic R. B. Oost suggests that these narrative twists have an effect on the reader that is not only disorientating, but almost persecutory; the reader becomes, in encountering this novel, a Gothic victim racing through various textual labyrinths in search of a 'truth' that never quite comes into view.[17]

The Unreliable Narrator

In an influential essay entitled 'Gothic and the Madness of Interpretation', Scott Brewster argues that the narrative strategies of Gothic fiction produce the possibility of so many conflicting interpretations that Gothic textuality can have a near maddening effect on the reader. Brewster observes that 'Gothic does not merely transcribe disturbed, perverse or horrifying worlds: its narrative structures and voices are interwoven with and intensify the madness they represent'.[18] The device of the frame narrative, often overlapping with multiple accounts of a novel's events, contributes to the textual 'madness' associated with Gothicism; so does another strategy that can again overlap with the techniques of narration discussed above: the use of an 'unreliable narrator'. Such a narrator is one who either does not know, or who chooses not to relate all of the facts pertaining to their circumstances. An example has been considered already: Henry James's *The Turn of the Screw* (1898) is narrated by a governess whose grasp of events as they unfold is tenuous and this unreliability is indeed foregrounded in James's frame narrative through the introduction provided by the frame narrator and his friend, Douglas.

The use of the unreliable narrator in Gothic fiction is frequently a device through which the emotional instability of the protagonist is conveyed, and such instability (often bordering on madness or paranoia) is frequently tied to the common Gothic motif of persecution and punishment. William Godwin's *Caleb Williams* (1794) is an early Gothic text that in this regard anticipates later developments in Gothic narrative style and structure. The protagonist is a man who early on in the novel establishes a close relationship with his employer, the aristocratic Falkland. When Caleb discovers that Falkland is the murderer of another nobleman, Tyrrel, he is forced to leave Falkland's service and Falkland proceeds to pursue Caleb across the country in an attempt to ensure that Caleb does not reveal his crime. Falkland even goes to the lengths of inventing stories to discredit Caleb and distributing them in pamphlet form; wherever Caleb goes, Falkland's various persecutions follow, driving Caleb deeper into despair and paranoia.

The novel is a powerful critique of the powerlessness of ordinary individuals before systems of law that invariably side with men such as Falkland. However, the Gothic qualities of the narrative complicate a straightforward interpretation of the text as merely a vehicle for the communication of a radical political message. The relationship between Caleb and Falkland is emotionally intense and, as some critics have suggested, verging towards homo-eroticism. The two men appear to be bound together by what George Haggerty defines as a dysfunctional 'sado-masochistic configuration' of power.[19] Caleb's account of events is compromised by the emotional intensity and complexity of his relationship with his employer. Early on, Caleb admits to possessing an active imagination influenced by his reading of romance fiction. When he begins to suspect Falkland of murder, he appears to cast Falkland as the villain of a romance and is driven by 'insatiable curiosity' to resolve the mystery. Whatever Caleb's motivations (and they remain unclear even to Caleb himself), he desperately wants to find that Falkland is guilty of murder. He admits that as soon as the idea occurs to him, it becomes fixed in his mind. He determines 'to place myself as a watch upon my patron' and clearly relishes the prospect: 'To be a spy upon Mr. Falkland! That there was a danger in the employment served to give an alluring pungency to the choice.'[20] When Caleb begins to feel that his conjectures are being confirmed, he is elated:

> My blood boiled within me. I was conscious to a kind of rapture for which I could not account. I was solemn, yet full of rapid emotion, burning with indignation and energy. In the very tempest and hurricane of the passions, I seemed to enjoy the most soul-ravishing calm. I cannot better express the then state of my mind than by saying, I was never so perfectly alive as at that moment. (p. 135)

This is not to say that Falkland is innocent of the murder of Tyrrel, but rather that Godwin offers no independent confirmation of this crime beyond a first-person account compromised by the narrator's repeated admissions that he has a considerable emotional investment in believing his employer guilty. Thus, whilst Falkland's eventual confession of murder to Caleb appears quite unequivocal, it must be remembered that this confession is narrated by Caleb, and given his state of mind it is not inconceivable that he has embellished this account in order to perpetuate that 'kind of rapture' induced in him by the prospect of Falkland's disgrace. By positing Caleb as an unreliable narrator, Godwin opens up a range of interpretations of the events recounted and the motivations behind them, and thus introduces into the text an element of uncertainty (and the possibility of what Scott Brewster calls 'the madness of interpretation') that is typical of Gothic fiction.

Postmodern Gothic

The French philosopher Jean-François Lyotard defined post-modernism as an 'incredulity towards meta-narratives'.[21] A meta-narrative is an overarching theory or discourse that purports to give a comprehensive, all-encompassing account of an intellectual discipline or aspect of experience. Postmodernism contends that such accounts are illusory, that 'truths' are necessarily incomplete and provisional. Postmodern fiction tends to foreground the artificiality and contingency of its own literary strategies, insisting especially upon the problematic relation between fiction and other cultural and historical discourses. One could argue that this postmodern perspective was anticipated at least a century ago by some of the Gothic novels discussed in this chapter – novels which draw attention to, and simultaneously undermine, what might be termed the 'truth value' of a text. It finds fuller expression in new forms of literary Gothicism in Britain and America at the end of the twentieth century and in the first decade of the twenty-first.

A text that exemplifies the textual strategies of postmodern Gothic in many ways is the Scottish writer Alasdair Gray's novel *Poor Things* (1992). This text is subtitled, 'Episodes from the Early Life of Archibald McCandless M. D., Scottish Public Health Officer, edited by Alasdair Gray'. Gray thus invokes the standard Gothic device of posing as the 'editor' of his own narrative, but Gray's interventions do not cease with a 'preface'; Gray interposes elsewhere his commentary on the events narrated. Moreover, the novel is an exercise in intertextuality; it is an elaborate, playful reworking of Mary Shelley's *Frankenstein*. The protagonist is a scientist named Godwin Bysshe Baxter (the name evokes Shelley's father, William Godwin, and her husband, Percy Bysshe Shelley). The narrative also utilises the technique of multiple narration that Shelley employs in her novel (see above): Gray writes an introduction, Archibald McCandless narrates part of the novel, and Gray as 'editor' includes commentary on the text. The complex mode of narration complicates the 'truth-value' of texts which ostensibly describe an experiment by Baxter whereby he replaced the brain of a woman named Bella Baxter with that of a child. The unreliability of the narrative's parts is sharply foregrounded by another of the text's interventions, this time by McCandless's wife:

> My second husband's story positively stinks of all that was morbid in that most morbid of centuries, the nineteenth. He has made a sufficiently strange story stranger still by stirring into it episodes and phrases to be found in Hogg's Suicide's Grave with additional ghouleries from the works of Mary Shelley and Edgar Allan Poe. What morbid Victorian fantasy has he NOT filched from? I find traces of *The Coming Race*, *Dr. Jekyll and Mr. Hyde*, *Dracula*, *Trilby*, Rider Haggard's *She*, *The Case-Book of Sherlock Holmes* and, alas, *Alice Through the Looking-Glass;* a gloomier book than the sunlit *Alice in Wonderland*. He has even plagiarized work by two very dear friends: G. B. Shaw's *Pygmalion* and the scientific romances of Herbert George Wells.[22]

Whether Mrs McCandless's contribution is any more reliable than the others, however, is impossible to ascertain. The text resists any form of interpretative closure that might reveal the 'truth' about Dr Baxter and his creation (if she is, indeed, his creation).

The American writer Mark Danielewski's first novel, *House of Leaves*, was published to considerable critical acclaim in 2000.[23] The novel, like Gray's, appropriates many of the narrative conventions developed in earlier Gothic fictions and combines them with textual innovations that reflect contemporary cultural contexts. Like Maturin's *Melmoth the Wanderer*, *House of Leaves* is a multi-layered, multi-framed narrative in which various accounts of events are embedded one within the other. Developments in reprographic and printing technology enable Danielewski to take strategies of narrative 'embedding' to a wholly new level, however. The narratives in *Melmoth the Wanderer* switch back and forth with disorientating fluidity, but the form of the text – the sequential presentation of each segment of narrative on the page – remains conventional. In *House of Leaves*, the physical form of the text, the presentation of words and segments of narrative on the page, becomes chaotic and often breaks down completely. Squares of text appear randomly distributed on certain pages; other pages contain only a few words; some passages are struck out or appear upside down. In order to engage with the narrative, therefore, the reader must engage physically with the text, flicking between pages and moving the book around. The novel thus insists not only upon the artificiality of its own textual conventions, but upon its materiality. The text of *House of Leaves* becomes a kind of Gothic space requiring the reader to make various physical twists and turns in order to reach the end of the narrative.

The narrative structure of the novel is similarly complex. Three narrative 'frames' exist side by side, involving three central characters: Johnny Truant, the blind writer Zampanó and Will Navidson. Johnny Truant appears first as the 'editor' of Zampanó's manuscript, *The Navidson Record*. This manuscript, which Truant finds in Zampanó's apartment following his death, is a critical essay on a film also entitled *The Navidson Record*. Like the lost manuscripts so frequently invoked in earlier Gothic fictions, the origin of this film is obscure; the reader encounters it only through the editor's rendition of Zampanó's text. The film *The Navidson Record* documents Will Navidson's terrifying experiences in his family home, a house that undergoes massive, inexplicable spatial distortions that Navidson resolves to investigate with the help of a famous explorer named Holloway Roberts. The men mount several expeditions into the labyrinthine and constantly changing interior of the house until Roberts disappears. Navidson finds a tape of Roberts's final, distraught hours: Roberts has clearly gone insane and the tape ends with his suicide.

Running parallel with the Zampanó/Navidson narrative is Johnny Truant's life story rendered as footnotes to *The Navidson Record*. Truant narrates his early life with a violent foster father, his mother's incarceration in a mental hospital (her letters from hospital in fact form another layer of narrative within the text) and his own increasing descent into madness as he tries to make sense of the manuscript he is editing. Here, however, Danielewski deploys another stock convention of Gothic fiction: Johnny is an unreliable narrator who admits to adding parts to the manuscript he is editing and to making things up about his own past. The novel's textual and spatial distortions are thus mirrored by (and are possibly a product of) the distorted imagination of this narrator. There is no way of knowing the truth since the narrative structure of *House of Leaves* – the constant, visually disorienting interplay between various, often conflicting narrators and narratives – effaces the 'truth value' of every segment of the text.

In her study of Gothic postmodernism, Maria Beville asserts that, 'if any contemporary novel was to define the genre "Gothic-postmodernism" as it manifests itself today, none could do so more succinctly than Bret Easton Ellis' *Lunar Park*'.[24] Published in 2005, Ellis's novel constitutes a complex engagement with the tradition of literary Gothicism and with Ellis's own personal history and writing career (his contentious novel *American Psycho* (1991) is discussed in Part Three: 'Twentieth-century American Gothic'). The work self-consciously alludes to the circumstances of its textual production, as Gothic fictions often do in their prefaces and frame narratives. *Lunar Park*'s first 'chapter' functions as a kind of preface commenting on the origin of the narrative that is to follow and its relation to other contemporary literary and cultural phenomena, including Ellis's own earlier novels:

'You do an awfully good impression of yourself'

> This is the first line of *Lunar Park* and in its brevity and
> simplicity it was supposed to be a return to form, an echo of
> the opening line from my debut novel, *Less than Zero*.[25]

This opening indicates that, amongst other things, *Lunar Park* is an
exercise in intertextuality – the process whereby texts are compiled
out of borrowings from and allusions to other texts (like Gray's *Poor
Things* discussed above). The intertextual elements that shape *Lunar
Park* are rather unusual, however, in so far as they consist to a large
extent of borrowings from the author's own body of work. Just as
early Gothic fictions often borrowed extensively from previous texts,
Ellis becomes indebted to his own literary corpus in the production
of this novel. This peculiarly personal deployment of intertextuality
allows Ellis to revisit, from a new critical perspective, his earlier
fictions, especially the controversial 1991 novel *American Psycho*. The
introductory chapter to *Lunar Park* discusses the negative critical
reaction to that novel and Ellis's own motivation for writing such a
vivid and controversial text. The author confesses that the creation of
the psychopathic protagonist was 'an extremely disturbing
experience'; that it seemed in some way to emanate out of Ellis's
conflicted relation with his father, and that the character of Bateman
acquired an uncanny and traumatic reality for Ellis during the
writing of the novel: 'Someone – *something* – else took over and
caused this new character to be my only reference point during the
three years that it took to write the novel' (p. 18). Ellis in this
account could be said to 'Gothicise' the process of writing the earlier
novel; he cites himself as a victim of a form of haunting whereby he
became obsessed with, in a sense almost persecuted by, his own
fictional creation.

The 'proper' fictional narrative of *Lunar Park* begins in Chapter 2,
though Ellis's narrative structure and style do make it difficult to
determine conclusively where the 'facts' end and the 'fiction' begins.
The protagonist is named after the author and references to the

author's real life and literary output continue throughout the novel. *Lunar Park* is a narrative about various forms of haunting and this is reflected in the narrative strategies adopted by Ellis to communicate, but also to complicate events. 'Ellis' (the protagonist will be referred to in inverted commas to distinguish him from the author) is a typically unreliable Gothic narrator who even ironically comments at one point that, 'I felt like an unreliable narrator, even though I knew I wasn't' (p. 183). Various events occur that appear supernatural in origin: the malevolent toy that comes to life; the footsteps in ash across the carpet; the strange alterations to the appearance of the house; the apparent haunting of the house by the father of 'Ellis'. The likely explanation of these events, however, is that 'Ellis' imagines them – he is, he admits, given to hallucinations and panic attacks, and ever more so as his relationship with his wife disintegrates during the course of the novel.

'Ellis' is also haunted, as the introductory chapter suggests, by Ellis's earlier creation, the murderous Wall Street broker Patrick Bateman. At a Halloween party, the narrator is unnerved by a guest who attends in the guise of Patrick Bateman. Later, a detective appears in the office of 'Ellis' with a copy of *American Psycho* to discuss a spate of murders that seem to be copies of Bateman's killings in that earlier novel. The detective observes that the killer leaves behind no signs of his presence in the form of hairs or fingerprints, and 'Ellis' responds: '*Like a ghost.* That was the first thing I thought. *Like a ghost*' (p. 184). 'Ellis' becomes concerned that the serial killer might target him, but is reassured by the officer that this is unlikely since the murderer only seems interested in victims with the same names as characters in *American Psycho*. The following passage can be read as an ironic, postmodern commentary on the problematic relationship between the author, his fictions and the demarcation between 'fact' and 'fiction':[*]

---

[*] This is further underscored by the fact that Bret Easton Ellis created seemingly genuine websites for the character 'Ellis' and his wife, Jayne Dennis, presented as a former model and actress rumoured to have had an affair with real-life American actor, Keanu Reeves.

'Why do you think this person isn't gonna come after me or my family?' I asked again. By now I was rocking back and forth in the swivel chair.

'Well, the author of the book isn't in the book,' Kimball said, offering a pointlessly reassuring smile that failed utterly. 'I mean, Bret Ellis is not a character in the book, and so far the assailant is only interested in finding people with similar identities or names of fictional characters.' Pause. 'You're not a fictional character, are you, Mr. Ellis?' (p. 185)

Lunar Park presents Ellis/'Ellis' almost as a 'ghost' in his own work, pushing further the capacity of Gothic fiction to generate narrative strategies capable of contesting what a reader understands by fiction, history, narrative authority and authorial control.

Notes

1   Maurice Blanchot, *The Gaze of Orpheus* (New York: Station Hill, 1984), p. 156.
2   See, for example, Jacques Derrida, *Dissemination* (London: Athlone Press, 1991).
3   David Punter, *Gothic Pathologies: The Text, the Body and the Law* (London: Macmillan, 1998).
4   Horace Walpole, *The Castle of Otranto* (Oxford: Oxford University Press, 1996), p. 5.
5   Montague Summers, *The Gothic Quest: A History of the Gothic Novel* (New York: Russell & Russell, 1964), p. 186.
6   April Alliston, Introduction to *The Recess* (Lexington: University Press of Kentucky, 2000).
7   Sophia Lee, *The Recess* (Lexington: University Press of Kentucky, 2000), p. 5.
8   Ann Radcliffe, *Gaston de Blondeville* (New York: Arno Press, 1972), p. 49.
9   Angela Wright, *Gothic Fiction: A Reader's Guide to Essential Criticism* (London: Palgrave, 2007), p. 9.
10 Walpole, *The Castle of Otranto*, p. 9.

11 William Godwin, *St Leon* (Oxford Oxford University Press, 1994), p. xxxiii.

12 Charles Robert Maturin, *Melmoth the Wanderer* (London: Penguin, 2000), p. 5.

13 Gregory O'Dea, 'Framing the Frame: Embedded Narratives, Enabling Texts and *Frankenstein*', *Romanticism on the Net* (2003), 31, accessed from http://www.erudit.org.

14 Oscar Cargill, '*The Turn of the Screw* and Alice James', *PMLA*, 78 (1963), pp. 238–49.

15 Beth Newman, 'Narratives of Seduction and the Seductions of Narrative: The Frame Structure of Frankenstein', in Fred Botting (ed.), *New Casebooks: Frankenstein* (London: Macmillan, 1995), p. 170.

16 Maturin, *Melmoth the Wanderer*, p. 293.

17 R. B. Oost, '"Servility and Command": Authorship in *Melmoth the Wanderer*', *Papers in Language and Literature*, 31:3 (1995), pp. 291–312.

18 Scott Brewster, 'Seeing Things: Gothic and the Madness of Interpretation', in David Punter (ed.), *A Companion to the Gothic* (Oxford: Blackwell, 2000), p. 281.

19 George Haggerty, 'The End of History, Identity and Dissolution in Apocalyptic Gothic', *Eighteenth Century: Theory and Interpretation*, 41 (2000), p. 225.

20 William Godwin, *Caleb Williams* (London: Penguin, 1988), p. 112.

21 Jean-François Lyotard, *The Postmodern Condition: A Report on Knowledge* (Minneapolis: University of Minnesota Press, 1984), p. 15.

22 Alasdair Gray, *Poor Things* (London: Bloomsbury, 1992), p. 272.

23 Mark Danielewski, *House of Leaves* (London: Random House, 2000).

24 Maria Belville, *Gothic Postmodernism: Voicing the Terrors of Postmodernity* (New York and Amsterdam: Rodopi, 2009), p. 171.

25 Bret Easton Ellis, *Lunar Park* (London: Picador, 2005), p. 3.

Female Gothic

Since the 1970s, the term 'female Gothic' has acquired considerable critical significance, first, in identifying a distinct mode – or more accurately modes – of Gothic associated with women writers from Ann Radcliffe and Sophia Lee in the 1790s through to Angela Carter, Fay Weldon and Margaret Atwood in the late twentieth century.* Second, a body of criticism concerned with female Gothic has developed that has offered from various theoretical perspectives ways of conceptualising how women writers have used and developed key conventions, tropes and motifs of literary Gothicism in order to represent and interrogate aspects of female experience within different social and cultural contexts.

The term has its origin in currents of feminist literary criticism that arose out of the women's liberation movements of the 1960s and 1970s. Critics such as Kate Millet (see *Sexual Politics*, 1968) began to examine the extent to which male-authored texts within the Western literary canon tended to reflect and reproduce what such critics viewed as the social stereotypes and often blatantly misogynistic assumptions of the prevailing patriarchal culture. Other critics were concerned more with the recuperation and validation of

---

* The key conventions, tropes and themes of female Gothic, discussed in this chapter, can be appropriated by male authors also: see Wilkie Collins's *The Woman in White* (discussed in Part Three: 'Nineteenth-century Gothic'), for example.

works by women writers that they argued constituted an alternative, female canon of literature: Elaine Showalter's *A Literature of Their Own* (1978) and Ellen Moers's *Literary Women* (1976) are key critical works in this regard and, indeed, it was in Moers's influential study of nineteenth- and twentieth-century women's writing that the term 'female Gothic' first appeared. Moers's definition of the term was relatively straightforward: she posited 'female Gothic' as embracing 'the work that women have done in the literary mode that, since the late-eighteenth century, we have called "the Gothic"'.[1] This categorisation has since come to be considered as rather too general to account for the many varieties of Gothicism produced by women since the late eighteenth century,[2] but Moers's analysis of the specific ways in which early Gothicism functioned in women's fiction remains influential. This chapter considers the origin of female Gothic in the work of Ann Radcliffe in the 1790s and follows its development with reference to various themes over the following two centuries: madness, the family, science, monstrosity and feminist Gothic.

The Literary Origin of the Female Gothic

Critics such as Eve Kosofsky Sedgwick and Diana Wallace have identified in female Gothic a 'set of connected metaphors'[3] through which women in the late eighteenth century began to express aspects of female experience that could not easily be articulated elsewhere within a patriarchal culture. In particular, Wallace contends that the aesthetic and thematic concerns of Gothicism as it began to develop from the mid-eighteenth century onwards were especially effective in enabling women to conceptualise their experiences within a society in which they were more often than not silenced, marginalised and closely confined.[4] The key conventions associated with Gothic from Horace Walpole onwards included imprisonment, persecution, disinheritance and various forms of haunting that were often related to the protagonist's precarious social and cultural position. In

Walpole's *The Castle of Otranto* (1764), for example, the patriarchal seat of ancestral power is haunted by a spectre that demands the restitution of the correct male line of inheritance: Theodore must be substituted for Manfred (see the extended commentary in Part Three: 'Eighteenth-century Gothic'). Women are peripheral to this line of inheritance and the system of power it supports and it is arguably the women in this novel who, by virtue of their enforced passivity, suffer most from the spectral apparitions and the chain of events they set in motion. Manfred's wife, Hippolita, is nothing other than a chattel of her husband capable of being disregarded when Manfred formulates his plot to marry again to secure himself an heir. Both Isabella and Matilda are terrorised by Manfred's plotting, and neither has the power to counteract his paranoid machinations. Isabella's flight from Manfred through the labyrinthine passages of the haunted castle establishes a key convention of Gothic literature that women writers were to use to considerable effect in later decades in order to narrate symbolically the position of the marginalised, terrorised woman within a male-dominated society.

Indeed, critics from Ellen Moers onwards have argued that it was not really until women writers such as Sophia Lee and, especially, Ann Radcliffe began to develop Walpole's Gothicism specifically in order to narrate the experiences of women that the Gothic emerged as a mature, recognisable literary form. Lee's *The Recess* (1783–5) begins with the confinement of two sisters (the daughters of Mary Queen of Scots in this fictional reworking of history) in a recess beneath a ruined abbey; the confinement is necessary since the very existence of these young daughters of the Catholic Queen poses a threat to the Protestant monarchy. Unable to establish any form of legitimate identity within a public sphere defined and controlled by men the women move between various confined spaces and suffer various persecutions that have a distinctly Gothic aspect even in the absence of any of the supernatural machinery associated with Horace Walpole. In Radcliffe's more extensive and influential Gothic oeuvre, what Margaret Anne Doody terms 'the trappings of [Walpole's] Gothic story'[5] acquire a new thematic coherence as they are used to narrate the isolation and persecution of women within patriarchal power structures symbolised by the imposing Gothic castles in which these young women are invariably imprisoned. For feminist critics such as Doody, the setting of these fictions outside England and often in the past should not obscure their contemporary political relevance; in a period in which women had no legal status separate from that of their father, husband or appointed male guardian the vulnerability of the Radcliffean heroine to various forms of physical and psychological abuse cannot be read as a consequence of the tyrannical laws of other cultures. Diana Wallace makes this clear in her discussion of the legal and political contexts that form the backdrop to female Gothic writing in this period. In relation to the law, women experienced a kind of 'civil death'.[6] They were unable to hold or inherit property independently unless either single or widowed (and even then their sphere of activity was more tightly regulated than that of single and married men) and it was virtually impossible for a woman to divorce her husband; whereas a man could obtain divorce on the single ground of adultery, for example, a woman could not. Moreover, one of the most draconian laws of the period regarded the murder of a husband by a wife as akin to treason and women found guilty of such a crime could be sentenced to execution not by hanging, as was the norm, but by burning. The perilous position of women before the law made it entirely natural, says Wallace, for women to employ the Gothic tropes of incarceration, family violence and persecution to address their predicament either directly (in the work of Mary Wollstonecraft, for example), or implicitly in the less overtly political romances of Sophia Lee or Ann Radcliffe. Wallace cites the opening paragraph of Wollstonecraft's *Maria, or The Wrongs of Woman* (1798) as an example of the way in which female Gothic was deployed in a variety of literary contexts to interrogate injustices against women:

> Abodes of horror have frequently been described, and castles, filled with spectres and chimeras, conjured up by the magic spell of genius to harrow the soul and absorb the wondering

mind. But, formed of such stuff as dreams are made of, what were they to the mansion of despair, in one corner of which Maria sat.[7]

In Wollstonecraft's fiction, the chimeras of Gothic romance (its claustrophobic settings, mysterious disappearances and so on) become the concrete expression of the sufferings of Maria who has been incarcerated in an insane asylum by her tyrannical aristocratic husband. The novel (unfinished at the time of Wollstonecraft's death) narrates the stories of two women: Mary herself (who writes her account of her tragic life to her daughter) and a former servant girl named Jemima who is also an inmate in the asylum. Jemima was raped by her employer, turned out of his house whilst pregnant with his child and finally imprisoned after turning to prostitution. By narrating the tragic circumstances of women from two very different social backgrounds, the novel intimates that the oppression of women crosses boundaries of social class and, whilst she seems rather dismissive here of the intangible 'dreams' of the romances which came to be identified with female Gothic, the fact that Wollstonecraft appropriates the devices of Radcliffean romance in this context displays the potential for female Gothic to articulate a radical political, proto-feminist position.

One of the key concerns of early female Gothic, then, is the traumatic consequences for women of their inability to defend themselves against forms of abuse that are if not directly authorised, at least permitted by patriarchal systems of power. However, female Gothic does often open up even in the oppressive climate of the late eighteenth century spaces within which women can claim a certain degree of self-sufficiency and influence. Ellen Moers points out that Radcliffe's plots invariably revolve around the disputed property rights of women, as well as the tendency for women to be treated as property by abusive fathers and father-figures. The typical Radcliffean heroine is engaged in a struggle to take back her inheritance from men who seek to misappropriate it, and these legalistic struggles acquire a wider cultural significance in terms of women's struggle for autonomy. As Kate Ferguson Ellis argues, 'the heroine exposes the villain's usurpation and thus reclaims an enclosed space that should have been a refuge from evil but has become the very opposite, a prison'.[8] Moreover, Radcliffe's novels often prioritise the recovery by women of lost female genealogies which prove crucial to their recovery of disputed estates. In Part Three: 'Eighteenth-century Gothic', Radcliffe's *The Mysteries of Udolpho* (1794) was considered from this perspective. A text that arguably pushes this thematic concern further is Radcliffe's novel of 1790, *A Sicilian Romance*.

The epigraph to *A Sicilian Romance* is a quotation from Shakespeare's Hamlet: 'I could a tale unfold.' These are the words spoken to Hamlet by the ghost of his father during their encounter in Act I of the play when Hamlet is being enjoined to avenge his father's death. Shakespeare's tragedies were a major influence upon early Gothic fiction,[*] and Radcliffe's epigraph reflects this influence; she is invoking Shakespeare as a precedent here, as Walpole does more extensively in his second preface to *The Castle of Otranto*. However, it could be argued that Radcliffe's female Gothic novel reworks from a feminine perspective a Shakespearean precedent that is concerned primarily with the perversion of a male bloodline through the murder of the king (see Shakespeare's *Hamlet*, *Macbeth* and *Richard III*, for example). The 'tale' that 'unfolds' in Radcliffe's text, by contrast, does not relate to a lost patrilineal bloodline, but to the concealment of the maternal origin of the two protagonists, Julia and Emilia. This is a work concerned with the denial of the mother rather than the usurpation of the father's 'name', and the contestation of the particular injustices perpetrated by the Marquis of Mazzini against his daughters and their mother constitutes a potent critique of an order of law premised upon institutional violence.

The Marquis has imprisoned his first wife – the girls' mother – in the disused southern quarter of the Castle of Mazzini and declared her dead in order to marry the second Marchioness. The thematic and symbolic structure of *A Sicilian Romance* nevertheless allows this order of governance eventually to be contested. Julia escapes from

---

[*]   See Part Two: 'A Cultural Overview' and Part Three: 'Eighteenth-century Gothic'.

the castle and is pursued by her father deeper and deeper into the caverns beneath it. Here, she finds her mother whose liberation not only restores her to her daughters, but by exposing the iniquity of the Marquis frees them from his malevolent influence. Critics who have approached this text from a psychoanalytic perspective have attributed considerable symbolic importance to the recovery of a 'hidden' mother: it represents the need for the female protagonist to reclaim a maternal point of origin that is often diminished in importance, if not denied outright (as symbolised through the fiction of Louisa's death in this novel) within patriarchal societies. Alison Milbank contends that it is the 'buried experience' of maternal influence that the Radcliffean heroine brings to light in order to assert her own identity and autonomy.[9]

Women, Madness and the Family

Part Three discussed in various contexts how adept the Gothic has become at narrating madness. The technique of 'terror' associated first with Ann Radcliffe often depends for its effect upon the portrayal of mental disorientation caused by the extreme circumstances in which protagonists are situated. From the nineteenth century onwards, madness becomes an explicit theme in Gothic fiction and frequently its treatment is highly gendered: late nineteenth-century scientific interest in female 'hysteria', for example, is reflected in Bram Stoker's treatment of the feminine response to the vampire (as discussed in Part Three: 'From the *Fin de Siècle* to Modern Gothic'). In female Gothic, the treatment of madness arguably acquires a political urgency and a cultural specificity that is less evident elsewhere in the Gothic tradition. In the two nineteenth-century texts considered in detail in this chapter – Charlotte Brontë's *Jane Eyre* (1847) and Charlotte Perkins Gilman's 'The Yellow Wallpaper' (1892) – women are portrayed as susceptible to madness, but their mental trauma is not depicted as somehow innate to their femininity; rather, it is related to and emanates from social situations that render the female protagonist vulnerable, alienated and desperate. Both of these texts have been recognised as central to the female Gothic canon. Indeed, the Gothic's capacity to represent states of hallucination and paranoia (through the evocation of the supernatural, the use of uncanny Gothic 'doubling', the manipulation of Gothic spaces and so on) becomes in these texts a potent tool for the interrogation of a woman's place within patriarchal culture.

Brontë's *Jane Eyre* can be described as a female *Bildungsroman*.* Jane begins as an orphan in the care of her wealthy aunt, Mrs Reed. Jane moves from a rather hostile childhood home to various locations each of which poses a fresh challenge to her as she struggles to assert her own identity and autonomy. The fact that Jane eventually marries the man she loves, Edward Rochester, suggests that the novel follows a rather predictable nineteenth-century trajectory of feminine self-development, but as many contemporary critics realised this was not the case at all. Brontë uses a variety of Gothic tropes and motifs (unjust incarceration, madness, doubling, the family home as a site of violence) in order to disassociate Jane from, and to radically call into question, the social structures, conventions and mores of a stifling Victorian patriarchy that threatens at various stages in Jane's life to eliminate the very sense of self that makes her a worthy subject of a narrative of self-development: what Jane struggles against in a more contemporary domestic context (she moves through the ordinary domestic spaces of Victorian England, not the castles of medieval Italy) is that sort of 'civil death' that placed the heroines of eighteenth-century Gothic romance in such peril.

In 1855, the critic and novelist Mrs Oliphant made an observation in relation to Brontë's novel that is illuminating not only in terms of

---

*   A *Bildungsroman* is a novel of self-development (the term in German means precisely that) that charts the growth to maturity of a protagonist who must overcome various obstacles to material success and psychological self-realisation. Two well-known examples contemporaneous with *Jane Eyre* are Charles Dickens's *David Copperfield* (1849–50) and *Great Expectations* (1860–1).

the public reaction to *Jane Eyre*, but with regard to the wider cultural status of Gothic fictions. She contended:

> Ten years ago we professed an orthodox system of novel making. Our lovers were humble and devoted and the only true love worth having was that chivalrous true love which consecrated all womankind. When suddenly, without warning, *Jane Eyre* stole upon the scene, and the most alarming revolution of modern times has followed the invasion of *Jane Eyre*.[10]

In the 1790s, in the immediate aftermath of the French Revolution, Gothic fictions were associated with 'terror' not simply because their authors strove to generate fear in the reader, but because these fictions were considered to be disruptive and subversive of the status quo.* The reaction of Mrs Oliphant to Brontë's novel establishes a similar relation between *Jane Eyre* and the prospect of revolution; the novel has entered new and dangerous territory, challenging conventional representations of 'true love' and 'consecrated womankind'. The same association was made even more explicitly by Elizabeth Rigby in the conservative magazine, the *Quarterly Review* in 1848: 'The same tone of thought which has fostered Chartism and rebellion is the same which has also written Jane Eyre.'[11]

In one of the most influential late twentieth-century readings of Jane Eyre, Sandra Gilbert and Susan Gubar contend that what most disturbed Victorian critics about this novel was its 'rebellious feminism'. They describe the novel as:

> a distinctively female bildungsroman in which the problems encountered by the protagonist as she struggles from the imprisonment of her childhood toward an almost unthinkable goal of mature freedom are symptomatic of difficulties Everywoman must meet and overcome.[12]

---

* They were aligned with the 'terrors' of revolution, as discussed in Part Three: 'Eighteenth-century Gothic' and 'Romantic-era Gothic'.

Gilbert's and Gubar's *The Madwoman in the Attic* (1979) is part of a wider feminist analysis of the place of the woman writer within patriarchal culture. They argue that the literary canon has been constructed by and for men, and that women have either been excluded from or denigrated within it. They cite a number of male writers and critics united in their assumption that literary creativity is incompatible with femininity; thus, the novelist Anthony Burgess is quoted as asserting that Jane Austen's novels are compromised because they 'lack a strong male thrust', whilst for the writer William Gas women can never fully succeed in literary endeavours because they 'lack that blood congested genital drive which energizes every great style'.[13] For Gilbert and Gubar, the highly sexualised language of such critics is revealing, asserting as it does a connection between male sexual generation and literary generation: women fail in the literary sphere because they cannot 'father' the text. In this context, the title of Gilbert's and Gubar's work is significant: their 'madwoman' alludes to Bertha Mason, the first wife of Edward Rochester who is imprisoned by him in the attic of Thornfield Hall. For these critics, Bertha becomes a 'double' of the woman writer in a culture so hostile to female self-realisation that a woman who steps outside prescribed feminine roles (as Bertha and Jane do) is considered dangerous, or even mad.

The Gothic trope of the double is used by Brontë at various points to narrate the inner conflict that afflicts Jane as she struggles to affirm an autonomous female identity. Jane also finds herself within various Gothic spaces that symbolise the culture against which Jane's 'feminist rebellion' is directed. As a child in Gateshead Hall, Jane is bullied by John Reed, the eldest son of the family who is depicted as a Gothic-style tyrant-in-the-making. Jane does not make a virtue out of quiet suffering, however; she flies into a rage against John and as a result is locked in the 'red room'. This Gothic chamber was the bedroom in which the family patriarch, Mr Reed, died. Jane is afraid that the room might be haunted and when she looks in a large mirror in the darkened room draped in red, she sees her own reflection as if it were a ghost: she experiences herself as her own spectral double.

Gilbert and Gubar interpret this scene as a reworking of Radcliffean female Gothic in which the protagonist experiences a kind of cultural 'haunting' that alienates her from society and from herself:

> [The chamber is haunted] more so than any chamber in, say, *The Mysteries of Udolpho*, which established a standard for such apartments. For the spirit of a society in which Jane has no clear place sharpens the angles of the furniture, enlarges the shadows, strengthens the locks on the door. And the death bed of a father who was not really her father emphasizes her isolation and vulnerability.[14]

Jane's confrontation here with her spectral, other 'self' prefigures a later episode in which she experiences further conflict between who she feels she is, and what others expect of her. The middle section of the novel narrates the developing relationship between Jane and Rochester after Jane is employed as governess at Thornfield. When Rochester proposes to Jane, she accepts but not without considerable misgivings which Brontë posits as entirely rational. First of all, in naming her male protagonist Edward Rochester, Brontë is alluding to a well-known seventeenth-century aristocrat – the Earl of Rochester – who was notorious for his sexual decadence. Whilst Edward is hardly as degenerate as his namesake, his youth was sufficiently dissolute to have apparently produced an illegitimate child (the text suggests, though does not make it explicit, that Rochester is the father of Jane's young charge, Adele) and a marriage to a woman that Rochester admits he hardly knew, let alone loved. Whilst Jane is unaware of Bertha's identity during their courtship, she knows enough of his history and of the circles he moves in to be disturbed by the prospect of marrying him, especially since his treatment of women (including herself) continues to display at times a flirtatious insouciance that borders on arrogance. Moreover, whilst Edward insists that he regards Jane as a soulmate and an equal, Jane is well aware that this is not how the law views a wife: as Mrs Rochester, Jane's identity will be absorbed into that of her husband

and she will be entirely dependent upon his good will for the continuation of the equality and comradeship that defines their period of engagement. Jane's inner conflict comes into sharp focus on the day of her wedding; looking at herself in her bridal gown she appears once more as other to herself: in the mirror, she sees 'a robed and veiled figure, so unlike my usual self that it seemed almost the image of a stranger'.[15] When Jane's marriage to Rochester is interrupted by the revelation that Rochester is still married, Bertha can be read as another double of Jane – the first bride who enacts physically, through her madness, the repressed hostility that Jane feels towards Rochester. Bertha's 'madness' becomes the projection of Jane's self-alienation and her legitimate rage against Rochester and, more importantly, what Rochester represents, at least at this point in the novel: a society that seems intent upon making a cruel mockery of a woman's desires and aspirations for equality and freedom.

At the end of the novel, Bertha Mason burns down Thornfield, killing herself and maiming Rochester in the process. The rage and madness of Jane's double harms Rochester physically and destroys the material embodiment of his patriarchal, aristocratic power: his ancestral family home. The novel thus dismantles the symbolic and social structures that underpin the authority of men like Rochester over women like Jane and Bertha. Moreover, the destruction of Thornfield and the transformed circumstances in which the previously vigorous, socially powerful Rochester finds himself open up a space for a truly egalitarian marriage. This is not necessarily because Rochester is, as some critics have suggested, 'symbolically castrated' by the fire such that he no longer poses a sexual threat to Jane; rather, it can be argued that the fire effects an internal transformation in Rochester, rendering him 'paradoxically stronger than he was when he ruled Thornfield, for now, like Jane, he draws his powers from within himself, rather from inequity, disguise, deception'.[16] As Jane draws her story to a close, she makes one of the most famous asides to the reader in English fiction: 'Reader, I married him.' As Gilbert and Gubar admit, this observation can be interpreted as signifying Jane's final absorption into a conventional patriarchal marriage at the expense of the autonomy she has struggled throughout the novel to achieve, and at the expense of Brontë's 'rebellious feminism'. However, the revised terms of this marriage (suggested by Jane's assertive pronouncement, 'Reader, *I* married *him*', and not '*he* married *me*') suggest a more unorthodox closure to the novel which is possibly why some contemporary critics continued to regard this female Gothic heroine, in spite of her eventual marriage, as 'the personification of an unregenerate and undisciplined spirit'.[17]

Madness and Medicine

The disciplines of psychiatry and, later, of psychoanalysis developed in their recognisably modern forms in the mid-to-late nineteenth century when certain physical and psychological symptoms came to be interpreted according to various theories of neurosis, psychosis and, especially with regard to women, hysteria. In the early twentieth century, Freud offered a comprehensive account of the unconscious according to which almost all symptoms of mental disorder could be interpreted as manifestations of repressed memories and sexual conflicts that could not be admitted into the conscious domain of the ego, the day-to-day, functional self. Freud's conceptualisation of femininity was especially influenced by prevailing notions of womanhood as constituting a state that was almost defined in terms of psychological dysfunction: female reproductive biology was considered to destabilise the bodies and minds of women to the extent that femininity itself emerged almost as inherently psychopathic. The work of Jean-Martin Charcot is discussed in Part Three: 'From the *Fin de Siècle* to Modern Gothic'. His late nineteenth-century work with female patients defined as 'hysterics' had a considerable influence upon cultural representations of femininity, not least in Gothic fictions that depicted the 'hysteric' female as a dangerous other in need of control and, if necessary, elimination.

These constructions of femininity in terms of latent or actual hysteria had a particular impact upon women whose behaviour transgressed social and cultural norms: put simply, they were labelled 'mad'. Elaine Showalter's influential study of the discourse of hysteria from the 1880s onwards draws attention to this negative cultural construction of the female intellectual at the *fin de siècle*. According to the Viennese doctor Fritz Wettels (a contemporary of Freud), 'Hysteria is the basis for a woman's desire to study medicine, just as it is the basis of women's struggle for equal rights.'[18] Showalter also cites the American psychologist Silas Weir Mitchell:

> For me, the grave significance of sexual difference controls the whole question [of female nervous illness]. The woman's desire to be on a level of competition with man and to assume his duties is, I am sure, making mischief, for it is my belief that no length of generations of change in her education and modes of activity will ever really alter her characteristics. She is physiologically other than man.[19]

In 1892 the American writer Charlotte Perkins Gilman published a Gothic short story, 'The Yellow Wallpaper', which narrates the devastating impact on its female protagonist of the contemporary discourse of female hysteria. The story fictionalises an aspect of Gilman's own experience; following the birth of her first child, she suffered what would later be understood as post-natal depression. At that time, however, her condition could be understood only in terms of prevailing accounts of the susceptibility of women (especially intellectual women) to hysteria. Gilman was prescribed the 'rest cure' popularised by Dr Silas Weir Mitchell. Mitchell's cure prohibited any form of physical or mental exertion and during Gilman's treatment she was unable to write or engage in any form of intellectual activity. The consequences of the rest cure are explored through Gilman's appropriation of the female Gothic mode in the narration of her protagonist's descent into total madness.

Critics such as Showalter have read Gilman's short story as something close to a psychoanalytical case study of female madness, except that, unlike Mitchell and his contemporaries, Gilman foregrounds the social and cultural conditions that generate the woman's trauma. The protagonist is nameless throughout the narrative which signifies the extent to which she constitutes a blank, an absence, in her own personal history. She and her husband move to an archetypal Gothic space and immediately the narrative reveals Gilman's knowing treatment of the conventions of Gothic fiction and their importance in terms of the symbolisation of female experience:

> It is very seldom that mere ordinary people like John and myself secure ancestral halls for the summer.

> A colonial mansion, a hereditary estate, I would say a haunted house, and reach the height of romantic felicity – but that would be asking too much of fate![20]

The protagonist is confined by her husband to an unused nursery at the top of the house. She attempts to portray John as well-meaning, but what emerges from her narrative is a sense of her husband as an exceptionally controlling, insensitive physician who has diagnosed his wife's condition to his own satisfaction and makes no attempt to communicate meaningfully with her. The text explicitly aligns John with doctors such as Weir Mitchell and casts these men of science in the role of archetypal Gothic villains:

> John says if I don't pick up faster he shall send me to Weir Mitchell in the fall.

> But I don't want to go there at all. I had a friend who was in his hands once, and she says he is just like John and my brother, only more so! (p. 105)

Confined in the nursery-prison (it has bars on the windows, a vivid evocation of the alignment common in female Gothic fiction between domesticity and imprisonment), the protagonist has nothing to do but stare at the walls. She becomes obsessed with the intricate pattern of the yellow wallpaper and begins to hallucinate. She sees behind the pattern the figure of a woman who appears to be struggling to get out. Throughout the narrative, the voice of the narrator remains ostensibly lucid; at no point does her account become incoherent. Moreover, she remains aware of her own position in her marriage, and in wider society, as a woman who must observe certain standards of proper conduct even as she descends into insanity; thus she contemplates suicide, but dismisses the prospect since, 'I know well enough that a step like that is improper and might be misconstrued' (p. 116). The contrast between what is being narrated and the style in which it is recounted adds to the sense that this narrator is thoroughly incorporated into – and imprisoned by – a patriarchal ideology that constructs her as 'mad'. She is aware of herself as a 'case study' in feminine hysteria (referring to the complexities of 'my case', for example) and she enacts what is expected of her according to this discourse.

Her madness, however, ultimately exceeds her husband's appraisal of his wife's nervous condition and here the key Gothic tropes of paranoia and incarceration acquire a particular psychological intensity and cultural significance: the woman becomes one with the prisoner behind the wallpaper and turns against her husband whom she suddenly perceives as violent and tyrannical, but also as absurd and naive. She ends up creeping around the edge of the room whilst he cries out for an axe to break down the door, only to fall silent and finally faint when he sees his wife crawling over the wallpaper she has ripped off the walls. The old, patriarchal Gothic space that at the beginning of the narrative harks back to the eighteenth-century Gothic romances of Ann Radcliffe ('ancestral hall, hereditary estate') becomes in Gilman's *fin de siècle* female Gothic a site of trauma in which the medical man replaces the aristocratic tyrant as the persecutor of women.

Female Gothic in the Mid-twentieth Century

During the twentieth century, women writers continued to deploy the conventions of female Gothic writing discussed so far in this chapter in order to interrogate the position of women within family structures posited as claustrophobic, oppressive and even dangerous. A key mid-century work of female Gothic is *The Haunting of Hill House* (1959) by American writer Shirley Jackson. This is a text in which the Radcliffean Gothic (with its vulnerable heroine and malevolent Gothic spaces) is reworked to produce a psychologically intense, bleak narrative of vivid hauntings that are intimately related to the mental instability and eventual breakdown of the protagonist, Eleanor Vance. The novel begins with a tense encounter between Eleanor and her sister during which Eleanor seeks permission to take the family car on a trip to Hill House. Eleanor has been invited thence by scientist Dr Montague, who is conducting research into paranormal activity. It is clear that the unmarried Eleanor is regarded as infantile and irresponsible by her married sister in spite of the fact that Eleanor has spent the previous decade of her life caring alone for their sick mother (who has recently died). When Eleanor is refused permission to take the car – which, as she keeps plaintively pointing out, she jointly purchased – she takes the car anyway and drives to her appointment at the haunted Hill House.

Eleanor becomes the focus for intense paranormal activity thereafter. The text intimates that Eleanor feels guilt over her mother's death, but also resentment at having devoted so much of her young adult life to the care of a hostile, peevish woman. Given that the haunting of the house is related to the death of a similarly irascible matriarch, it is suggested that the house has somehow 'chosen' Eleanor as its special victim. In spite of the house's victimisation of Eleanor, she feels a strong sense of belonging to it and, following her death in a car crash at the end of the novel, it is suggested that the lonely and vulnerable protagonist has been incorporated into the supernatural economy of Hill House (though the repetition of the novel's opening in this closing sequence – the insistence that whatever occupies Hill House 'walks alone' – could be taken to mean that Eleanor's sense of belonging was a delusion cruelly fostered by the house and its ghost).[21] The novel is a dark meditation upon the extent to which unmarried women in mid-twentieth-century America remained marginalised and open to manipulation by virtue of the assumption that the role of the self-abnegating carer was rightfully theirs whether they wanted it or not.

Daphne du Maurier's *Rebecca* (1938) reworks the female Gothic theme of the vulnerable young woman in a marriage that threatens her psychological and (implicitly) physical well-being, and it does so through the use of complex instances of haunting and doubling. The young Mrs de Winter narrates the events that took place early in her marriage at Manderley, the stately home of her aristocratic husband, Maxim. The young bride is psychologically haunted by Maxim's first wife, the assertive and sophisticated Rebecca. Echoes of Rebecca abound at Manderley and are deliberately evoked by the servant, Mrs Danvers, who remains deeply loyal to her former mistress. In one of the novel's most Gothic moments, Danvers contrives to have Mrs de Winter wear a gown that was last worn by Rebecca to a fancy dress ball; Danvers thus orchestrates a scene in which the second wife appears as the double of the first, to the terror and consternation of Maxim. The narrator becomes increasingly disconcerted by the spectral presence of Rebecca and by her growing assumption that Maxim still loves his first wife. Maxim eventually reveals, however, that his marriage was loveless and turbulent; that Rebecca taunted him with the fact of her numerous lovers; and that he eventually killed her in a fit of passion prompted by her assertion that she was pregnant with another man's child. The narrator accepts her husband's account and even feels some relief that her insecurities as to his affections for his first wife are unfounded. Nevertheless, the text to some extent undercuts the narrator's apparently ready emotional acceptance of Maxim's account of Rebecca's death. In an evocation of the burning down of Rochester's mansion in *Jane*

Eyre, the narrator's reminiscence ends with Manderley in flames. Just as the fire in that earlier female Gothic novel can be read as the externalisation of Jane's (and Bertha Mason's) rage against Rochester (see the discussion above), so the burning of Manderley might be interpreted as symbolising the rage of the narrator (and possibly her spectral double, Rebecca) against Maxim de Winter. It is telling in this regard that the narrator is never given her own name; so completely is her identity effaced by marriage to the patriarch, de Winter, that she is only ever referred to as Mrs de Winter.

Women and Monstrosity: New Transformations

Mary Shelley's *Frankenstein* (1818) is not only an iconic text within the Gothic tradition generally, it is also (as Ellen Moers acknowledges in *Literary Women*) one of the most influential examples of female Gothic that articulates through its narrative of monstrous transformation the problematics of feminine identity in a patriarchal culture which appropriates, and perverts, processes of physical generation (see Part Three: 'Romantic-era Gothic'). Fay Weldon's *The Lives and Loves of a She-devil* (1983) can be read as a modern reworking of Mary Shelley's *Frankenstein*. Many of Weldon's novels engage with issues raised by the women's liberation movement in the 1970s and 1980s and in this text Weldon uses the Gothic tropes of monstrosity, disguise and doubling in order to question and, especially, to satirise societal pressures that her novel shows to be deeply damaging to women.

The novel's protagonist and, for the most part, its first-person narrator, is Ruth, a woman who is judged to be quite grotesque in appearance by society and by herself. She is over six feet tall, plump and muscular; she has a loud, deep voice and is socially awkward and physically clumsy. Her husband, Bobbo, is a handsome, successful accountant who married her only because she was pregnant and who constantly belittles her whilst feeling sorry for himself. Ruth's nemesis is a woman named Mary Fisher who conforms exactly to the ideal of feminine manners and beauty that so elude Ruth. She is, moreover, a writer of romance fiction, and thus she perpetuates through her work the stereotypes that she conforms to so successfully in her personal life. The novel opens with a description of Mary Fisher that evokes and subverts the conventions of romance and of Gothic fiction; Mary lives in a Gothic space – a 'High Tower' – and she seems to possess the refined sensibility of the eighteenth-century Gothic heroine, except that she is duplicitous, scheming and promiscuous:

> Mary Fisher lives in the High Tower, on the edge of the sea: she writes a great deal about the nature of love. She tells lies.
>
> Mary Fisher is small and pretty and delicately formed, prone to fainting and weeping and sleeping with men while pretending that she doesn't.[22]

Mary is having an affair with Bobbo and it is this that triggers Ruth's transformation into a 'she devil'. It is not so much the knowledge of this affair that initiates Ruth's rebellion, however, but her husband's reaction to her knowledge of it. When she steps momentarily out of her role as passive, long-suffering wife – revealing to Bobbo's parents that he is having an affair – Bobbo loses his temper and names her a 'she devil' before walking out to live with Mary. The novel then ironically turns Bobbo's pronouncement against him. Since he believes he has the power to define Ruth's identity, then his construction of her will become his reality: Ruth becomes his monstrous creation – the she-devil that turns against him and destroys him:

> So. I see. I thought I was a good wife tried temporarily and understandably beyond endurance, but no. He says I am a she devil.

I expect he is right. In fact, since he does so well in the world and I do so badly, I really must assume he is right. I am a she devil.

But this is wonderful! This is exhilarating! If you are a she devil the mind clears at once. The spirits rise. There is no shame, no guilt, no dreary striving to be good. There is only, in the end, what you *want*. And I can take what I want. I am a she devil. (p. 49)

Ruth proceeds to ruin the lives of Mary and Bobbo. She burns down the family home and takes the children to live with Bobbo and the horrified Mary at the High Tower. She then creates a number of new identities for herself in order to take revenge on her husband, managing to frame him for fraud and manipulate the judge into giving him the maximum sentence. Her final transformation, however, is the most Gothic and the most ambivalent from a feminist perspective. By means of extensive cosmetic surgery, Ruth turns herself into her rival; she becomes the physical double of Mary Fisher and appropriates her identity. Ruth's transformation into the 'perfect' woman, however, is a monstrous transformation as the novel intimates through the characterisation of Ruth's surgeon as a modern Victor Frankenstein playing God with women's bodies:

Mr Ghengis enjoyed his work. It seemed to him that it was one of the few occupations in the world which could not be faulted. Social work could be seen as system bolstering; ordinary doctoring as fostering the interest of the pharmaceutical companies; teaching as the enslavement of the young mind; the arts as idle elitism; business of any kind as grinding the world's poor beneath the capitalist heel, and so forth: but cosmetic surgery was pure. It made the ugly beautiful. To transform the shell of the soul was, Mr Ghengis felt, the nearest a man could get to motherhood: moulding, shaping, bringing forth in pain and anguish. True the pain and anguish were not strictly his but his patients'. Nevertheless he felt it. Nothing was for nothing. (p. 229)

Ruth's 'pain and anguish' are such that she can hardly walk after her numerous operations; nevertheless, she interprets her transformation as a victory and certainly it is a powerful, ironic comment on the culture whose values Ruth exploits for her own vengeful ends. Within this culture, femininity as such is monstrous in one way or another, the novel suggests. Ruth begins and ends the novel as a 'monster'; the only difference, as she makes clear, is that at the outset she was 'comic', utterly disempowered and pitiful, and at the end she is 'serious', self-actualised as a 'she devil' and in total control of the High Tower and her now grovelling, 'poor confused creature' of a husband (p. 256).

Feminist Gothic

From the 1970s onwards, women writers of Gothic fiction began to appropriate Gothic conventions in order to confront certain problematic representations of women within Western culture and, in a sense, to rewrite key narratives from a feminist perspective. Fay Weldon's novel discussed above can be read as a feminist transformation of the Gothic trope of the monstrous body. The Canadian writer Margaret Atwood has also used the Gothic mode to explore the oppression of women and the possibilities of female liberation: see *The Robber Bride* (1993) and *The Handmaid's Tale* (1985). The 1993 text features an exceptionally ambivalent central character named Zenia who uncannily re-appears after her own funeral to disrupt the comfortable, middle-class, professional lives of three college friends, now in their fifties. Zenia had long been a thorn in the side of these women (with a special talent for stealing their husbands) and she becomes even more of a burden and a danger after her 'death'. Like Ruth in Weldon's novel, Zenia is remarkably adept at self-invention and throughout the text she seems to lack any stable, material identity. Zenia emerges as a Gothic anti-heroine, dangerous yet charismatic and powerful and not reducible to the patriarchal stereotype of the wicked woman. Indeed, she may be read as embodying the repressed desires of her three college friends for female empowerment and self-transformation.

The earlier novel is Atwood's most famous and it exemplifies the close links between Gothic and science fiction explored already in Part Three: 'From the *Fin de Siècle* to Modern Gothic'. *The Handmaid's Tale* is a dystopian fantasy set in a future America which is controlled by religious fundamentalists. The text's Gothicism lies in its depiction of the intense, paranoiac persecution that women suffer psychologically and physically. Women have become entirely the sexual and reproductive servants of men and are given such names as 'Offred' – or 'Of Fred' – to signal their belonging to a male. The novel ends bleakly and abruptly with the narrator about to be carried off to an unknown fate following various attempts by her to counter her subjugation. Atwood 'Gothicises' the lives of women in *The Handmaid's Tale* in order to allegorise the various forms of oppression from which they suffer.

A writer closely associated with the feminist reworking of older narratives – especially myth and fairy tale – is Angela Carter, whose novel *The Magic Toyshop* (1967) is discussed in Part Three: 'British Gothic in the Late Twentieth Century'. Carter had a strong literary and academic interest in fairy tale; in 1977 she translated into English the fairy tales of the French writer Charles Perrault and she went on to produce two compilations of fairy tales for the feminist press Virago. For Carter, European myths and fairy tales – Beauty and the Beast, Little Red Riding Hood, Cinderella and so on – have had a powerful effect upon the collective imagination of Western societies and have reproduced certain stereotypes of femininity that need to be addressed from a feminist perspective. They encourage the notion that femininity is essentially passive, that female sexuality is simultaneously vulnerable and dangerous, and that young women must undergo certain rites of passage designed to teach them how to control their bodies and their desires. In her collection of short stories *The Bloody Chamber* (1979), Carter offers various interpretations of some of the most vivid and powerful fairy tales of the Western cultural tradition, especially Snow White, Little Red Riding Hood and Beauty and the Beast. This analysis focuses on the story that opens the collection and that gives it its name.

'The Bloody Chamber' recounts the marriage of a young woman to a wealthy Marquis who inhabits an archetypal Gothic castle. The Marquis is a good deal older than his bride and the opening of the tale foregrounds especially the narrator's sexual inexperience compared to her husband; she is both fascinated and repelled by sex, and by the Marquis whose sexual charisma intrigues and frightens her. It is clear that the nameless narrator exists as the embodiment of the Marquis's (and, by extension, the wider culture's) sexual fantasies and early on he begins to manipulate his bride so that she conforms ever more closely to this ideal. He has her wear a tight ruby necklace – almost like a collar, a mark of sexual ownership – which he instructs her never to remove; he places her in front of numerous mirrors in which her image as sexual object is given back to her (and to the reader) hundreds of times. It becomes quickly apparent that the Marquis's sexuality is sadistic; the bride finds a collection of violent pornography which clearly she was meant to discover; the Marquis is aroused by her having found them, makes fun of her reaction, then proceeds rapaciously to take her virginity. The narrator's response reveals the extent to which this enactment of the Marquis's macabre sexual fantasy corrupts her own developing sexual imagination: her language becomes coarse and violent as she envisions 'a dozen husbands impaling a dozen brides'.[23]

'The Bloody Chamber' is most explicitly a retelling of the Blue Beard tale which is one of Charles Perrault's stories translated by Carter in 1977. According to this myth, Blue Beard married many women whom he then violently murdered, locking their corpses in a secret chamber. Blue Beard took delight in playing on the curiosity of each new wife, tempting them into unlocking the chamber and discovering his secret whereupon the new wife would herself be killed. This is exactly what happens to Carter's protagonist. Whilst her husband is away on business, she discovers a set of keys which gives her access to a forbidden chamber; this vault is, of course, the 'bloody chamber' in which the narrator finds several implements of medieval torture and, finally, the mutilated corpses of each of the Marquis's previous wives, one still wearing a bridal veil. His most recent bride is discovered in an 'iron maiden', a contraption in which metal spikes fixed to the inside of the door kill the victim locked inside. The narrator takes note of a particularly gruesome detail: the dead woman's blood is still flowing from her wounds; hence, she must have died very recently.

When the Marquis discovers his bride's transgression he decides to kill her. The symbolism of the ruby choker becomes apparent: he intends to decapitate her. In bringing the narrative to a close, however, Carter radically departs from the traditional narrative of Blue Beard. As the narrator kneels before the Marquis's guillotine, her mother appears on a white horse and shoots the Marquis. She appears in this scene as the hero of a typical fairy tale, riding in on a white charger to save the heroine. This gesture subverts the Blue Beard original in a number of ways. First, the appearance of the mother[*] is so at odds with the conventions of fairy tale, so comical in fact, that it appears to parody the sinister, moralising content of myths such as Blue Beard in which the curiosity and self-assertion of young women are invariably punished. Moreover, by positioning the narrator's mother as her 'macho' rescuer, Carter radically reworks the traditional fairy tale representation of the maternal figure: in fairy tales, the mother appears as the wicked stepmother of Snow White, for instance; or as the passive mother who is unable to protect her daughter (in Red Riding Hood, for example, it is the woodcutter who intervenes to save the girl and her grandmother from the wolf); or as the fairy godmother whose benevolence nevertheless operates within strict patriarchal limits (Cinderella's fairy godmother ensures that Cinderella becomes the bride of the prince, her ambition never exceeds this goal). Read as feminist Gothic, 'The Bloody Chamber' can be seen to offer an

---

[*] It would probably be more accurate to describe the mother as the macho hero of a Western movie – a sharp-shooting cowboy.

alternative to traditional narratives that perpetuate the notion that girls must repudiate self-assertion in order to survive.

Critics have not been unanimous in interpreting Carter's work as subversive in the manner suggested by the above analysis. For critics such as Patricia Duncker, traditional fairy tale is simply too implicated within and compromised by patriarchal ideologies of femininity and sexuality to be appropriated subversively by women writers. The function of fairy tale as 'a carrier of ideology', argues Duncker, 'proves too complex and pervasive to avoid. Carter is rewriting the tales within the strait-jacket of their original structures'.[24] For Duncker, Carter's protagonists, even when they do narrate their own stories (itself a radical departure from the conventions of fairy tale) remain 'abstractions' caught up within patriarchal systems of power. Carter's feminist Gothic remains a contested category within contemporary literary criticism and it might be read, as critic Lucy Armitt suggests, as exemplifying the 'complex trickery' inherent within Gothic narrative *per se*.[25] As discussed in the preceding chapter, the narrative instability and, as Armitt puts it, the trickery of Gothic fictions often render interpretation according to preconceived critical categories rather difficult. The diverse responses to Carter's Gothic certainly suggest that it escapes interpretation according to any single late twentieth-century feminist critical perspective.

Notes

1   Ellen Moers, *Literary Women* (London: Women's Press, 1976), p. 90.
2   For an overview of the criticism, see the introduction to Diane Wallace and Andrew Smith (eds), *The Female Gothic: New Directions* (London: Palgrave, 2009).
3   Eve Kosofsky Sedgwick, *The Coherence of Gothic Conventions* (New York and London: Methuen, 1986), p. 7.
4   Diane Wallace, 'The Haunting Idea: Female Gothic Metaphors and Feminist Theory', in Wallace and Smith (eds), *The Female Gothic*, pp. 26–41.
5   Margaret Anne Doody, 'Deserts, Ruins and Troubled Waters: Female Dreams in Fiction and the Development of the Gothic Novel', *Genre*,

10 (1977), p. 552.

6   Wallace, 'The Haunting Idea', p. 33.

7   Mary Wollstonecraft, *Maria, or The Wrongs of Woman* (London: Penguin, 1992), p. 61.

8   Kate Ferguson Ellis, *The Contested Castle: Gothic Novels and the Subversion of Domestic Ideology* (Chicago: University of Illinois Press, 1989), p. xiii.

9   Alison Milbank, Introduction to Ann Radcliffe, *A Sicilian Romance* (Oxford: Oxford University Press, 1993), p. xxiii.

10 Cited in Sandra M. Gilbert and Susan Gubar, *The Madwoman in the Attic: The Woman Writer and the Nineteenth-century Literary Imagination* (New Haven, CT, and London: Yale University Press, 1979), p. 337.

11 Ibid., p. 337.

12 Ibid., p. 339.

13 Anthony Burgess, 'The Book is Not for Reading', *New York Times*, December 1966, and William Gas, 'Review of Norman Mailer, *Genius and Lust*', *New York Times*, October 1976, both cited in Gilbert and Gubar, *The Madwoman in the Attic*, p. 9.

14 Gilbert and Gubar, *The Madwoman in the Attic*, p. 340.

15 Charlotte Brontë, *Jane Eyre* (London: Penguin, 1985), p. 315.

16 Gilbert and Gubar, *The Madwoman in the Attic*, p. 369

17 Elizabeth Rigby, *Quarterly Review*, 1848, cited in Gilbert and Gubar, *The Madwoman in the Attic,* p. 337.

18 Elaine Showalter, *Hystories: Hysterical Epidemics and Modern Culture* (New York: Columbia University Press, 1997), p. 50.

19 Ibid.

20 Charlotte Perkins Gilman, 'The Yellow Wallpaper', in Elaine Showalter (ed.), *Daughters of Decadence: Women Writers of the Fin de Siècle* (London: Virago, 1993), p. 98.

21 Shirley Jackson, *The Haunting of Hill House* (London: Penguin, 1984), p. 246.

22 Fay Weldon, *The Lives and Loves of a She-devil* (London: Hodder & Stoughton, 1983), p. 7.

23 Angela Carter, 'The Bloody Chamber', in *The Bloody Chamber* (London: Vintage, 2006), p. 14.

24 Patricia Duncker, 'Re-imagining the Fairy Tales: Angela Carter's Bloody Chambers' , *Literature and History*, 10:1 (1984), pp. 6–7.

25 Lucy Armitt, 'The Fragile Frames of The Bloody Chamber', in Joseph Bristow and Trev Lynn Broughton (eds), *The Infernal Desires of Angela Carter: Fiction, Femininity, Feminism* (London: Longman, 1997), p. 96.

Gothic Bodies

A key theme of Gothic literature since its inception has been the mutability and monstrosity of the body. Bodies in Gothic fiction have the disturbing capacity to appear as *dis*embodied, as hovering between categories of the human and the animal (the werewolf, or vampire), or as entirely and monstrously unhuman (the grotesque shapes that populate the short stories of H. P. Lovecraft discussed in Part Three: 'From the *Fin de Siècle* to Modern Gothic', for example). As Gothic literature has entered into the mainstream of academic study since the 1980s, critics have offered a range of perspectives on Gothic representations of the body and several of the most influential are discussed in this chapter. Kelly Hurley, in her study of the body in *fin de siècle* Gothic, observes:

> Within this genre one may witness the relentless destruction of 'the human' and the unfolding in its stead of what I will call 'the abhuman'. The abhuman subject, characterized by its morphic variability, continually in danger of becoming not-itself, becoming other.[1]

This is an excellent starting point for an understanding of a certain type of Gothic body that emerged out of the conflicted cultural contexts of the late nineteenth century: the 'monster' that transforms the 'human' into something radically 'other'. Dr Jekyll's transformation into his abhuman other, Mr Hyde, can be understood from this perspective, for example (see the extended commentary in Part Three: 'Nineteenth-century Gothic').

Other critics have drawn upon various aspects of psychoanalytic theory to interpret different forms of the Gothic body. Freud's essay 'The Uncanny' (1919) is often invoked in analyses of ghosts and doubles in Gothic fiction, for example, whilst the theory of abjection developed by the French psychoanalyst and philosopher Julia Kristeva has proved particularly useful in interrogating the status of the Gothic monster in its various forms. This chapter gives an account of some representations and interpretations of the Gothic body from the eighteenth century onwards under various headings, including the 'Double'; the 'Spectre'; the 'Monster', 'Abjection' and 'Fear and Desire'.

The Double

The figure of the double is prevalent within Gothic fiction and it takes a variety of forms. In some instances, the double exists as a character distinct from the protagonist who nevertheless comes to represent an aspect of the protagonist's often conflicted, unstable identity. The extent to which Victor Frankenstein's monster doubles its creator has been discussed already in Parts Three and Four. Roderick, in Edgar Allan Poe's 'The Fall of the House of Usher' (1839), can be read as doubled by his sister whose live burial symbolises Roderick's repression of aspects of his self (see Part Three: 'Nineteenth-century Gothic'). A more recent example of Gothic doubling is found in the series of *Alien* films in which the identity of the heroine, Ripley, merges with that of the alien to the extent she herself becomes alien (or abhuman, to employ Kelly Hurley's term) by the fourth and final film in the series.

Another form of the double as it appears in Gothic fiction can be described by the German term *Doppelgänger*, meaning 'walking double'. Such a creature is the physical replica of an individual that is, in popular folklore, invariably regarded as an ill omen, usually as a harbinger of death. Two texts discussed in more detail below offer vivid instances of this type of Gothic double: James Hogg's novel *The Private Memoirs and Confessions of a Justified Sinner* (1824) and Edgar Allan Poe's short story 'William Wilson' (1839). The double here appears as the uncanny 'twin' of the protagonist and can be read as externalising a repressed component of the protagonist's own troubled psyche. The *Doppelgänger* thus tends in Gothic fiction to embody the split identity of the main character and the destruction that it visits upon its double is in reality the self-destruction of a deeply troubled protagonist.

The final type of double in the Gothic novel is the creature that appears to emanate out of the protagonist such that the protagonist becomes his or her own double. The monstrous transformation of Jekyll into Hyde, or of Oscar Wilde's Dorian Gray into the full manifestation of his debauched self (initially represented by Dorian's inanimate double – the portrait) can be understood in these terms (see Part Three: 'From the *Fin de Siècle* to Modern Gothic'). Mutations such as those of the werewolf – where the individual exists as both human and animal – also entail a monstrous doubling of the self by the (altered) self, as opposed to by an entity that appears (however ambivalently) to exist separately from the main subject.* Other instances of this type of transformation involve less dramatic forms of physical mutation, but they can still be understood as a form of the Gothic doubling of the self. Stephen King's novel *The Dark Half* (1989) is a vivid example of this form of doubling. The protagonist, Thad Beaumont, is a recovering alcoholic and failing novelist who begins to enjoy considerable success when he adopts the pseudonym George Stark and invents a serial killing protagonist named Alexis

---

* In Stephen King's *The Cycle of the Werewolf* (1983), in which the small American town of Tarker's Mills is terrorised by a werewolf that turns out to be the town's Baptist minister, Reverend Lowe, the transformation of man into wolf is used to explore some of the central preoccupations of King's oeuvre: the struggle between good and evil and the capacity of the human to mutate into something monstrously alien to itself.

Machine. When Beaumont is revealed to be Stark, he stages a mock funeral for his literary alter ego. A murderous rampage follows seemingly perpetrated by Stark (who doubles the protagonist, Alexis), but in reality carried out by Beaumont: Thad becomes the violent alter ego that initially guaranteed the success of the struggling, paranoid author.

The Gothic Double and the Freudian Uncanny

Many critics, as suggested, have sought to understand the Gothic double in terms of Freud's theory of the uncanny. The fundamentals of the Freudian uncanny are considered briefly in Part Two: 'A Cultural Overview' where it is noted that Gothic fictions of the nineteenth century seemed to anticipate Freud in their representation of dysfunctional family relationships and repressed psycho-sexual impulses that return to traumatise the individual. Freud's theory of the uncanny points to the continuing importance to the individual of aspects of early childhood experience that have of necessity to be repressed if the child is to progress to functioning adulthood. Chief amongst these is the child's experience of sexual desire for the parent of the opposite sex; in young boys (and Freud is very much of his time in focusing almost exclusively upon male experience), this desire leads to a terror of punitive castration at the hands of a jealous and vengeful father. The young girl on the other hand perceives herself as already having been castrated since she lacks male genitalia. A key moment in the psychological development of the child is the first perception of sexual difference, bound up as it is for Freud with the trauma of the 'Oedipal complex':[2] the boy and girl interpret the lack of a penis as a 'punishment' for forbidden desire – the girl has been punished, the boy most likely will be if he fails to repudiate his desire for the mother. For both sexes, then, an experience of lack (either the fear of it, or the reality of it) is essential to identity formation, but the memory of its origin in sexual desire for a parent has to be repressed. For Freud, however, nothing is ever lost within the human psyche; what is repressed has the capacity to return and terrorise, or 'haunt' (to employ a Gothic term entirely appropriate to Freud's theory of the uncanny) the individual. The return of the repressed is the key source of the phenomenon that Freud describes as the uncanny. When a repressed memory intrudes into the safe, familiar world of the adult – rendering it suddenly and radically unfamiliar, or uncanny – the individual experiences a moment of trauma that threatens the very basis of coherent adult identity.

Freud's theory of the uncanny has proved immensely influential in the production and interpretation of Gothic fiction since the early twentieth century. Indeed, Freud himself conceived of the uncanny in Gothic terms: it is, he writes, that which 'arouses dread and creeping horror ... that class of the terrifying which leads us back to something long known to us, once very familiar'.[3] Moreover, the uncanny has a particular relevance to an understanding of how the double functions in Gothic fiction. Freud accepts the phenomenon of the double as a source of the uncanny. He writes (drawing on his contemporary Otto Rank's theory of the double which was close to his own):

> The theme of the 'double' has been very thoroughly treated by Otto Rank (1914). He has gone into the connections which the 'double' has with reflections in mirrors, with shadows, with guardian spirits, with the belief in the soul and with the fear of death; but he also lets in a flood of light on the surprising evolution of the idea. For the 'double' was originally an insurance against the destruction of the ego, an 'energetic denial of the power of death', as Rank says; and probably the 'immortal' soul was the first 'double' of the body ... Such ideas ... have sprung from the soil of unbounded self-love, from the primary narcissism which dominates the mind of the child and of primitive man. But when this stage has been surmounted, the 'double' reverses its aspect. From having been an assurance of immortality, it becomes the uncanny harbinger of death ... The 'double' has become a thing of terror, just as after the

collapse of their religion the gods turned into demons.[4]

The double poses a terrible threat to the self-contained, functioning identity of the individual. For Freud, the threat occasioned by the appearance of the double in its various forms has its roots in what is called 'primary narcissism'. This technical psychoanalytic term refers to the state in early childhood where the infant perceives of itself as immortal and invincible, as the centre of its universe. The child experiences everything in terms of and with reference to its own emerging self; thus the child projects the 'self' outwards, acquiring multiple 'selves' that represent aspects of the child's experience of external reality. The child's other selves are, as Freud says above, 'an insurance against the destruction of the ego'. The child must overcome this stage of primary narcissism, however, and this entails a traumatic encounter with its own mortality especially at the point at which the child enters the Oedipal phase of development: at this point, the double shifts from providing a support to the emergent ego, to potentially destroying it, and the memory of these childhood projections must be repressed ('the double has become a thing of death', says Freud). This stage of development is not deleted from the mental life of the individual, however; it can return to consciousness bringing with it that uncanny experience of 'dread and creeping horror'. This is what happens when the individual confronts the double as an alternative version of the self; the double is a traumatic evocation of the fragility of human identity and the possibility of its annihilation by an external, punitive force (see the discussion below of Hogg and Poe). Moreover, the individual will tend to project on to this double those aspects of the psyche with which the adult cannot be reconciled.* Thus, the double emerges as a monstrous entity that is potentially fatal to the sanity, if not the very life, of the protagonist of Gothic fiction.

James Hogg's *The Private Memoirs and Confessions of a Justified*

---

* An example is the self-destructive violence, rooted in childhood experiences of the violence of the father, latent in the personality of Stephen King's Jack Torrance in *The Shining*, discussed in Part Three: 'Twentieth-century American Gothic'.

Sinner (1824) narrates the gradual corruption of the protagonist Robert Wringhim* at the hands of a mysterious, sinister stranger named Gil-Martin. Robert, ostensibly the son of a Scottish nobleman, is adopted by a Protestant minister also named Robert Wringhim (and the text suggests that this man might be Robert's real father). The elder Wringhim is a severe preacher who adheres to the doctrine of predestination. According to this doctrine, a person's eternal destination – whether they are saved or damned by God – is already determined at the moment of their birth. They are predestined to go either to heaven or hell and no action on their part can alter this immutable, divinely ordained fact. At least, this is the austere version of predestination that the elder Wringhim preaches to his adopted son, and the young Robert absorbs it without question. His father is convinced that the boy is one of the 'elect', one of those people predestined to be saved, and thus Robert comes increasingly to believe, under the satanic influence of Gil-Martin, that no sin, however heinous, can alter this fact. Hence, the narrative is the confession of a justified sinner.

The novel, however, is not exclusively or arguably even predominantly an exploration of the flaws of the doctrine of predestination. It narrates the psychological breakdown of the protagonist and uses a complex scheme of doubling to reveal the inner conflict of Robert Wringhim. While Wringhim's legitimate identity is that of the son of an influential Scottish lord, it is profoundly undermined by Robert's status within this noble family. Unofficially adopted by the preacher, Robert is an outsider within his own family. To return to Freud's theory of self-development, a boy must overcome the terror and rage he feels towards his father as he negotiates the Oedipus complex: he must eventually identify with his father. Robert's alienation from his father (and the possibility that he might in fact be illegitimate) prevents him from productively making this transition. In particular, he is in competition with his brother, George, who represents within this text a privileged,

---

* The name of the protagonist is sometimes given as 'Wringham', but in most editions it is rendered 'Wringhim' and this is the version used here.

powerful form of masculine aristocratic power that Robert cannot hope to emulate. Robert is crippled by paranoia and unable to assert any kind of potent self-identity. Within this context, Robert's belief in predestination and the inevitability of his own salvation becomes a compensatory mechanism whereby he achieves some kind of self-validation. Gil-Martin plays on this conviction, pushing it towards a diabolical determination to sin on Robert's part. Indeed, the identity of Gil-Martin (who is able to morph into other shapes at will) increasingly merges with that of Robert rendering it unclear whether the perpetrator of various crimes (including the murder of Robert's brother) is Robert or Gil-Martin. As the critic Eve Kosofsky Sedgwick argues, Robert's repressed hatred of the 'fountainhead of male prestige' represented by George returns in the form of the Gothic double, Gil-Martin.[5]

Poe's 'William Wilson' (1839) is narrated by a man haunted by a *Doppelgänger* who first appears at the protagonist's boarding school and who shares the narrator's name. This double appears to be the opposite of the protagonist in temperament; whereas the narrator is assertive, irrationally capricious and almost bullying, the other William is rational, quietly confident, apparently assured of his own understated superiority and impervious to the narrator's attempts to dominate him. This infuriates the narrator, whose imposing persona masks (by his own admission) a deep insecurity. Increasingly, the other William comes, at least in the mind of the narrator, to resemble him physically and this is a source of 'intolerable horror' as the narrator confronts in this uncanny version of himself qualities at odds with his aggressive, increasingly debauched personality: the characteristics of the second William appear to challenge and even threaten to annihilate the narrator's own outwardly potent, yet inwardly precarious self-identity.

William's double does not represent a monstrous embodiment of the repressed drives of an ostensibly 'civilised' character; rather (and this demonstrates the versatility of the Gothic trope of the double), it is the narrator who is under the sway of drives and desires that he has not managed to overcome successfully in the course of his childhood development. He admits that he is and has always been 'addicted to the wildest caprices, and a prey to the most ungovernable passions'.[6] In this context, the double represents William's 'civilised' self, and William becomes the monstrous other to this model of self-restraint. In Freudian terms, it might be said that the double represents the narrator's 'super-ego'* that exists to control desires that might otherwise overwhelm the individual. The narrator admits that his father played no effective part in his development; William might be said, in Freudian terms, to lack a fully formed super-ego and the other William emerges in order to fulfil this role. After boarding school, the narrator is followed persistently by his double whose mysterious appearances invariably contrive to 'frustrate those schemes, or disturb those actions, which, if fully carried out, might have resulted in bitter mischief' (p. 127). The narrator is beyond reformation, however, and in his final encounter with the other William, he kills him only to perceive that all along this *Doppelgänger* was an aspect of his own self.

Spectres

One of the key generic markers of Gothic fiction is the presence of spectres. Whilst a novel need not necessarily include a ghost in order to be considered 'Gothic',† the ghost story is unequivocally a Gothic mode of fiction.‡ The appearance of a ghost in whatever form is often crucial to a narrative's generation of terror or horror, and since the late eighteenth century the capacity of a text to provoke these responses

---

* The super-ego may be theorised as the authoritative voice of the father internalised by the child.

† Some of the most iconic Gothic texts do not contain spectres in the traditional sense – consider Mary Shelley's *Frankenstein* (1818) and Stevenson's *The Strange Case of Dr Jekyll and Mr Hyde* (1886).

‡ The ghost story has become popular again as a Gothic mode in contemporary British fiction: see Susan Hill's *The Woman in Black* (1983) and Sarah Waters's *The Little Stranger* (2009), discussed in Part Three: 'British Gothic in the Late Twentieth Century'.

has been deemed crucial to the Gothic aesthetic. The importance of the spectre to Gothic writing is not limited to its effect on the reader, however. (Although the emotional volatility associated with a reader's reaction to a ghost story accounted for much of the hostility towards Gothicism in the early years of its development – see Part Three: 'Eighteenth-century Gothic'.) The presence of a spectre – like that of a Gothic double (and the two are often closely related) – may articulate deep-seated cultural anxieties and psychological traumas that emanate out of certain historical circumstances. In *The Castle of Otranto* (1764), for example, the spectre of the former Prince Alfonso appears to ensure that the principality returns to the proper order of succession (see the extended commentary in Part Three: 'Eighteenth-century Gothic'). Written within eighty years of the Act of Settlement (1701) which settled the succession to the English throne, and at a time when questions of governance and inheritance were by no means fully resolved, the return of the spectre of Alfonso signifies a powerful preoccupation on Walpole's part with history and lineage. The past haunts the present, much as the turbulent events of the mid-seventeenth century (the execution of Charles I and the English Civil War) haunted Walpole's imagination: he had pinned to the wall above his bed a copy of the execution warrant of King Charles.

Freud's concept of the uncanny has again proved central to critical interpretations of the place of the spectre in Gothic fiction. The spectre is a Gothic 'body' that blurs the boundaries between life and death, and between matter and spirit. The spectre is always out of place in the familiar contexts of domestic family life into which it invariably intrudes and this accounts for its uncanny quality. It is worth observing here that the term 'canny', and therefore its opposite 'uncanny', have a peculiar double meaning in German which Freud discusses at length: *heimlich* can mean familiar and agreeable (or 'homely'), or concealed and unfamiliar ('unhomely'). The term *unheimlich* (uncanny) thus suggests for Freud the return of something that has been kept hidden.[7] It marks the return into the safe, stable space of the home something that is at the same time familiar and unfamiliar: a shape, for example, that is seemingly human, but not living. In Gothic fiction, this uncanny body that is not a body often signifies the breakdown of homeliness, rationality and sanity: it marks, in Freudian terms, the return of the repressed.

Elizabeth Gaskell is a writer most often associated with Victorian realist fiction, but in 1852 she published a short story which exemplifies the representation and symbolic significance of the spectre in Gothic fiction: 'The Old Nurse's Story'. A nurse, Hester, narrates to a group of children a terrifying episode from the childhood of their mother, Rosamond, who was placed in the nurse's care following the death of her parents. Rosamond and her nurse go to live at Furnivall Manor, the ancestral home of a wealthy branch of Rosamond's family. The manor is occupied by Miss Grace Furnival, a rather imposing and not especially welcoming woman who seems constantly melancholic. Shortly after their arrival, Rosamond begins to experience visions of a small girl locked out in the snow who beckons Rosamond to join her. The child is the ghost of Grace's niece. Her presence is the spectral reminder of an appalling injustice in the family's history. As young women, Grace and her sister Maude fell in love with a foreign musician employed by their father. The man seduced and secretly married Maude; she bore his child only then to be deserted by him. Out of jealousy, Grace let it be known that her sister had borne a child, but in the absence of the husband it was assumed that the offspring was illegitimate. The sisters' tyrannical father had both mother and child thrown out in the middle of a snow storm and both of them died.

The ghosts of mother and child return at the end of the narrative and both are unequivocally malevolent; Gaskell does not portray these spectres as seeking justice, but vengeance. Hester protects Rosamond against their influence, but Grace is stricken with a fatal fever and dies some time later muttering, 'What is done in youth can never be undone in age!'[8] Through the figure of the spectre Gaskell's fiction articulates a key theme of the genre: that the past will always return; it can neither be undone, nor forgotten. Moreover, as is often the case in Gothic, the spectre that haunts the family in this narrative can be related to wider social and cultural contexts: it is not merely symbolic of a single family's dysfunction. The mother is sent to her death because she transgresses the code of the patriarchal family in giving birth outside its authorised structures. Along with her child, she becomes in death a force of pure malevolence, an uncanny realisation of the evil that her sexual misconduct was deemed to represent when she was alive. Thus the return of the repressed operates at a cultural as well as an individual level. The body of this transgressive woman is subjected to a process of cultural repression analogous to the individual's 'forgetting' of forbidden sexual drives: the woman is outcast and forgotten, but returns to haunt the father's house, the locus of Victorian patriarchal power.

One of the most famous Victorian ghost stories is Edgar Allan Poe's 'The Black Cat' (1843) which introduced a different variety of spectre: the ghostly animal of the title that returns, as Gothic spectres often do, to avenge an injustice. The narrator, who owns the black cat, attacks the animal in an insane drunken rage and gouges out one of its eyes. In its depiction of the psychological effect of drink and the violence that flows from it this is a very modern Gothic narrative, more concerned than Gaskell's tale with the emotional perversity of its protagonist.[*] The narrator regrets his act when he recovers, but is nevertheless infuriated by the cat's understandable terror of him after the attack. In another moment of pure frenzy, the narrator grabs the animal, takes it into the garden and hangs it. As one would expect from a Gothic narrative, this irrational outburst in fact constitutes a displacement of anger which is shortly to find another focus.

A series of inexplicable events ensues: the narrator's house catches fire and a giant image of the hanged animal is found emblazoned on the building's only remaining wall. The reader, alive to the conventions of the supernatural tale, is thus given to understand that the black cat has already made a kind of spectral return and this is reinforced when the narrator finds in a tavern a cat identical to the dead animal except for a white mark on its chest. The narrator takes the cat home, but soon begins to find it loathsome; he believes the

---

[*] One can appreciate in this respect the influence of Poe over later writers such as Stephen King.

animal is in some sense tormenting him and starts to imagine that the mark on its chest resembles a gallows. Eventually, he attacks the cat with an axe, and when his wife intervenes to protect the animal, the narrator, by this point quite deranged, kills her instead and inters her body in the wall of the cellar. As the police investigate her disappearance and find nothing to implicate him in his wife's murder, the narrator is quite confident that he has evaded detection until a high-pitched wail emanates from the cellar wall. When the bricks are removed, the corpse is found with the black cat sitting on its head.

The critic Ed Piacentino observes an affinity in this tale between the narrator's wife and the black cat;[9] she intervenes to protect it and the narrator appears to turn his rage against her without a moment's thought; the woman and the cat become doubles of each other, as signified by the cat's uncanny intervention on behalf of the dead wife when its wails reveal her corpse to the police.[*] What the cat represents for the narrator, and the symbolic significance of the animal's spectral return, is hinted at in the opening pages. The narrator describes his tale as, 'the most wild, yet the most *homely* narrative' (my emphasis).[10] The uncanny is defined by its capacity to appear as simultaneously familiar and strange, as 'wild' and 'homely'. This tale thus seems to present itself as uncanny and the spectral apparitions it narrates are fundamental in comprehending the obscure, confused motivations of the protagonist.

The narrator begins his narrative with a description of his temperament in childhood, which was characterised by such 'docility and humanity' that he became the butt of jokes amongst his peers (p. 271). The narrator as a child had a special fondness for animals which he delighted in caring for and caressing. The narrator's disposition here is marked as feminine: these qualities of gentleness and nurturing are not qualities that would have been considered especially legitimate in a male at this time, hence the ridicule suffered

---

[*] For a contemporary reworking of Poe's tale, which makes even more explicit the affinity between the cat and the wife, see Joyce Carol Oates's 'The White Cat' (1987). Unlike Poe, Oates makes the wife (whom she names Alissa – Poe leaves his narrator's wife nameless) a powerful personality within her narrative.

by the narrator during childhood. As an adult, his fondness and compassion for animals begin to fade, to some extent under the influence of drink, but the narrator is careful to note that his intemperance is not the major cause of his cruelty; rather, the narrator falls victim to a 'spirit of perverseness' that compels him to 'offer violence to his own nature' (p. 273). He seems intent upon destroying the humane, docile aspect of his self, the aspect culturally coded as feminine. The critic Terry Heller argues that the second cat and ultimately the narrator's wife become images of what Heller terms the narrator's 'lost self' – the repressed, 'feminine' self of his childhood.[11]

In twentieth-century Gothic, spectres continue to signify the return of the repressed on an individual and a cultural level. The extended commentary in Part Three: 'Twentieth-century American Gothic', for example, considers the extent to which the ghosts of the Overlook Hotel in King's *The Shining* (1977) could be regarded as manifestations of Jack's repressed psychological trauma, and as signifying the hidden violence and corruption that marked aspects of American political and cultural life in the early to mid-twentieth century. Another significant example of the use of spectrality to explore repressed cultural memories is provided by Toni Morrison's *Beloved* (1987). This novel narrates the lives of a community of ex-slaves who remain in various ways traumatised by their experience of slavery. Some of the characters seek actively to fight against the legacy of slavery, whereas others – including the main protagonist, Sethe – try to repress memories too painful to be entertained. Sethe vividly reveals the way in which repression operates in the psyche of the individual by employing the term 'disremember' instead of 'forget': to disremember is actively to push a memory out of the conscious mind, which is precisely how repression functions.[12] Into this context of psychological pain and disremembering, the text introduces a powerful spectral presence: the ghost of Sethe's daughter, Beloved. Beloved was murdered by Sethe following Sethe's escape from her slave master. Sethe enjoyed only twenty-eight days of freedom before being recaptured, but rather than deliver her children back into slavery she tries to kill all of them, and does in fact kill Beloved. Beloved's return to the house that Sethe occupies after the civil war marks the return to Sethe of the trauma and violence that she had sought to disremember. Moreover, Beloved's return has a wider cultural and political importance, signifying a haunting of the American national psyche by the legacy of slavery.

Monsters

Unlike the spectre, the monstrous bodies that have proliferated within Gothic fiction since the early nineteenth century are characterised by gross materiality; the monster is not a disembodied entity signifying the return of the dead, but invariably a creature defined by its perverse physicality. To appreciate the difference between monstrosity and spectrality in the Gothic, it is worth considering the difference between a ghost and a zombie[*] as these entities are generally represented. The ghost is a disembodied spirit of a dead person that returns often to redress a past injustice, or simply to terrorise an individual who has become the focus of the spectre's malign energy. The ghost invariably displays supernatural powers which defy rational explanation: the ability to pass through solid objects, to render itself visible or invisible at will, to manipulate objects from a distance and so on. The zombie, on the other hand, is a physical body returned from the dead and its physical form is usually subject to the same spatial and temporal limitations that restrict ordinary bodies. Similarly, a vampire (although it possesses certain supernatural powers that distinguish it from the zombie) is an embodied creature, a form that physically returns from the dead and that, crucially, requires physical sustenance in order to survive.

---

[*] The term 'zombie' is thought to be of West African origin. Referring initially to a snake-type deity, it acquired the meaning 're-animated corpse' in relation to voodoo ritual. Another possible derivation is the Spanish *sombre*, meaning 'shade', or 'phantom'.

Many critics have argued that the monster thus reflects specific anxieties concerning the material form of the body and its relationship to the mind; the monster poses the question, in fact, of what it means to be human. The zombie, for example, is a human form lacking any attribute of personality: it represents the raw material of the body stripped of intellect and emotion, and given over to senseless destruction. The fact that the zombie typically feeds on the brains of its victims is revealing here: it destroys the organ associated with the production and organisation of identity. The zombie thus interrogates what it means to be human in a modern, secular milieu.*

In his analysis of what he calls 'monster culture', Jeffrey Jerome Cohen asserts, 'The monster's body is a cultural body ... an embodiment of a certain cultural moment' and its prevailing tensions and anxieties.[13] The paragraph above discusses the zombie, in general terms, as this type of 'cultural body'. A further analysis of the changing representation of the zombie in contemporary culture gives support to Cohen's thesis. The figure of the zombie has become almost as ubiquitous in late twentieth- and early twenty-first-century culture as the vampire. The success of George Romero's zombie films† and of zombie novels by writers such as S. D. Perry (the *Resident Evil* series), David Wellington (the online *Monster* trilogy), Max Brooks (*World War Z*) and Stephen King (*Cell*) appears to reflect certain anxieties that centre upon the influence of modern technologies on the human body (consider contemporary concerns regarding genetic cloning, for example), and threats of pandemic illness and invasion. In this respect, current zombie narratives resemble the Gothic of the Victorian *fin de siècle* and the mid-twentieth-century Cold War period in which fears of national or global catastrophe are mediated through the figure of the invading alien.‡ In Wellington's *Monster Planet* (2005) and Max Brooks's

---

* In a secular society the 'soul' does not define what it is to be distinctively human.
† See, for example, *Night of the Living Dead* (1968) and *Dawn of the Dead* (1978).
‡ See, for example, H. G. Wells's *The War of the Worlds* (1898) and Jack Finney's *The Body Snatchers* (1955).

influential *World War Z* (2006), for example, the zombie threat is combined with the prospect of global apocalypse; in Stephen King's *Cell* (2006), a mysterious signal emitted over the mobile phone network (referred to as 'The Pulse') transforms cell phone users into zombies. The film *28 Days Later* (2002), meanwhile, links the phenomenon of zombie transformation to the threat of deadly virus transmission and to contemporary concerns regarding the status of the animal and the human: a group of animal rights activists frees a monkey from a laboratory that turns out to be infected with a disease known as 'Rage'; the disease spreads through the human population initiating the familiar scenario of zombie transformation and apocalypse.

Because monsters invariably reflect the concerns of a particular historical moment, it is difficult to generalise about what such monsters might signify in a broader, theoretical sense, but Cohen offers various useful theses for interrogating those qualities that always seem to characterise the monster beyond the specific cultural contexts of any given time. He asserts, for example, that monsters invariably 'refuse easy categorization'. Indeed, he argues that monsters initiate a crisis in categorical forms of thinking that seek to define an entity in terms of rational, coherent physical and conceptual qualities:

> [Monsters] are disturbing hybrids whose externally incoherent bodies resist attempts to include them in any systematic structuration. And so the monster is dangerous, a form suspended between forms that threatens to smash distinctions.[14]

Victor Frankenstein's monster is dangerous, therefore, not only because of its macabre origin in Victor's corpse-strewn laboratory, or its capacity for violence once it turns against its creator, but because its 'externally incoherent body' – a living thing made of dead matter – frustrates its incorporation into rational schemes of thought. The same is true of zombies and vampires both of which are described using terms that point to their conceptual, as well as their physical incoherence: the 'living dead' and the 'undead'.

Cohen also sees in the monstrous body an embodiment of cultural difference and a reflection of power relationships through which difference may be rendered monstrous in order to expel it from a social group that seeks homogeneity. Thus, representations of monstrosity within white, Christian cultures have often functioned to depict the racial other as dangerously subhuman. In her analysis of Gothic horror and monstrosity Judith Halberstam makes a similar point, arguing that the figure of the vampire in the 1890s can be understood as reflecting a certain cultural construction of the 'Jewish body'. She writes:

> [P]arasitism was linked specifically to Jewishness in the 1890s ... the Jewish body was constructed as a parasite, as the difference within, as unhealthy dependence, as a corruption of the spirit that reveals itself upon the flesh.[15]

Halberstam sees in Stoker's Count Dracula an embodiment of the animalistic, devious qualities attributed to European Jews within European, Christian culture.

Femininity, Monstrosity, Vampirism

Sheridan Le Fanu's *Carmilla* (1872) was in many ways a precedent text for *Dracula* (1897), though Stoker changed the vampire's place of origin from Styria to Transylvania and, crucially, he changed the sex of his vampire. Le Fanu's monster is a female vampire who embodies various aspects of cultural difference. The woman, Carmilla, infiltrates the house of a well-to-do family* in order to victimise their young daughter, Laura. The vampiric threat in this novel is posited as implicitly sexual such that the text, through its

---

* There are strong echoes of Coleridge's female vampire, Geraldine, here – see Part Three: 'Romantic-era Gothic'.

narration of what is essentially a vampiric seduction, condenses various contemporary anxieties concerning unregulated female sexuality* and especially female homoeroticism. Carmilla's beauty is exceptional, but also dreadfully mesmerising; her appearance, actions and speech are strange and often incomprehensible to her victim and thus Carmilla is constructed not only in terms of irresistible erotic power, but of profound cultural otherness:

> She used to place her pretty arms about my neck, draw me to her, and laying her cheek to mine, murmur with her lips near my ear, 'Dearest, your little heart is wounded; think me not cruel because I obey the irresistible law of my strength and weakness; if your dear heart is wounded, my wild heart bleeds with yours. In the rapture of my enormous humiliation I live in your warm life, and you shall die--die, sweetly die--into mine. I cannot help it; as I draw near to you, you, in your turn, will draw near to others, and learn the rapture of that cruelty, which yet is love; so, for a while, seek to know no more of me and mine, but trust me with all your loving spirit.'
>
> And when she had spoken such a rhapsody, she would press me more closely in her trembling embrace, and her lips in soft kisses gently glow upon my cheek.
>
> Her agitations and her language were unintelligible to me.[16]

Laura construes Carmilla's attentions as similar to the courtship of a male lover and even wonders if 'a boyish lover had found his way into the house and sought to prosecute his suit in masquerade' (p. 105).† Carmilla is a mannish female, possibly even a man in disguise, who therefore blurs stable categories of identity and

---

* This is a key theme in *Dracula* – see Part Three: 'From the *Fin de Siècle* to Modern Gothic'.

† For a modern reworking of this theme, see Angela Carter's 'The Lady of the House of Love' in *The Bloody Chamber* (1979) collection of short stories.

representation (in this case masculine and feminine) in the manner suggested by Cohen and Halberstam as characteristic of the monstrous Gothic body. And yet Le Fanu's text insists that in spite of her masculine 'masquerade', Carmilla remains essentially feminine and, significantly, the mark of her femininity is her 'melancholy' and her 'languor' ('her movements were languid – *very* languid', p. 102). Carmilla is identifiably feminine in so far as she displays these signs of mental weakness and instability and thus this text, like many examples of *fin de siècle* Gothic fiction, reflects the prevailing interpretation of femininity as in some sense disordered (see Part Three: 'From the *Fin de Siècle* to Modern Gothic'). Whether as a romantically assertive pretend male, or as a melancholic and languid female, Carmilla's Gothic body functions to disrupt 'easy categorization' and 'systematic structuration'.

Abjection

The theories of Cohen and Halberstam draw upon the work of the influential French theorist, Julia Kristeva, whose *Powers of Horror* (1982) developed an idea that has proved central to late twentieth- and early twenty-first-century Gothic criticism: the concept of 'abjection'. An experience of abjection, says Kristeva, arises when an individual confronts an object that 'disturbs identity, system, order. What does not respect borders, positions, rules'.[17] Like the Freudian uncanny, abjection has its roots in early infancy when a child is undergoing a complex and traumatic process of identity formation that requires it to repress the chaotic, though deeply pleasurable drives associated with the pre-Oedipal phase. The abject differs from the uncanny, though, in the materiality of its causes and effects. An experience of abjection is triggered by something that strikes the individual not only as strange and unfamiliar, but as so physically repulsive as to trigger an adverse physical response: nausea, trembling, even vomiting. It should therefore be clear why, in Gothic criticism, abjection has tended to be associated with monstrosity, and spectrality with the uncanny. Spectres bear all the hallmarks of the uncanny; they are strange, unfamiliar and unsettling, but rarely physically repulsive. Monsters, on the other hand, are so physically perverse as to sicken the onlooker; their frustration of 'system' and 'order' powerfully evoke the chaotic impulses that define early childhood and that must be repressed if a secure adult identity is to be established and maintained.

The fiction of H. P. Lovecraft and Stephen King offers exemplary representations of the abject Gothic body in twentieth-century fiction. The monsters that populate Lovecraft's short stories are entirely removed from the domain of the human and trigger violent responses of physical horror in the protagonists. As has been observed already (see Part Three: 'From the *Fin de Siècle* to Modern Gothic'), narrators are frequently driven mad by their encounters with abjection in Lovecraft's tales. The common scenario is that a traveller visits a distant and hostile land – quite unlike any human environment – out of which emerge monsters that can be read, in Kristeva's terms, as a manifestation of chaotic drives that threaten to annihilate the individual. Thus, says the narrator of 'Dagon' (1919), 'it darted like the stupendous monster of nightmares ... I think I went mad then';[18] the narrator of 'The Call of Cthulhu' (1928) observes, 'when I think of the extent of all that may be brooding down there I almost wish to kill myself' (p. 165). Lovecraft's tales, moreover, reveal another quality of the Gothic monster that Cohen identifies as central to its characterisation and cultural significance: it invariably seems to escape. The monster at the end of 'The Call of Cthulhu' 'still lives' and in 'Dagon' it even infiltrates the domesticated domain of mid-twentieth-century America: the narrator hears it pressing against the door as he concludes his tale and rushes for the window.

Stephen King's *Pet Sematary* (1983) uses the abject body (in the form of creatures returning, zombie-like, from the dead) in order to explore trauma at the individual and wider cultural level. This novel is considered by King to be his scariest horror fiction (see King's introduction to the 2000 edition of the text). It centres on the figure of Louis Creed, a doctor and committed family man who nevertheless feels a certain ambivalence, if not outright hostility, towards his domestic and professional commitments. Like many of King's protagonists,* Louis has been and remains conflicted by childhood experiences that he seeks to repress, and this repression becomes the catalyst for murderous violence against the central character and his family. At the beginning of the novel, he arrives in the small town of Ludlow with his wife and two small children; irritated by what he perceives as their incessant, suffocating demands, he momentarily indulges in a fantasy of escape from his family responsibilities: the 'wild but not unattractive idea' of abandoning his family in Bangor on the pretext of getting something to eat, and driving away 'without so much as a look back'.[19] The abject powers that overwhelm Creed and his family in this novel can be read as a symbolic expression of Creed's failure to live up to his own conceptualisation of what constitutes a good father and husband. Significantly, the novel opens with the statement that Creed 'lost his father at three and had never known a grandfather' (p. 3). The text emphasises from the outset that Creed has always lacked a male role model and, by implication, a functioning sense of his own masculine identity; he is therefore only too keen to adopt his neighbour, the elderly Judson Crandall, as a surrogate father. Crandall – a former railroad worker, veteran of the First World War, strong and faithful husband and father – conforms to Creed's notion of the ideal man (the man who 'should have been his father', p. 9), but it transpires that Crandall had affairs with prostitutes in his youth. Reality constantly collides with Creed's attempts to construct for himself a version of masculinity capable of protecting his family and empowering himself. Creed's tragic attempts to keep his family together become, in fact, the direct cause of the supernatural violence that rips the family apart; his actions are underscored by his and Crandall's conflicted, ultimately destructive masculinity.

---

* Consider, for example, Jack Torrance in *The Shining* (1977) – see Part Three: 'Twentieth-century American Gothic'.

The 'Pet Sematary' of the novel's title is a burial site established by the town's children (hence the misspelling of cemetery) to bury their pets. The pet cemetery is on the outskirts of an ancient Indian burial ground haunted by a spirit that has the power to resurrect the bodies buried there. The location of the Indian burial ground on the margins of Ludlow introduces another theme that complements the novel's treatment of masculine anxiety and dysfunction. This site, sacred to a race nearly exterminated and then dispossessed by white settlers, is appropriated and abused by a white community that allows its children to bury their pets on its outskirts and then seeks to bend its powers to its own purposes. The motif of burial thus operates on a number of levels in this text. The literal burial of animals becomes a metaphor for the burial of the traumatic, violent national history of America's colonisation; at an individual level it is a metaphor for the character's own burial of disavowed desires. Crandall knows the secret of the burial ground and, when the Creeds' pet cat dies, he convinces Louis whilst his wife and children are away to bury the animal in the Indian cemetery. The cat is indeed resurrected, though in a repellent form. The animal embodies the repulsive qualities associated with abjection; it stumbles about like a zombie, its fur is matted and rank, and its smell nauseates the family. An instructive comparison to be made here is between King's zombie cat and Edgar Allan Poe's black cat discussed above: the black cat is a strange spectral entity, simultaneously familiar and unfamiliar to its owner – it is an uncanny Gothic body. The Creed family cat is, on the other hand, indisputably abject.

After Gage, the son of Louis and Rachel, is killed in a road accident (for which Louis tellingly blames himself as an incompetent father who failed to stop his son as he raced towards the road) Louis decides to exhume Gage's body and rebury it in the Indian cemetery. What is resurrected, however, is a demonic, murderous and, again, abject version of Gage that violently kills Crandall and Rachel before being killed in turn by Louis. The novel concludes ominously with a version of Rachel (the novel refers to her as 'It') returning to the family home after her burial in the Indian cemetery by the desperate and by now utterly deranged Louis. King's figuration of abject bodies in this text thus allows him to interrogate the complex, conflicted individual history of Louis Creed and the traumatic, 'buried' cultural memories of contemporary America.

Fear and Desire

Kristeva insists that abjection triggers not only horror, but a dreadful and conflicted fascination precisely because it is associated with the pleasure of unregulated childhood desires and drives. Cohen makes a similar point in observing that 'the fear of the monster is really a kind of desire'.[20] The monster is incoherent and unregulated in its appearance and in the enactment of its desires: it represents a dreadful, yet compelling state of freedom from every restraint. From this perspective, it is possible to understand why monsters may become 'sites of identification' in Gothic horror fiction (see Part Three: 'Twentieth-century American Gothic'). This approach helps to explain why monster narratives are often framed by episodes of forceful escape at the outset (the monster breaks frenziedly out of a confined space – a cage or coffin, for example) and the uncompromisingly violent destruction of the monster at the end.[*] The monster's escape signifies a catastrophic, yet liberating breakdown of systems of repression and restraint that must be violently, unambiguously restored.

Sheridan Le Fanu's *Carmilla*, see above, can be read as signifying the dreadful attraction/repulsion that characterises abjection. Laura's seduction by Carmilla, and what this represents in terms of the cultural 'otherness' attributed to the vampire, has been considered. The text also makes clear that the vampire's capacity to manipulate human

---

[*] An iconic example of this from twentieth-century cinema is King Kong (in the film of 1933) breaking out of captivity to terrorise New York City. He climbs the Empire State Building before being shot down by aircraft.

desire is not because she is unequivocally attractive, but precisely because she both disturbs and attracts her prey. Laura's conflicted response to Carmilla's embraces can be read as a manifestation of abjection, of what Kristeva terms 'the power of horror':

> From these foolish embraces, which were not of very frequent occurrence, I must allow, I used to wish to extricate myself; but my energies seemed to fail me. Her murmured words sounded like a lullaby in my ear, and soothed my resistance into a trance, from which I only seemed to recover myself when she withdrew her arms.

> In these mysterious moods I did not like her. I experienced a strange tumultuous excitement that was pleasurable, ever and anon, mingled with a vague sense of fear and disgust. I had no distinct thoughts about her while such scenes lasted, but I was conscious of a love growing into adoration, and also of abhorrence. This I know is paradox, but I can make no other attempt to explain the feeling.[21]

The threat represented by the abject body has to be violently repudiated in order to regulate the chaotic desires ('I was conscious of a love growing into adoration, and *also of abhorrence*', says Laura) that threaten the breakdown of stable individual and cultural identity. Carmilla is violently murdered in a manner that anticipates the killing of the vampire Lucy in Bram Stoker's *Dracula*. Still, however, there is a sense that the monster might make a return. As Cohen points out the monster always seems to escape the mechanisms of control imposed upon it, and what Carmilla represents in psychological and cultural terms is not capable of unequivocal destruction/repression. Thus Laura observes at the close of her narrative:

> It was long before the terror of recent events subsided; and to this hour the image of Carmilla returns to memory with

ambiguous alternations--sometimes the playful, languid, beautiful girl; sometimes the writhing fiend I saw in the ruined church; and often from a reverie I have started, fancying I heard the light step of Carmilla at the drawing room door. (p. 148)

Notes

1   Kelly Hurley, *The Gothic Body: Sexuality, Materialism and Degeneration at the Fin de Siècle* (Cambridge: Cambridge University Press, 1996), p. 3.
2   See Sigmund Freud, *The Interpretation of Dreams* (New York: Avon Press, 1980). Freud's Oedipus complex derives its name from the Greek myth of Oedipus, king of Thebes, who killed his father and married his mother.
3   Sigmund Freud, *Writings on Art and Literature* (Stanford, CA: Stanford University Press, 1997), p. 195.
4   Ibid., p. 210.
5   Eve Kosofsky Sedgwick, *Between Men: English Literature and Male Homosocial Desire* (New York: Columbia University Press, 1985), p. 102.
6   Edgar Allan Poe, 'William Wilson', in *The Fall of the House of Usher and Other Writings* (London: Penguin, 2003), p. 111.
7   Freud, *Writings on Art and Literature*, p. 195.
8   Elizabeth Gaskell, 'The Old Nurse's Story', in *Nineteenth-century Stories by Women* (Peterborough, Ontario: Broadview Press, 1993), p. 306.
9   Ed Piacentino, 'Poe's "The Black Cat" as Psychobiography: Some Reflections on Narratological Dynamics', *Studies in Short Fiction*, 35:2 (1998), p. 156.
10 Edgar Allan Poe, 'The Black Cat', in *The Fall of the House of Usher and Other Writings* (London: Penguin, 2003), p. 271.
11 Terry Heller, *The Delights of Terror: An Aesthetics of the Tale of Terror* (Chicago: University of Illinois Press, 1987), p. 103.
12 Toni Morrison, *Beloved* (New York; Alfred A. Knopf, 1987), p. 118.
13 Jeffrey Jerome Cohen, 'Monster Culture (Seven Thesis)', in *Gothic Horror: A Guide for Students and Readers* (London: Palgrave, 2007), p. 199.
14 Ibid., p. 201.

15   Judith Halberstam, *Skin Shows: Gothic Horror and the Technology of Monsters* (Durham, NC: Duke University Press, 1995), pp. 96–7.

16   Sheridan Le Fanu, *Carmilla*, in *Three Vampire Tales* (Athens: University of Georgia Press, 2004), p. 104.

17   Julia Kristeva, *Powers of Horror: An Essay on Abjection* (New York: Columbia University Press, 1982), p. 4.

18   H. P. Lovecraft, 'Dagon', in *The Call of Cthulhu and Other Weird Stories* (London: Penguin, 1999), p. 5.

19   Stephen King, *Pet Sematary* (London: Hodder & Stoughton, 2007), p. 4.

20   Cohen, 'Monster Culture', p. 212.

21   Le Fanu, *Carmilla*, p. 104.

Nation and Empire

Gothic writing has been concerned often, indeed one might say invariably, with representations of 'otherness' and with the power relationships that define the identity and status of the 'other'. This volume has considered various ways in which Gothic literature reflects and sometime interrogates (in female Gothic writing, for example) cultural understandings of gender, sexuality and social class. This chapter considers the Gothic's engagement with questions of race, nationhood and empire which were significant especially to the formation of the Gothic in the eighteenth century (when the anti-Catholicism of certain Gothic fictions helped to confirm Protestant nationhood in England) and to its development throughout the Victorian period, particularly during the height of British imperialism in the Victorian *fin de siècle*. Certain Gothic fictions during these periods of intense nation-building and colonial expansion can be seen to have reproduced discourses that constructed racial identities through representations of otherness that supported the colonial project. This has been touched upon already: Judith Halberstam's analysis of anti-Semitism in late Victorian vampire fiction is considered in the preceding chapter, for example.

On the other hand, in the twentieth century and beyond the flexibility and mutability of the Gothic has enabled writers to appropriate Gothicism in order to contest colonial discourses.

Writers such as Jean Rhys, Mayra Montero and Jamaica Kincaid have developed a distinct postcolonial Gothic voice which often functions to challenge colonial practices through the utilisation of Gothic tropes and motifs of haunting, paranoia, monstrosity and the uncanny. Postcolonial Gothic novelists also offer complex rewritings of some of the key texts in the Gothic tradition, texts that are often reworked in order to critique Western conceptualisations of the racial other (Bertha Mason in *Jane Eyre*, for example) and to give a voice to persons traditionally silenced within Western nations and their colonies.

Religion and Nationhood in the Eighteenth Century

In the mid- to late eighteenth century, a political and cultural understanding of Gothicism emerged that associated the Gothic not with the barbarism of the ancient Visigoth tribe that had invaded and destroyed Ancient Rome, but with an emerging Protestant nation that was seen to have its origin in north European 'Goths' depicted as heroic, liberty-loving, industrious peoples (see Part Three: 'Eighteenth-century Gothic'). The Gothic in this particular political and cultural context became a crucial component of an emerging ideology of nationhood that sought, amongst other things, to establish a clear national identity for Protestant Britain against the Catholicism of most of the rest of Europe.* It should be remembered that during this period matters of politics were invariably bound up with matters of religion. The English reformation had established the country as a Protestant state under the headship of a monarch – Henry VIII – who was also leader of the English church. For the country to continue as Protestant, however, it was necessary to ensure that every monarch ascending to the throne was Protestant and this required various interventions by parliament to exclude Catholics from the line of succession. The Bill of Rights (1689)

---

* The ideology of nationhood was associated especially with the Whig party to which the Gothic novelist Horace Walpole belonged.

ensured that the Catholic James II was replaced by the Protestant William of Orange and his wife Mary. In the absence of any obvious heir from the line of William and Mary (and at a time when the descendants of the deposed King James could still argue a legitimate claim to the throne), the Act of Settlement of 1701 ensured that the English throne passed to George I and thereafter to his Protestant heirs who were forbidden from converting to Catholicism and from marrying Catholics (a provision that remains in force in the early twenty-first century).

The disputes over monarchical succession in this period demonstrate that the country's status as a Protestant nation was hardly a given; the political establishment worked hard to ensure that Britain did not revert to Catholicism. In this context, the Gothic became implicated in a political–religious discourse that was often vehemently anti-Catholic. Catholicism was assumed to pose a threat not only to the Church of England, but to the political integrity of the state and Catholics were thus placed under various restrictions designed to limit their social and political influence.* Catholicism was also subject to negative cultural representations that sought to depict the religion as at odds with Enlightenment values: it was considered irrational, steeped in superstition and decadent in its emphasis on extravagant religious spectacle. The Protestant understanding of Catholicism is clearly articulated in Walpole's *The Castle of Otranto* (1764). The first preface (discussed in Part Four: 'Narrative Instability and the Gothic Narrator') posits the tale as the product of what it perceives as an uncivilised, medieval Catholic culture, the text of which was found in the library of a Catholic family in the north of England. There is a sense, then, that the barbarism of medieval Europe (and, as Walpole and others saw it, the Catholic past of England itself) lives on in the form of texts such as this, preserved in obscure 'unreformed' corners of the nation. This 'Gothic story' (in which the Catholic church becomes complicit with the persecutory schemes of Manfred) is thus implicated in a Protestant

---

* Catholics were excluded from most public appointments and could not own or inherit property, for example.

project of nation-building which constructs the Catholic as other to a rational eighteenth-century reader who can be relied upon to dismiss intellectually (and politically) what were deemed the irrationalities of Catholicism (and its claim to the English throne).

Although some legal and political restrictions affecting Catholics were lifted towards the end of the eighteenth century, anti-Catholicism in many ways intensified in England in the immediate aftermath of the French Revolution in 1789 as Catholics (the political loyalties of whom had long been suspect to Protestants) became associated with the revolutionary threat. Revolutionaries were often referred to as 'Jacobins' in reference to the deposed King James II* and one of the most influential revolutionary groups in France was called the Jacobin Club. Gothic novels, which exploded in popularity during the 1790s (see Part Three: 'Eighteenth-century Gothic'), display anti-Catholic sentiments that can be related to wider anxieties concerning the Jacobin revolutionary threat. Leslie Fiedler observed in 1960 that the Gothic novel in the late eighteenth century was 'the most blatantly anti-Catholic of all [forms of fiction], projecting in its fables a consistent image of the Church as the enemy'.[1]

The protagonist of Matthew Lewis's *The Monk* (1796) is the corrupt, and ultimately murderous and rapacious, monk Ambrosio. The beginning of Lewis's text presents Ambrosio as an exceptionally charismatic and gifted preacher who draws crowds to the cathedral in Madrid to hear him speak. The novel opens with a large congregation gathered to receive Ambrosio's sermon; the emphasis is upon the visual elements of the scene, the extravagant dress of the congregants and the lush interior of the church. The Catholic faith here is displayed in terms of its emphasis on sensuous spectacle and the crowds that have flocked to hear the priest are depicted as venal, superstitious, superficial and vain. By virtue of his rhetorical gifts, charisma and Machiavellian intelligence Ambrosio is able easily to manipulate these devotees, especially the coarse and ambitious Leonella, the aunt of Antonia (Ambrosio's sexual prey whom he finally rapes and kills). Virtually every representative of Catholic

---

* The Latin rendition of James is Jacobus.

authority is depicted as corrupt in this novel and the characters who ultimately prevail against such debauched authority are those (Raymond, Lorenzo and Agnes) who ideologically represent, in spite of their location within a Roman Catholic culture, a liberty-loving, rational English Protestantism.

Similarly, Ann Radcliffe's heroines in novels such as *The Mysteries of Udolpho* (1794) and *The Italian* (1797) are located in Catholic cultures and profess the Catholic faith, but essentially they exemplify qualities associated by English Protestants with English Protestantism: moderation, rationality, a love of liberty, self-discipline and an emphasis on interior faith against external religious ritual. Angela Keane observes that Radcliffe's protagonists are English 'liberals' embroiled in conflict with autocratic systems of power that are both religious and political.[2] This conflict is frequently mediated through representations of Gothic space: the convent or church becomes a nightmarish, physically overwhelming site of oppression in opposition to which the landscapes of nature emerge as authentic spiritual spaces in which Radcliffean heroines experience the divine.[*] Natural landscape in Radcliffe's fiction is the location of a God who does not reside within the Gothic structures and autocratic institutions of the Catholic church, but in sublime, open spaces that signify for the Protestant reader in the 1790s the open, democratising, 'natural' religion of a freedom-loving nation.

There remains, however, a certain ambivalence in the Gothic's treatment of Catholicism in the late eighteenth century which Leslie Fiedler has interpreted in terms of the Protestant fascination with its other. It was through negative representations of the Catholic church (lascivious priests, venal abbesses, vulnerable novices, haunted abbeys and so on) that the Gothic often sought to generate its key aesthetic effect: terror. Moreover, as many critics hostile to Gothicism in the 1790s appreciated, what readers of Gothic were seeking was not only terror, but a certain amount of titillation. The notion that sexual corruption was rife within the Catholic church allowed Gothic novelists

---

[*] See the discussion of Radcliffe's *A Sicilian Romance* (1790) in Part Three: 'Romantic-era Gothic', for example.

to represent a degree of sexual transgression that would not have been appropriate in a realist fiction dealing with late eighteenth-century English social life. Having asserted (as quoted above) that Gothic novels often were 'blatantly anti-Catholic', Fiedler observes:

> [The] Gothic imagination feeds on what its principles abhor, the ritual and glitter, the politics and pageantry of the Roman church. The ideal of celibacy and its abuses particularly intrigue the more prurient Gothic fictionists, as do the mysteries of the confessional, where for ages – into the ear of God knows what lustful priest – was whispered 'this secret sin, this untold tale', which they had made the subject of their art.[3]

Gothic fiction allowed Protestant readers to consume the extravagant pleasures associated with Roman Catholicism surreptitiously, under the banner of a mode of fiction that proclaimed its anti-Catholic credentials loudly. It is certainly Lewis whom Fiedler has in mind here as an especially 'prurient Gothic fictionist', though Radcliffe also plays with the potential for a perverse eroticism to emerge out of 'the ideal of celibacy' – in her depiction of the young Ellena persecuted by the monk Schedoni in *The Italian*, for example. Schedoni is modelled on Lewis's Ambrosio in a novel that is meant to repudiate the excesses of *The Monk* precisely through a duplication of Lewis's plot and character types – the corrupt monk, the virginal heroine who is his potential victim but who turns out to be related to him, and so on. Even by alluding to Lewis's notorious scenes of sexual violence in order to reject his Gothic aesthetic, however, Radcliffe's work becomes implicated in a complex economy of religious spectacle and sexual desire; the scene, then, in which Schedoni approaches the sleeping Ellena in order to murder her has the capacity to be read as implicitly, perversely sexual through its allusion to the scene in which Ambrosio rapes and murders Antonia. As several critics have observed, the 'enticing call of sensuous Catholic splendour' lends an ambivalent, double-edged quality to Gothic fictions ostensibly committed to the values of Protestant England.[4]

Gothic Orientalism

The philosopher Edward Said's influential work *Orientalism* (1978) explores the ways in which the Orient was exploited by imperialist powers from the eighteenth century onwards for its material resources, but also for what it represented culturally to the Western imagination. During the Romantic era, a variety of texts can be seen to be implicated in the ideological project that Said terms 'Orientalism'. Byron's poem *The Giaour* (1813), for example (see Part Three: 'Romantic-era Gothic') is an instance of the cultural figuration of the Orient as a space that is intriguing, yet potentially dangerous and to an extent incoherent. This is a space that produces charismatic figures that border on, and sometimes directly assume, monstrous forms, much as the othered space of Catholic Europe produces monsters such as Matthew Lewis's Ambrosio. Byron's poem is a Gothic narrative in which the Giaour is a vampiric creature, compelling yet deadly.[*]

Gothic fiction of this period reveals a similar fascination with the Orient as an othered space. Exemplary of this construction of the East in Gothic fiction is William Beckford's *Vathek* (1786, considered briefly in Part Three: 'Eighteenth-century Gothic') and, indeed, the life of Beckford himself is illuminating in terms of the Orientalism he reproduces in his novel. Beckford was an exceptionally wealthy man who owned slave plantations in the West Indies; he was thus implicated directly in the colonial projects of the moment (as was his friend Matthew Lewis, a plantation owner also). He lived an extravagant lifestyle, even by the standards of the English upper classes at the time, and the excesses of his protagonist Caliph Vathek can be read as a fictional rendering of the extremes of appetite and delusions of grandeur to which Beckford himself was subject.[†]

---

[*] The poem forms part of a series by Byron entitled 'Turkish Tales' which includes *The Bride of Abydos* (1813), *The Corsair* (1813), *Lara* (1814), *The Siege of Corinth* (1816) and *Parasina* (1816).

[†] Beckford's grandest gesture was the construction of his manor house, Fonthill Abbey, which cost more than £250,000 in the early nineteenth century (about £25 million in the early twenty-first century).

Vathek was inspired by *The Arabian Nights*, a collection of tales of ancient Middle Eastern origin translated into French by Antoine Galland in the early eighteenth century. This translation introduced the tales to a European readership and helped to motivate the growing European interest in Arabia and the East that gave rise to the Orientalist literature of the Romantic period. *Vathek* narrates the adventures of the Caliph Vathek as he enters into a 'Faustian pact' with the devil (named Eblis in this text) through the devil's intermediary, the hideous Giaour.* This demonic pact enables Vathek to pursue without restraint his extraordinary appetites, though the reader is left in no doubt that Vathek is moving towards his damnation.

In this respect, one interesting point about Beckford's novel is that its engagement with Islam, the religion of the Arabian caliph, is not entirely unsympathetic; indeed, Islam often functions in the novel to provide a moral framework within which the increasingly debauched antics of Vathek can be appraised. Vathek constructs elaborate mansions each devoted to the gratification of one of the five senses; not satisfied with these venal pursuits, however, he resolves to build a gigantic tower to reach to heaven. The Prophet Mohammed, like the Old Testament God confronted with mankind's construction of the tower of Babel in the book of Genesis, is angered by the pride of the caliph and responds thus:

> The great prophet Mahomet, whose vicars the caliphs are, beheld with indignation from his abode in the seventh heaven the irreligious conduct of such a vicegerent. 'Let us leave him to himself,' said he to the genii, who are always ready to receive his commands; 'let us see to what lengths his folly and impiety will carry him; if he run into excess we shall know how to chastise him. Assist him, therefore, to complete the tower which, in imitation of Nimrod, he hath begun, not, like

---

* Here the direct influence of Beckford on Byron is apparent – Byron took Beckford's representation of the Giaour as the model for the vampiric creature he depicts in his poem.

that great warrior, to escape being drowned, but from the insolent curiosity of penetrating the secrets of Heaven; he will not divine the fate that awaits him.'

His pride arrived at its height when, having ascended for the first time the eleven thousand stairs of his tower, he cast his eyes below, and beheld men not larger than pismires [ants], mountains than shells, and cities than bee-hives.[5]

At this point, Vathek emerges as an Oriental version of the Romantic anti-hero who later became a central figure in Romantic and Gothic literature. Vathek appears in this passage, one could argue, as a prototype of Mary Shelley's Victor Frankenstein, or Byron's Manfred (see Part Three: 'Romantic-era Gothic').[6] In this 1786 text, however, the monstrous embodiment of overreaching, almost Satanic, ambition is projected outwards, into the 'othered' space of the Orient; in later Gothic and Romantic texts, the satanic other enters into the reader's home territory.

The Giaour preys upon Vathek's insatiable appetite for power, convincing him to 'abjure Mahomet' and offer child sacrifices to the dark powers, after which he will receive unimaginable treasures. Vathek, in the novel's darkest and most Gothic moment, offers fifty young boys as a sacrifice having convinced them and their parents that they have been specially chosen to present him with gifts and receive rewards in their turn. In front of a large audience of his subjects, Vathek throws the boys into a chasm that symbolises the hell to which Vathek is shortly to be consigned. At this point, the Orient emerges as a deeply othered Gothic space in which the most grotesque atrocities are committed by the Oriental tyrant.

Critics and theorists such as Edward Said have construed the Western Orientalism that manifests itself in Beckford's novel as part of a wider imperialist project* whereby the Orient is constructed as the binary opposite of Western culture, a site of cultural difference that embodies a barbarism deemed to have no place within the

---

* Beckford himself was a member of the British parliament and a plantation owner.

civilised European nation; indeed, the function of the European nation – and this was one of the key ideological justifications of European imperialism throughout its history – was to 'civilise' the Orient. As the critic Eric Meyer observes, however, this civilising imperialist project was threatened by the possibility that the West might become contaminated in some sense by the barbarism of the Orient in the process of attempting to reform it (and, indeed, the trope of invasion and corruption by alien forces that symbolises the colonial other is prevalent in Gothic fiction from the late eighteenth century onwards). Meyer's analysis focuses upon the West's representation of Oriental sexual practices, especially the institution of the harem. The harem plays a key role in *Vathek*, becoming a signifier of Vathek's uncontrollable sexual appetites and, by extension, of the unregulated sexuality associated with the Oriental male. Meyer's point is that the unruly sexuality associated with the East (that allows it to be constructed as an undisciplined feminine space in need of Western, masculine, imperialist control) becomes an object of disgust and desire for the Western colonialist:

> Vathek's passion for the Eastern girl Nouronihar [who becomes his lover in the novel] and the many subpornographic harem episodes that punctuate the text, serve to solicit the gaze of the reader toward an Orient that is conceived as a feminine space of languid sensuality and riotous passion. The Orient is thus (re)figured as the harem fantasy of a militant European imperialism that places 'the East' as the obscure object of Western desire. Vathek's long and rather aimless quest into the mysterious lands of the East in search of nameless gratifications is a displaced version of imperial travel narratives and the accounts of missionary colonialism; and, like these generic equivalents, the narrative structure of *Vathek* positions the Orient as a feminized space invaded by the masculine subject, one who undergoes the risk of being feminized by the experience, of 'going native' when subjected to the sensual lures of the East.[7]

Vathek becomes, according to this analysis, a version of the Western male colonialist who is susceptible to absorbing, through his imperialist adventures, a tantalising, dangerous otherness that is both racial and sexual. From this perspective, we can return to the point made above in respect of Beckford's own life in England: in view of his extraordinary extravagance and devotion to pleasure, it is possible to posit this pillar of the British imperialist establishment as a version of Caliph Vathek himself.

Charlotte Dacre's novel *Zofloya, or The Moor* (1806) is another example, in a different context, of Gothic Orientalism that reveals the extent to which representations of the East were coloured by contemporary constructions of feminine sexuality and the sexuality of the Oriental male. Dacre was a controversial Gothic writer by virtue of the fact that her style often conformed closely to the 'horror' mode of Gothic initiated by Matthew Lewis in the 1790s. There was considerable outrage against Lewis's publication of *The Monk* in 1796; its explicit scenes of violence and sex saw the text condemned as obscene and blasphemous (see Part Three: 'Eighteenth-century Gothic'). Dacre's *Zofloya, or The Moor* is modelled to quite a considerable extent on Lewis's earlier novel and, though it eschews some of Lewis's more graphic moments, it met with a similar degree of public disapprobation not least because in this instance the author was a female. One 1806 reviewer in an essay ironically entitled *The Flowers of Literature* commented:

> The *fair* author of *Zofloya* had before *distinguished* herself, in the annals of literary libertinism; and she has now *treated* HER admirers with the development of such scenes, as, we had hoped, no female hand could be found to trace. But, as we wish not to initiate our readers in the mysteries of brothels, or in the more secret vices of the cloister, we dismiss the ungrateful subject.[8]

Dacre's novel narrates the adventures of a female libertine named Victoria who, like Lewis's rapacious monk Ambrosio, engages diabolical help in pursuing her lustful desires. Married to a man she becomes quickly bored with after a brief flirtation, Victoria becomes increasingly attracted to her husband's younger brother, Henriquez, who is betrothed to a thirteen-year-old orphan named Lilla. As Victoria's lust for Henriquez increases, she falls under the influence of his servant – the Moor, Zofloya – who promises to help her rid herself of her rival and seduce Henriquez. Zofloya provides poisons which enable Victoria to murder first her husband, and then the elderly chaperone of Lilla. Zofloya then drives Victoria to commit the most violent act in the novel – the repeated stabbing of Lilla – in a scene that reproduces closely the horror Gothic style associated with Lewis: although devoid of sexual content, the episode evokes the violent murder of the young, virginal Antonia by Ambrosio.

Dacre's novel has a strong sexual dimension, however. It is evident in Victoria's quasi-incestuous lusting over her husband's brother, but also in the seductive power of Zofloya over Victoria. Victoria has dreams in which it is Zofloya who seems to appear as the love object, not Henriquez; as Victoria implicates herself more deeply in the diabolical plans formulated by Zofloya, he appears (often in the setting of sublime mountain landscapes) as the charismatic Gothic anti-hero towering above her whilst she comes close to fainting like a breathless, blushing heroine of a romance fiction. In these scenes, the Moor Zofloya emerges as the racially othered male whose blackness becomes the signifier of a dangerous, irresistible sexual prowess. Within the symbolic scheme of this novel, it is clear that Victoria is as corrupted by Zofloya's exotic racial and sexual otherness as she is by her own lustful desires. By the end of the text, Victoria and Zofloya are living as lovers on the run amongst bandits in the Italian mountains and, as Victoria begs Zofloya to save her from the consequences of her crimes, he finally reveals his demonic identity:

> a figure, fierce, gigantic, and hideous to behold! – Terror and despair seized the soul of Victoria; she shrieked, and would have fallen from the dizzying height, had not his hand, who

appeared Zofloya no longer, seized her with a grasp of iron by the neck!⁹

What occurs here is what Diane Long Hoeveler terms a 'demonization of difference': the sexually irresistible Moor becomes the very devil himself. This is not to say, however, that the novel unapologetically articulates the racist stereotypes of its historical moment; as Hoeveler suggests, Zofloya can be read as the embodiment of Victoria's own excessive sexual longings such that the novel becomes more a critique of aristocratic decadence than an anxious depiction of 'demonic' racial difference. Moreover, the scene in which Zofloya is revealed to be demonic strongly smacks of hyperbole, of what Hoeveler terms 'parody [and] self-conscious deflation'.¹⁰ The hyperbolic transformation of the racial other literally into a demonic other might thus itself be interpreted as a parodic interrogation of the imperial nation's 'demonization of difference'.

The Gothic and Imperialism at the *Fin de Siècle*

Britain's political and commercial power over its colonies increased markedly during the nineteenth century and along with this increase in the material influence of the Empire over most of the globe came the development of various cultural discourses that sought to position colonial subjects as subordinate and other to the British. In his two major works on European colonialism, *Orientalism* (referred to above) and *Culture and Imperialism* (1993), Edward Said argues that the West (or the 'Occident' to use a term frequently employed in this context) developed in the nineteenth century an imperialist ideology whereby the diverse peoples and native cultures of colonised territories were constructed against white European colonists in terms of oppositional categories (black/white, civilised/savage, modern-scientific/primitive-occult, and so on) that exerted considerable ideological control over the colonised. Said contends, furthermore, that Western literature throughout this period was complicit in the development of these imperialist discourses: see his influential reading of Jane Austen's *Mansfield Park* (1814) in *Culture and Imperialism*, for instance.*

Part Three: 'From the *Fin de Siècle* to Modern Gothic' discusses the influence of theories of 'degeneration' over Gothic fictions of the *fin de siècle*. The notion that Europe had reached a more advanced evolutionary stage than that achieved by other nations and races was accompanied by an anxiety that European culture could nevertheless degenerate to a more primitive state under certain conditions (some of which, paradoxically, were seen to be generated by the technologies and cultural processes of modernity itself – see H. G. Wells's *The Island of Dr Moreau* (1896), for example). In terms of the colonial ideology of the moment, this fear of degeneration translates into an anxiety concerning what Stephen Arata terms 'reverse colonization', a process whereby 'what has been represented as the "civilized" world is on the point of being colonized by "primitive" forces'.[11] The critic Patrick Bratlinger goes further in identifying a mode of *fin de siècle* Gothic that he terms 'Imperial Gothic'. This form of Gothicism, he argues, often represents 'atavistic descents into the primitive' through its narration of colonial encounters with racial difference; it 'expresses anxieties about the ease with which civilisation can revert to barbarism or savagery and thus about the weakening of British imperialist hegemony'.[12] For Bratlinger, the Victorian *fin de siècle* and the early decades of the twentieth century saw the publication of various fictions in which the deeply othered territories of the Empire – notably Africa and Asia – form the setting for narratives of colonial adventures gone awry. Many of these fictions have certain Gothic elements, even if they do not warrant the designation 'Gothic' in their entirety: Joseph Conrad's *Heart of Darkness* (1902), for example (although it is in some ways critical of

---

* The wealthy patriarch Sir Thomas Bertram, who owns Mansfield Park in Austen's novel, also owns slave plantations in the West Indies and spends time away from England administering his estate abroad. Said points out that the novel does not interrogate his involvement in the slave trade in spite of the fact that it was written at the time when the trade (having been abolished in Britain in 1807) was one of the most hotly contested issues of the moment.

European colonial practices), portrays the Congo as effectively a Gothic space – a space in which the Westerner encounters an atavistic savagery that threatens his own rather precarious subjectivity. Rider Haggard's *She* (an immensely popular fiction first published in serial form in the *Graphic* magazine in 1886–7) is in many respects a more overtly Gothic text, identified by Sheila Egoff as a forerunner of the fantasy genre.[13] Fantasy literature, with its 'intrusion of something unreal' into the domain of an otherwise seemingly normal world, is a close relation of modern Gothic literature and in Haggard's text it is late nineteenth-century Africa that serves as the strange, Gothic landscape that confronts the Western adventurer with 'something unreal'.[*]

The novel's protagonists – Horace Holly and Leo Vincey – embark on a bizarre colonial quest to avenge the murder of Leo's ancestor, an Egyptian priest named Kallikrates. By virtue of his unusual ancestry, Leo is thus implicated in the otherness – the 'something unreal' – that is attributed to Africa and its peoples. Vincey and Holly enter into an uncharted region of the continent where they encounter the 'She' of the novel's title, a seemingly all-powerful magician and queen (possibly even a goddess) named Ayesha who rules tyrannically over the Amahagger tribe. Ayesha, who is thousands of years old, was responsible for the death of Killikrates (whom she murdered in a jealous rage), and on seeing Vincey she becomes obsessed with him, believing him to be the reincarnation of the priest. She seeks to persuade Vincey to join her in immortality by stepping into an eternal flame – the Spirit of Life – but Vincey desists. As Ayesha enters the fire, her extraordinary beauty dissolves as she reveals her true age and what is posited as her essentially animalistic, savage nature: 'She raised herself upon her bony hands, and blindly gazed around her, swaying her head slowly from side to side as a tortoise does. She could not see, for her whitish eyes were covered with a horny film.' The flames appear to destroy Ayesha, but she utters the ominous warning to Vincey that, 'I die

---

[*] An influential example in popular culture through its film adaptations is Edgar Rice Burroughs's novel *Tarzan* (1912).

not ... I shall come again.'[14] Indeed, this novel is underscored by the threat that what Ayesha represents in terms of the inhuman otherness of this remote African territory has the potential to return and to invade the European homeland of the protagonists. Holly observes, for example, that 'evidently the terrible *She* had determined to go to England and it made me shudder to think what would be the result of her arrival' (p. 193).*

It is clear that Ayesha represents not only the colonial other of British imperialism, but the feminine other of Victorian patriarchy. She embodies the destructive, irrational energy associated with female sexuality in this period and often conceptualised medically in terms of hysteria. The implication is that when women are not carefully controlled, they have the potential to assume monstrous forms: Haggard's Ayesha, Stoker's female vampires in *Dracula*, the diabolical female murderer in Arthur Machen's *The Great God Pan* (1894, see Part Three: 'From the *Fin de Siècle* to Modern Gothic'). Another novel of the period in which colonial anxieties are aligned powerfully with patriarchal constructions of 'good' and 'bad' womanhood is Bram Stoker's *The Jewel of Seven Stars* (1903), a text which can be credited with inaugurating one of the key tropes of Gothic fiction in the later twentieth century: the resurrected Egyptian mummy as Gothic monster.

This novel is narrated by a barrister, Malcolm Ross, who falls in love with Margaret Trelawny, whose genteel modesty epitomises the Victorian ideal of virtuous femininity. Margaret seeks Ross's help when her father is discovered in his study, apparently in a kind of trance, with a peculiar pattern of cuts to his left wrist. The mystery appears to be related to Mr Trelawny's investigations of ancient Egyptian tombs, especially that of the queen Tera whose tomb he was exploring at the time Margaret was born. The novel manifests a

---

* This might be compared with Count Dracula's arrival in England as an instance of the infiltration of the nation by the racial other: see the preceding chapter and Part Three: 'From the *Fin de Siècle* to Modern Gothic'. See also a contemporary text, Richard Marsh's *The Beetle* (1897), in which an androgynous, hypnotic, shape-shifting creature arrives in Britain from the Orient.

growing contemporary interest in Egyptology (Egypt was a British colony at this time) and a fascination with the supposedly occult powers associated with Egyptian scripts and artefacts. In an attempt to investigate the mystery associated with Tera, Margaret's father, and increasingly Margaret herself (who is especially susceptible to the occult influence of the queen), Ross reads an account of Trelawny's adventures in Egypt and discovers various objects associated with Tera, including an elaborate ruby (the jewel of the novel's title) and the sarcophagus of the queen. When Trelawny eventually awakens from his trance, he explains to Ross that his life's work has been to employ the occult powers of the ruby to bring about the resurrection of Tera, and Ross agrees to help him. The result of the experiment – at least in the 1903 edition of the novel – is the monstrous apparition of Queen Tera and the death, at the moment of her resurrection, of everyone except Ross. Of particular note here is the fact that Margaret finally emerges as the double of Tera in a moment that aligns the Egyptian queen's racial otherness with Margaret's previously idealised femininity: the 'good' woman becomes the dangerous, occult female:

> I groped my way across the room to where I thought Margaret was. As I went I stumbled across a body. I could feel by her dress that it was a woman. My heart sank; Margaret was unconscious, or perhaps dead. I lifted the body in my arms [and laid it] in the hall, and groped my way to Margaret's room, where I knew there were matches, and the candles which she had placed beside the Queen. I struck a match; and oh! it was good to see the light. I lit two candles, and taking one in each hand, hurried back to the hall where I had left, as I had supposed, Margaret.

> Her body was not there. But on the spot where I had laid her was Queen Tera's Bridal robe, and surrounding it the girdle of wondrous gems. Where the heart had been, lay the Jewel of Seven Stars.[15]

In a later edition of the novel released in 1912, Stoker's ending is considerably less bleak. The horror of Tera's awakening is downplayed and the participants in the experiment survive, with Ross going on to marry Margaret. The foreign, occult power of Tera is thus minimised in this later version; racial (and sexual) difference is still demonised, but it is much more effectively controlled as Tera disappears into a pile of dust and the social structures of Victorian patriarchy are reasserted through conventional bourgeois marriage.[*]

It would be wrong to assume, however, that Gothic fictions concerned with colonial territories are invariably complicit with imperialist ideology. Rudyard Kipling, in spite of his reputation as the foremost writer of Empire in this period,[†] gives a much more ambivalent treatment of British colonialism in the short story 'The Mark of the Beast' (1890), a tale described by Paul Battles as 'one of his most forceful critiques of Empire: ... an allegory of the relationship of British colonizer and Indian colonized'.[16] The protagonist of the story is a deeply unattractive figure named Fleete – a friend of the story's first-person narrator – who at a New Year's party in India drunkenly defaces a statue of the Hindu god Hanuman by grinding his cigar into the statue's forehead and announcing triumphantly, 'Shee that? Mark of the B--beasht! I made it. Ishn't it fine?'[17] Fleete's drunken abuse of the statue attributes to the Hindu god the mark of Satan – the biblical 'Mark of the beast' from the book of Revelation. The desecration of the statue thus operates on two levels here: Hanuman is defiled physically by Fleete's drunken vandalism, and symbolically by Fleete's alignment of the Hindu god with the Judeo-Christian devil. This moment of colonial violence, however, is immediately reversed as a leper – the 'Silver Man' – steps from behind the statue and presses his face against Fleete's chest. Fleete is taken home by

---

[*] This happens in Stoker's earlier novel, *Dracula*, through the marriage of Jonathan Harker and Mina.

[†] Rudyard Kipling is well known for his patriotic texts that display a marked colonial sensibility – see the poems 'If' and 'The White Man's Burden'. The story under discussion here shows a different, more critical response to the British imperial project.

the narrator and another friend, Strickland, but it becomes clear that Fleete has been in some sense cursed by the Silver Man: he begins to transform into a wolf. The narrator and Strickland seek out the Silver Man, and capture and torture him in order to compel him to cure Fleete, which he eventually does. Far from closing the tale with a re-assertion of colonial authority over the 'savage', however, the tale ends with an extraordinary exposure of what is posited as the hollow hypocrisy of a colonial mission justified in terms of its civilising influence over the Orient:

> [Strickland] caught hold of the back of a chair, and, without warning, went into an amazing fit of hysterics. It is terrible to see a strong man overtaken with hysteria. Then it struck me that we had fought for Fleete's soul with the Silver Man in that room, and had disgraced ourselves as Englishmen for ever, and I laughed and gasped and gurgled just as shamefully as Strickland, while Fleete thought that we had both gone mad. We never told him what we had done. (p. 232)

The ideological opposition between an enlightened imperialist nation and its bestial other collapses entirely here; as Paul Battles observes, '[the narrator and his friends] are brought face-to-face with the Beast, and the Beast lies not within the Other, but within themselves'.[18] Note the name that Kipling gives to Strickland, the man who initiates the torture of the Silver Man: it seems to be a combination of 'Stricken' and 'England'.

Postcolonial Gothic

Postcolonial theory developed in the late twentieth century as a critical discourse that examines the ideological processes of colonialism, its material practices and the continuing impact of these on former colonial regions. Postcolonial fiction over the same period developed through the work of writers who either inhabit the former colonies, or who have emigrated (or whose families emigrated) to Europe and America. Indeed, the notion of diaspora (peoples dispersed from their country of origin to live elsewhere) is central to postcolonial literatures in which questions of displacement and cultural belonging are explored through the often dislocating, alienating experiences of diaspora communities.*

Postcolonial Gothic is a mode of fiction that puts into play the tropes, motifs and themes of Gothicism in order to interrogate the legacies of colonialism, especially its impact upon the subjectivity of individuals who have been displaced by colonial practices. This displacement is often figured in postcolonial fiction as simultaneously physical and existential in the sense that colonialism constructs it subjects as others and as homeless even when they adopt the citizenship of a former colonial power: they are depicted as never quite belonging either to their nation of origin (or their parents' nation of origin if they are second-generation immigrants), or to the country in which they have settled. The protagonist of Kureishi's *The Buddha of Suburbia* (not a Gothic text, but it exemplifies perfectly the point under discussion here) is considered British by his family in Pakistan and Asian by his white British peers. The fiction of Salman Rushdie also foregrounds the problematic negotiations of individual and cultural identity at work within immigrant communities, and Rushdie's work frequently contains elements of the Gothic that serve to represent the dislocation and alienation experienced by his protagonists. The controversial novel *The Satanic Verses* (1988) may be considered to conform to the genre of Magic Realist fiction.† Ian Netton points out that, 'Rushdie himself is on record as having claimed that his book was not about the Islamic faith, "but about migration, metamorphosis, divided selves"'.[19] The two central

---

* See, for example, Hanif Kureishi's *The Buddha of Suburbia* (1990) and Monica Ali's *Brick Lane* (2003).

† Magic Realist fiction has a broadly realist narrative that incorporates elements of the fantastical and supernatural in a manner that is often characteristic of Gothic narratives.

characters of the text – Gabreel Farishta and Saladin Camcha* – undergo supernatural transformations at the outset (Gabreel into the Archangel Gabreel and Saladin into a devil). Much of the rest of the narrative takes the form of dream sequences (again a common narrative device in Gothic fiction) which explore in various fantastical ways the fraught history of the relationship between East and West, and the role played by Western imperialism in the construction of the 'divided selves' of the novel's two main characters.

Postcolonial Gothic fiction can also be seen to engage explicitly with the Western tradition of Gothic literature in order to interrogate the ways in which Gothic tropes and motifs have been used to displace, silence and alienate colonial subjects constructed as other to white Western culture. A notable example of this deployment of 'Imperial Gothic' (to invoke Patrick Bratlinger's term once more) against itself is Jean Rhys's novel *Wide Sargasso Sea* (1966). This text is effectively a rewriting of Charlotte Brontë's *Jane Eyre* (1847, discussed in Part Four: 'Female Gothic') in which Rhys adopts as her protagonist the Creole woman Bertha Mason who is Edward Rochester's first wife in Brontë's novel. This is the woman, rejected by Rochester, who 'haunts' Thornfield Hall as the madwoman confined in the attic. Rochester in Brontë's text appears willing to repudiate Bertha's existence entirely in his desperation to marry Jane and he makes it clear that he loathes and fears his first wife. The novel, moreover, offers no alternative to Rochester's construction of his wife as insane and animalistic; Bertha seems to function throughout as a signifier of the mad, savage space of the colonies as they figure in the Western imperialist imagination. Rhys's novel offers a reclaimed history of Bertha on behalf of the silenced colonial subject. Bertha Mason becomes Antoinette Cosway, an engaging protagonist with a complex identity and personal history; the novel

---

* The choice of this name is significant. Salah ad-Din, who became known in the West as Saladin, was a twelfth-century Muslim military leader who recaptured Palestine from the crusaders. Saladin was regarded as a courageous and chivalrous leader by Muslims and Christians; it was only during colonial struggles over Palestine in the early twentieth century that Saladin came to be portrayed negatively in the West.

might be said to recreate Brontë's Bertha as a fully human subject, repudiating her status as the Empire's racial other through the nuanced and empathic narration of the painful story of Antoinette. Antoinette marries an Englishman who renames her Bertha, a gesture through which he seeks, as male coloniser, to take ownership of the Jamaican woman who has become his wife and therefore (Rhys's novel is set in 1834) his property.* Marriage is thus analogous in this novel to processes of colonisation whereby territories are accumulated and the identities of their people effaced. It is significant in this regard that Antoinette Cosway becomes Antoinette Mason following the remarriage of her mother. Her gradual transformation into Bertha Mason is thus effected through transactions of marriage that displace Antoinette's identity much as colonialism displaced the cultures which it appropriated.

Rochester removes Antoinette from her Jamaican home after their marriage and this physical displacement produces a crisis of identity for the protagonist who says about her new surroundings, 'there is no looking-glass here and I don't know what I am like now ... what am I doing in this place and who am I?'[20] The absence of the looking glass here symbolises the absence of any cultural reference point through which Antoinette might maintain for herself a coherent identity; she has an uncanny sense here of being unfamiliar to herself, of not knowing 'what I am like now'. This moment, moreover, establishes a connection between Antoinette and Brontë's protagonist, Jane; the novel may thus be read as an interrogation of patriarchy as well as imperialism (and, indeed, the two are closely linked throughout the text as its treatment of marriage transactions in a colonial context makes plain). Antoinette's comment about the looking glass evokes the episode in *Jane Eyre* when the protagonist sees her reflection in the large mirror in the 'red room' at Gateshead

---

*   The renaming of Antoinette is important in terms of the wider colonial context. Slaves brought to America were invariably given Anglo-American names in place of their African names. This is a key theme in the Black American writer Alex Haley's best-selling novel *Roots: The Saga of an American Family* (1976) in which great symbolic importance is attached to the recovery of slave 'Toby's' African name: Kunta Kinte.

Hall (discussed in Part Four: 'Female Gothic' in relation to the Gothic double). That moment for Jane is one of profound alienation: she fails to recognise her reflection and sees it as a ghost. Both protagonists thus experience moments of interior dislocation figured as the inability to see oneself, or as the misrecognition of oneself. A similar moment occurs later in Brontë's novel when Jane is wearing her wedding veil; again, her reflection appears as other to herself. It might be argued, though, that at least Jane eventually does come to 'see' herself, to establish for herself a coherent identity after a period of suffering (and significantly here it is Rochester who is blind at the end of Brontë's novel; his inability to 'see' himself implies a reconfiguration of his masculine subjectivity as Jane achieves greater independence). There is no such opportunity for Antoinette/Bertha to reclaim a coherent image of selfhood following her marriage; she is rejected by her husband and, like Brontë's Bertha, descends into madness. Rhys's postcolonial Gothic thus insists that Antoinette and Jane cannot be conflated into one instance of oppressed nineteenth-century womanhood: colonialism closes off for Antoinette the journey of self-development open to Jane.

Caribbean writers in the late twentieth century have developed a significant postcolonial Gothic literature that narrates the trauma of individuals and groups displaced and silenced, like Antoinette Cosway, by the material and symbolic structures of colonialism. Writers such as Mayra Montero and Jamaica Kincaid may portray former colonial territories as spaces that have been rendered 'Gothic' (violent, unhomely, alienating) by Western interventions. Montero's *In the Palm of Darkness* (1999) narrates the search by an American scientist, Victor Grigg, for an endangered species of bullfrog in Haiti. Victor[*] resembles the protagonists of the Imperial Gothic narratives considered in the above section – characters such as Holly and Vincey in Haggard's *She*, or Trelawny in Stoker's *The Jewel of Seven Stars* – who enter into dangerous colonial spaces on some kind of mission of discovery. Like Rhys's *Wide Sargasso Sea*, however, Montero's text writes against the tradition of Imperial Gothic in depicting the

---

[*] The name alludes to the high-point of British imperialism – victory/Victoria.

devastating impact of imperialism on an island that remains violently divided against itself. It is through the Haitian guide who accompanies Grigg, Theirry Adrien, that this alternative history emerges. Adrien's knowledge of the island and experience of Haitian culture take precedence over Grigg's scientific world-view. Whereas Grigg insists, very much in the manner of the rationalistic imperialist explorer, that 'nothing very serious can happen to a man when all he looks for, all he wants is a harmless little frog',[21] Adrien tries to dissuade him from the venture, insisting that Grigg's belief in his capacity to confront, unharmed, this traumatised landscape is entirely misplaced. Adrien knows, and Grigg soon discovers, that the mountains in which the 'harmless frog' is supposedly located are overrun by violent gangs of humans and zombies, and it is through the zombie motif especially that Montero signifies the extent to which a brutal colonial past (an 'undead' history, one might say) continues to traumatise the island.

Jamaica Kincaid's *The Autobiography of My Mother* (1996) is an account of the painful history of its Dominican protagonist, Xuela, who is of mixed European and Caribbean descent. Xuela throughout the novel inhabits a nightmarish Gothic landscape (a 'thick blackness of nothing', as she at one point describes it)[22] from which all emotional ties appear to have been erased in a potent metaphor for the brutalising effects of colonialism. The first words that Xuela remembers reading as a schoolgirl are the words 'British Empire' written on a map of the world, and the influence of empire is posited as having created an environment in which Xuela seeks to survive by eliminating the ties of affection and solidarity that often bind together oppressed groups in other postcolonial fictions.* This text is therefore a much bleaker Gothic exploration of racial and cultural identity than Rhys's text; as Cathleen Schine puts it, the novel 'simplifies the life around her main character, rendering it free of all everydayness, purifying it until it sparkles with hatred alone'.[23] The most potent symbolisation of Xuela's self-alienation is the novel's title and what it signifies with regard to the narrator's cultural and

---

* In Jean Rhys's novel, for example, Antoinette at least enjoys some material and emotional support within her native Jamaica.

existential situation. The title 'The Autobiography of My Mother' suggests that this narrative is a first-hand account of Xuela's life presented to the reader by Xuela's child, but Xuela has no child. Indeed, her only pregnancy at the age of sixteen ends in an abortion. The narrative thus renders itself spectral, positing itself as mediated through a child never born.* Xuela's own mother, moreover, died giving birth to Xuela and figuratively haunts her daughter in recurring dreams. The key Gothic tropes of the absent mother and the double (Xuela can be read as doubled by the unborn child who uncannily presents her life-story as the 'autobiography of my mother') are utilised vividly here to represent the trauma – political, cultural and psychological – of a colonial subject rendered other even to herself.

Notes

1   Leslie Fiedler, *Love and Death in the American Novel* (New York: Stein & Day, 1960), quoted in Angela Wright, *Gothic Fiction* (London: Palgrave, 2007), p. 79

2   Angela Keane, *Women Writers and the English Nation in the 1790s* (Cambridge: Cambridge University Press, 2001), p. 38.

3   Fiedler, *Love and Death in the American Novel*, p. 73.

4   Jerrold E. Hogle, *The Cambridge Companion to Gothic Fiction* (Cambridge: Cambridge University Press, 2002), p. 4

5   William Beckford, *Vathek* (Oxford: Oxford University Press, 1983), p. 6.

6   See also John Gilroy, *York Notes Companions: Romantic Literature* (London: Pearson Longman & York Press, 2010), for a discussion of Romantic heroes and anti-heroes.

7   Eric Meyer, '"I Know Thee Not, I Loathe Thy Race": Romantic Orientalism in the Eye of the Other', *ELH*, 58:3 (1991), p. 660.

---

*   Consider also Toni Morrison's novel *Beloved* (1987) in which (in a different context) a child returns to 'haunt' a protagonist also traumatised by colonial practices, in this instance slavery (see the preceding chapter for a discussion of the text).

8   See the Cardiff Corvey Electronic Database, British Fiction, 1800–1829: Production and Reception, accessed from www.cardiff.ac.uk.

9   Charlotte Dacre, *Zofloya, or The Moor* (New York: Arno, 1974), p. 232.

10   Diane Long Hoeveler, 'Charlotte Dacre's *Zofloya*: A Case Study in Miscegenation as Sexual and Racial Nausea', *European Romantic Review*, 8:2 (1997), p. 199.

11   Stephen Arata, *Fictions of Loss in the Victorian Fin de Siècle* (Cambridge: Cambridge University Press, 1996), p. 108.

12   Patrick Bratlinger, *Rule of Darkness: British Literature and Imperialism, 1830–1914* (New York and London: Cornell University Press, 1988), p. 229.

13   Sheila Egoff, *Worlds Within: Children's Fantasy from the Middle Ages to Today* (Chicago, IL: American Libraries Association, 1988), p. 7.

14   H. Rider Haggard, *Three Adventure Novels: She, King Solomon's Mines, Allan Quartermain* (New York: Dover, 1951), p. 210.

15   Bram Stoker, *The Jewel of Seven Stars* (Whitefish, MT: Kessinger Publishing, 2004), p. 207.

16   Paul Battles, '"The Mark of the Beast": Rudyard Kipling's Apocalyptic Vision of Empire', *Studies in Short Fiction*, 33:2 (1996), p. 333.

17   Rudyard Kipling, 'The Mark of the Beast', in *The Complete Works of Rudyard Kipling* (New York: Doubleday, 1921), p. 218.

18   Battles, '"The Mark of the Beast": Rudyard Kipling's Apocalyptic Vision of Empire', p. 343.

19   Ian Netton, *Text and Trauma: An East–West Primer* (London: Routledge, 1995), p. 22.

20   Jean Rhys, *Wide Sargasso Sea* (London: Penguin, 1968), p. 180.

21   Mayra Montero, *In the Palm of Darkness* (New York: Harper Collins, 1999), p. 37.

22   Jamaica Kincaid, *The Autobiography of My Mother* (New York: Farrar, Strauss & Giroux, 1996), p. 91.

23   Cathleen Schine, 'A World Cruel as Job's', *New York Times Book Review* (February 1996), p. 7.

Part Five
References and Resources

Timeline

	Historical events	Literary events
1751		Thomas Gray, *Elegy Written in a Country Church Yard*
1754		Thomas Warton, *Observations on the Faerie Queen of Spenser*
1756–63	Seven Years' War between England and France	
1757		Edmund Burke, *A Philosophical Enquiry into the Origin of Our Ideas of the Sublime and the Beautiful*
1760	George III crowned king	
1762		Richard Hurd, *Letters on Chivalry and Romance*
1764–5		Horace Walpole, *The Castle of Otranto*
1765		Thomas Percy, *Reliques of Ancient Poetry*
1776	American Declaration of Independence	
1778		Clara Reeve, *The Old English Baron*
1783		Sophia Lee, *The Recess*
1785		Clara Reeve, *The Progress of Romance*

Timeline

	Historical events	Literary events
1786		William Beckford, *Vathek*
1789	French Revolution begins	Ann Radcliffe, *The Castles of Athlin and Dunbayne*
1790		Edmund Burke, *Reflections on the Revolution in France*; Ann Radcliffe, *A Sicilian Romance*
1791		Ann Radcliffe, *The Romance of the Forest*
1792		Mary Wollstonecraft, *Vindication of the Rights of Woman*
1793	King Louis XVI executed	William Godwin, *Enquiry Concerning Political Justice*
1794	Robespierre executed	William Godwin, *Caleb Williams*; Ann Radcliffe, *The Mysteries of Udolpho*
1796		Matthew Lewis, *The Monk*
1797		Ann Radcliffe, *The Italian*; Samuel Taylor Coleridge, *Christabel*
1798		William Wordsworth and Samuel Taylor Coleridge, *Lyrical Ballads*; Charles Brockden Brown, *Wieland*
1799		William Godwin, *St Leon*
1803–15	Napoleonic Wars between Britain and France	
1806		Charlotte Dacre, *Zofloya, or The Moor*
1807	Slave trade in Britain abolished	

	Historical events	Literary events
1811	Regency Act transfers power to son of George III (as Prince Regent) owing to mental incapacity of the king	
1813		Byron, *The Giaour*
1816		E. T. A. Hoffmann, 'The Sandman'
1817		Byron, *Manfred*
1818		Mary Shelley, *Frankenstein*; Jane Austen, *Northanger Abbey*
1819		John Polidori, *The Vampyre*; John Keats, *Lamia*
1820	George IV crowned king	Charles Robert Maturin, *Melmoth the Wanderer*
1824		James Hogg, *The Private Memoirs and Confessions of a Justified Sinner*
1826		Ann Radcliffe, 'On the Supernatural in Poetry' and *Gaston de Blondeville*
1830	William IV crowned king	
1832	First Reform Act passed	
1838	Victoria crowned queen	
1839		Edgar Allan Poe, 'The Fall of the House of Usher' and 'William Wilson'
1841		Edgar Allan Poe, 'The Murders in the Rue Morgue'
1843		Edgar Allan Poe, 'The Black Cat'; Charles Dickens, *A Christmas Carol*

Timeline

	Historical events	Literary events
1847		Charlotte Brontë, *Jane Eyre*; Emily Brontë, *Wuthering Heights*
1850		Nathaniel Hawthorne, *The Scarlet Letter*
1852		Elizabeth Gaskell, 'The Old Nurse's Story'
1854–6	Crimean War between Britain and Russia	
1860		Wilkie Collins, *The Woman in White*
1861–5	American Civil War	
1864		Sheridan Le Fanu, *Uncle Silas*
1867	Second Reform Act passed	
1868		Wilkie Collins, *The Moonstone*
1872		Sheridan Le Fanu, *Carmilla*
1882	Married Women's Property Act passed	
1884	Third Reform Act passed	
1886		Robert Louis Stevenson, *The Strange Case of Dr Jekyll and Mr Hyde*
1887		Henry Rider Haggard, *She*
1891		Oscar Wilde, *The Picture of Dorian Gray*
1892		Charlotte Perkins Gilman, 'The Yellow Wallpaper'

	Historical events	Literary events
1893	Independent Labour Party founded	
1894		Arthur Machen, *The Great God Pan*
1895		H. G. Wells, *The Time Machine*
1896		H. G. Wells, *The Island of Dr Moreau*; Max Nordau, *Degeneration*
1897		Bram Stoker, *Dracula*; Richard Marsh, *The Beetle*
1898		Henry James, *The Turn of the Screw*
1899–1902	Boer War in the African Transvaal	
1901	Queen Victoria dies; Edward VII crowned king	
1903		Bram Stoker, *The Jewel of Seven Stars*
1904		M. R. James, *Ghost Stories of an Antiquary*
1911		Bram Stoker, *The Lair of the White Worm*
1917	Russian Revolution	
1914–18	First World War	
1918	British women over 30 gain right to vote	
1919		Sigmund Freud, 'The Uncanny'; H. P. Lovecraft, 'Dagon'
1922		F. W. Murnau (dir.), *Nosferatu*
1928	Voting age for women reduced to 21	H. P. Lovecraft, 'The Call of Cthulhu'

Timeline

	Historical events	Literary events
1929	Wall Street crash begins the Great Depression	
1931		M. R. James, *Collected Ghost Stories*; James Whale (dir.), *Frankenstein*; Tod Browning (dir.), *Dracula*
1933	Adolf Hitler appointed Chancellor of Germany	
1936		William Faulkner, *Absalom, Absalom!*
1938	Committee of Un-American Activities established by US House of Representatives	Daphne du Maurier, *Rebecca*
1939–45	Second World War	
1943		Jacques Tournier (dir.), *I Walked with a Zombie*
1945	Atomic bomb dropped by US Airforce on Japanese cities of Hiroshima and Nagasaki	
1947	India gains independence from Britain	
1950–3	Korean War	
1950	Senator Joseph McCarthy begins campaign against American communists	
1955		Jack Finney, *The Body Snatchers*
1958		Terence Fisher (dir.), *Dracula*
1959		Shirley Jackson, *The Haunting of Hill House*; Robert Bloch, *Psycho*

Gothic Literature

	Historical events	Literary events
1960		Alfred Hitchcock (dir.), *Psycho*
1963	President J. F. Kennedy assassinated in Dallas, Texas	
1965–73	Vietnam War	
1966		Jean Rhys, *Wide Sargasso Sea*
1967		Angela Carter, *The Magic Toyshop*
1968	American civil rights leader Martin Luther King assassinated	George Romero (dir.), *Night of the Living Dead*
1969	US moon landing	
1972	US Watergate scandal uncovered	Ira Levin, *The Stepford Wives* (1972)
1973		William Friedkin (dir.), *The Exorcist*
1974	President Richard Nixon resigns	J. G. Ballard, *Concrete Island*; Stephen King, *Carrie*
1975		Stephen King, *Salem's Lot*; J. G. Ballard, *High Rise*
1976		Anne Rice, *Interview with the Vampire*
1977		Stephen King, *The Shining*
1978		Ian McEwan, *The Cement Garden*
1979		Angela Carter, *The Bloody Chamber*; Ridley Scott (dir.), *Alien*
1982	Falklands War between UK and Argentina	Tennessee Williams, *A House Not Meant to Stand. A Gothic Comedy*

Timeline

	Historical events	Literary events
1983		Stephen King, *Pet Sematary*; Susan Hill, *The Woman in Black*; Fay Weldon, *The Lives and Loves of a She-devil*
1984		Iain Banks, *The Wasp Factory*; Wes Craven (dir.), *A Nightmare on Elm Street*
1985		Margaret Atwood, *The Handmaid's Tale*
1987		Toni Morrison, *Beloved*
1988		Thomas Harris, *The Silence of the Lambs*
1990–1	Gulf War	
1991		Bret Easton Ellis, *American Psycho*
1992		Poppy Z. Brite, *Lost Souls*; Francis Ford Coppola (dir.), *Bram Stoker's Dracula*; Alasdair Gray, *Poor Things*
1993		Margaret Atwood, *The Robber Bride*
1996		Robert Rodriguez (dir.), *From Dusk till Dawn*; Wes Craven (dir.), *Scream*; Jamaica Kincaid, *The Autobiography of My Mother*
1997		Poppy Z. Brite, *Exquisite Corpse*
1999		Eduardo Sánchez (dir.), *The Blair Witch Project*
2000		Mark Danielewski, *House of Leaves*
2001	Terrorist attacks on World Trade Center	

	Historical events	Literary events
2003	Iraq War begins	J. G. Ballard, *Millennium People*
2005	Terrorist attacks on London transport system	Hilary Mantel, *Beyond Black*; Bret Easton Ellis, *Lunar Park*; Eli Roth (dir.), *Hostel*; Stephenie Meyer, *Twilight*
2008		First series of television drama *True Blood*
2009		Sarah Waters, *The Little Stranger*
2010		Kevin Greutert (dir.), *Saw 3D*

Further Reading

Introductions, Cultural Overviews and Anthologies

Bloom, Clive (ed.), *Gothic Horror: A Guide for Students and Readers* (London: Palgrave, 2007)
>An anthology of Gothic writings and critical commentary from the early nineteenth to the late twentieth century

Botting, Fred, *Gothic* (London: Routledge, 1996)
>An introductory critical commentary on Gothic fiction from the eighteenth century to the late twentieth century

Byron, Glennis and David Punter (eds), *Spectral Readings: Towards a Gothic Geography* (London: Macmillan, 1999)
>An examination of the British, European and American historical and cultural contexts of Gothic literature

Clery, Emma J. and Robert Miles (eds), *Gothic Documents: A Sourcebook* (Manchester: Manchester University Press, 2000)
>An anthology of Gothic texts and writing related to the emergence of the Gothic from the eighteenth and early nineteenth centuries

Ellis, Markman, *The History of Gothic Fiction* (Edinburgh: Edinburgh University Press, 2000)
>Charts the cultural and historical development of Gothic fiction from the late eighteenth century through to the twentieth-century zombie film

Grixti, Joseph, *Terrors of Uncertainty: The Cultural Contexts of Horror Fiction* (London: Routledge, 1989)
>A study of twentieth-century horror fiction in its social, political and cultural contexts

Hogle, Jerrold E. (ed.), *The Cambridge Companion to Gothic Fiction* (Cambridge: Cambridge University Press, 2002)
>A collection of critical essays on Gothic literature from the eighteenth to the late twentieth century in a wide variety of national and cultural contexts

Horner, Avril (ed.), *European Gothic: A Spirited Exchange* (Manchester: Manchester University Press, 2002)
> A collection of critical essays on the development and varieties of Gothic literature in Britain and throughout Europe

Howells, Carol Ann, *Love, Mystery and Misery: Feeling in Gothic Fiction* (London: Continuum, 1995)
> A study of the importance of feeling and imagination in the development of Gothic fiction in Britain from the eighteenth to the mid-nineteenth century

Kilgour, Maggie, *The Rise of the Gothic Novel* (London: Routledge, 1995)
> An overview of the rise of Gothic fiction from the 1760s to the early nineteenth century

Lloyd-Smith, Allan, *American Gothic Fiction: An Introduction* (London: Continuum, 2004)
> A student's guide to the key texts, contexts and themes of American Gothic fiction from the nineteenth to the late twentieth century

MacAndrew, Elizabeth, *The Gothic Tradition in Fiction* (New York: Columbia University Press, 1979)
> Examines the literary and historical contexts of the origin of Gothic fiction in the eighteenth and early nineteenth centuries

Miles, Robert, *Gothic Writing, 1750–1820: A Genealogy*, 2nd edn (Manchester: Manchester University Press, 2002)
> An historical and theoretical study of the origin and development of Gothic literature during the Romantic period

Mulvey-Roberts, Marie (ed.), *The Handbook of the Gothic* (London: Palgrave, 2009)
> A comprehensive guide to Gothic literature containing entries addressing the key texts, themes, generic forms and contexts of the Gothic from its origins to the present day

Punter, David, *The Literature of Terror*, 2 vols (London: Longman, 1996)
> A comprehensive study of Gothic literature in its cultural, literary and sociological contexts from 1765 to the modern period

Punter, David (ed.), *A Companion to the Gothic* (Oxford: Blackwell, 2000)
> A collection of critical essays covering literary, cultural and historical aspects of Gothicism from the mid-eighteenth century to the present day

Punter, David and Glennis Byron, *The Gothic* (Oxford: Blackwell, 2004)
> A comprehensive guide to the Gothic covering key background materials and contexts, works, authors and themes

Sage, Victor (ed.), *The Gothick Novel: A Casebook* (London: Macmillan, 1988)
> An anthology of critical and literary sources relevant to the literary, cultural and historical origins and early development of Gothic fiction

Sedgwick, Eve Kosofsky, *The Coherence of Gothic Conventions* (London: Methuen, 1986)
> Examines the defining themes and literary conventions of Gothic fiction from the eighteenth to the mid-nineteenth century

Wright, Angela, *Gothic Fiction: A Reader's Guide to Essential Criticism* (London: Palgrave, 2007)
> A reader's guide to Gothic fiction that presents key primary materials alongside important critical commentaries from a variety of sources on major texts, themes and contexts

Eighteenth-century and Romantic-era Gothic

Brown, Marshall, *The Gothic Text* (Stanford, CA: Stanford University Press, 2004)
> An examination of the intellectual and cultural origins of Gothic literature in the pre-Romantic and Romantic periods that pays particular attention to the influence on Gothic fiction of the literature and ideas of German Romanticism

Bruhm, Steven, *Gothic Bodies: The Politics of Pain in Romantic Fiction* (Philadelphia, PA: Philadelphia University Press, 1994)
> An analysis of sensibility, selfhood and the articulation of pain in Romantic-era literature that sets Gothicism (though this is not the only subject of the study) in its wider philosophical and cultural contexts

Chaplin, Sue, *The Gothic and the Rule of Law, 1764–1820* (London: Palgrave, 2007)
> A study of the importance of various discourses of law and governance to the development of Gothic from Walpole to Mary Shelley

Clery, Emma J., *The Rise of Supernatural Fiction, 1762–1800* (Cambridge: Cambridge University Press, 1995)
> An examination of the key historical, cultural and political discourses that shaped the emergence and development of Gothic literature during the eighteenth century

Duggett, Tom, *Gothic Romanticism: Architecture, Politics and Literary Form* (London: Palgrave, 2010)`
> A wide-ranging artistic, cultural and historical study of forms of Gothicism in the late eighteenth and early nineteenth centuries and their relationship to the Romantic movement

Gamer, Michael, *Romanticism and the Gothic: Genre, Reception and Canon Formation* (Cambridge: Cambridge University Press, 2000)
> Examines the generic formation and cultural reception of the Gothic during the Romantic era and its relation to and appropriation by the literature of Romanticism

Mishra, Vijay, *The Gothic Sublime* (New York: State University of New York Press, 1994)
> A theoretical reading of key eighteenth- and nineteenth-century Gothic texts in terms of postmodern and psychoanalytical interpretations of the sublime

Napier, Elizabeth, *The Failure of Gothic Conventions: Problems of Disjunction in an Eighteenth-century Form* (Oxford: Clarendon, 1987)
> One of the first studies of Gothic to identify the generic and conceptual instability and ambiguity that appear to characterise the conventions and strategies of Gothic fiction

Norton, Rictor, *Gothic Readings: The First Wave, 1764–1840* (New York: Continuum, 2000)
> An anthology of works by major Gothic writers from Walpole to Poe that includes selections of cultural and historical material alongside literary texts

Townshend, Dale, *The Orders of Gothic: Foucault, Lacan and the Subject of Gothic Writing, 1764–1820* (New York: AMS Press, 2007)
> Employs the work of philosopher Michel Foucault and psychoanalyst Jacques Lacan to deliver a nuanced advanced theoretical study of diverse forms of Gothic literature from 1764 to 1820

Watt, James, *Contesting the Gothic: Fiction, Genre and Cultural Conflict* (Cambridge: Cambridge University Press, 1999)
> A study of the historical and cultural backgrounds of early Gothic fiction that emphasises its heterogeneous, often conflicting contexts and forms

Wein, Toni, *British Identities, Heroic Nationalism and the Gothic Novel, 1764–1824* (London: Palgrave, 2002)
> Examines the significant early relationship between Gothic fiction and formations and representations of British national identity

Nineteenth-century Gothic

Baldick, Chris, *In Frankenstein's Shadow: Myth, Monstrosity and Nineteenth-century Writing* (Oxford: Clarendon, 1987)
> A survey of the history of the Frankenstein myth in culture before the advent of cinema

Bloom, Clive (ed.), *Nineteenth-century Suspense: From Poe to Conan Doyle* (London: Macmillan, 1990)
> A collection of critical essays examining the literature of suspense and the supernatural in the mid-to-late nineteenth century

Briggs, Julia, *Night Visitors: The Rise and Fall of the English Ghost Story* (London: Faber, 1977)
> Examines the literary and cultural contexts of the Victorian ghost story and its reception

Crow, Charles, *American Gothic: An Anthology, 1787–1916* (Oxford: Blackwell, 1999)
> A collection of sources relevant to the development of American Gothic literature in the nineteenth century

Glover, David, *Vampires, Mummies and Liberals: Bram Stoker and the Politics of Popular Fiction* (Durham, NC: Duke University Press, 1996)
> An analysis of Stoker's novels, stories, essays and journalism in relation to the shifting political and commercial contexts of his period

Hughes, William and Andrew Smith (eds), *Bram Stoker: History, Psychoanalysis and the Gothic* (London: Macmillan, 1998)
> A collection of essays on Stoker's work from a variety of theoretical and critical perspectives

Mighall, Robert, *A Geography of Victorian Gothic Fiction: Mapping History's Nightmares* (Oxford: Oxford University Press, 1999)
> A study of the historical, geographical and political dimensions of Gothic fiction from Radcliffe to the Victorian *fin de siècle*

Robbins, Ruth and Julian Wolfreys (eds), *Victorian Gothic: Literary and Cultural Manifestations in the Nineteenth Century* (London: Palgrave, 2000)
> A collection of essays examining the literary and cultural forms and contexts of Victorian Gothic

Schmitt, Cannon, *Alien Nation: Nineteenth-century Gothic Fiction and English Nationality* (Philadelphia, PA: University of Philadelphia Press, 1997)
> A study of the extent to which Victorian Gothic fiction articulated various contemporary conceptualisations of English national identity

Smith, Andrew, *Victorian Demons: Medicine, Masculinity and the Gothic at the Fin de Siècle* (Manchester: Manchester University Press, 2004)
> An examination of *fin de siècle* Gothic in the context of contemporary crises in and demonisations of middle-class masculinity

Modern and Postmodern Gothic

Belville, Maria, *Gothic Postmodernism: Voicing the Terrors of Postmodernity* (New York and Amsterdam: Rodopi, 2009)
> An analysis of contemporary Gothic fiction and its relation to the cultural and political contexts of Western postmodernity

Clemens, Valdine, *The Return of the Repressed: Gothic Horror from The Castle of Otranto to Alien* (Albany, NY: Albany State University Press, 1999)
> An analysis of the origin and development of Gothic horror in terms of psychoanalytic theories of repression and the uncanny

Cohen, Jeffrey Jerome, *Monster Theory: Reading Culture* (Minnesota: University of Minnesota Press, 1996)
> A theoretical exploration of the construction and representation of monstrosity in modernity and postmodernity

Goddu, Teresa A., *Gothic America: Narrative, History and Nation* (New York: Columbia University Press, 1999)
> An analysis of American Gothicism in terms of national political, cultural and literary history

Magistrale, Tony and Michael Morrison (eds), *A Dark Night's Dreaming: Contemporary American Horror Fiction* (Columbia: University of South Carolina Press, 1996)
>   A collection of essays examining the cultural and literary forms and contexts of late twentieth-century American horror

Riquelme, John, *Gothic and Modernism* (Baltimore, MD: Johns Hopkins University Press, 2008)
>   A study of the complex and often critically neglected relationships between forms of Gothicism and Modernism in the early twentieth century

Sage, Victor and Allan Lloyd Smith (eds), *Modern Gothic: A Reader* (Manchester: Manchester University Press, 1996)
>   A collection of essays examining the presence of the Gothic in a range of contemporary cultural and literary contexts

Skal, David J., *The Monster Show: A Cultural History of Horror* (London: Penguin, 1994)
>   A study of the development of horror film from the 1920s to the 1990s

Smith, Andrew and Jeff Wallace (eds), *Gothic Modernisms* (London: Palgrave, 2001)
>   A collection of essays considering the relationship between Gothic and Modernism in literature and film

Key Debates

Narrative Instability and Criticism

Castricano, Jodey, *Cryptomimesis: The Gothic and Jacques Derrida's Ghost Writing* (Montreal: McGill University Press, 2001)
>   An analysis of the relationship between the work of philosopher Jacques Derrida and the central tropes, themes and textual strategies of the Gothic

Garrett, Peter K., *Gothic Reflections: Narrative Force in Nineteenth-century Fiction* (New York: Cornell University Press, 2003)
> Examines the relationships between the narrative strategies of Gothic fiction and other genres of literature in the nineteenth century

Punter, David, *Gothic Pathologies: The Text, the Body and the Law* (London: Macmillan, 1998)
> Examines the relationship between Gothic textuality and the law, arguing that Gothicism produces transgression and disruption within a range of modern and postmodern contexts

Wolfreys, Julian, *Victorian Hauntings: Spectrality, Gothic, the Uncanny and Literature* (London: Macmillan, 2002)
> Uses Jacques Derrida's theories of textuality and haunting to examine manifestations of haunting and spectrality in Victorian fiction

Female Gothic and Feminist Perspectives

Clery, E. J., *Women's Gothic: From Clara Reeve to Mary Shelley* (Tavistock: Northcote House, 2000)
> A study of the cultural and literary development of women's Gothic from the 1780s to the 1820s

DeLamotte, Eugenia C., *Perils of the Night: A Feminist Study of Nineteenth-century Gothic* (Oxford: Oxford University Press, 1990)
> Examines the extent to which female Gothic fiction of the Victorian period enabled women writers to express and explore anxieties around the fragility and instability of female selfhood

Ellis, Kate Ferguson, *The Contested Castle: Gothic Novels and the Subversion of Domestic Ideology* (Chicago: University of Illinois Press, 1989)
> An exploration of the cultural and political contexts of early female Gothic and its interrogation of the structures and symbols of patriarchal systems of power

Fleenor, Juliann E. (ed.), *The Female Gothic* (Montreal: Eden, 1983)
> A collection of essays examining the key tropes, themes and contexts of female Gothic writing

Gilbert, Sandra M. and Susan Gubar, *The Madwoman in the Attic: The Woman Writer and the Nineteenth-century Literary Imagination* (New Haven, CT, and London: Yale University Press, 1979)
>   A feminist study of nineteenth-century women's writing which includes chapters on key female Gothic texts of the period

Heiland, Donna, *Gothic and Gender: An Introduction* (Oxford: Blackwell, 2004)
>   Examines Gothic fiction from the late eighteenth to the mid-nineteenth century in terms of contemporary representations of gender and their political and cultural contexts

Hoeveler, Diane Long, *Gothic Feminism: The Professionalization of Gender from Charlotte Smith to the Brontës* (Liverpool: Liverpool University Press, 1998)
>   An analysis of female Gothic fiction from the 1780s to the mid-nineteenth century in terms of changing constructions of middle-class femininity in this period

Massé, Michelle A., *In the Name of Love: Women, Masochism and the Gothic* (New York: Cornell University Press, 1992)
>   A psychoanalytic study of aspects of women's identity as represented in British and American Gothic fiction from the eighteenth to the twentieth century

Milbank, Alison, *Daughters of the House: Modes of the Gothic in Victorian Fiction* (London: St Martin's Press, 1992)
>   An analysis from a feminist perspective of representations of femininity and domesticity in Victorian Gothic and sensation fiction

Moers, Ellen, *Literary Women* (London: Women's Press, 1976)
>   A wide-ranging study of women's writing from Austen to Woolf that includes a consideration of the origin and development of female Gothic fiction

Wallace, Diana and Andrew Smith (eds), *The Female Gothic: New Directions* (London: Palgrave, 2009)
>   A collection of essays addressing from diverse critical perspectives female Gothic fictions from the late eighteenth to the late twentieth century

Gender Criticism and the Gothic Body

Castle, Terry, *The Female Thermometer: Eighteenth-century Culture and the Invention of the Uncanny* (Oxford: Oxford University Press, 1995)
> Examines the origin of the Freudian concept of the uncanny in the diverse cultural, literary and scientific contexts of the eighteenth-century Enlightenment

Dryden, Linda, *The Modern Gothic and Literary Doubles: Stevenson, Wilde and Wells* (London: Palgrave, 2003)
> A study of the Gothic trope of the double and its varied cultural associations in the Victorian *fin de siècle*

Halberstam, Judith, *Skin Shows: Gothic Horror and the Technology of Monsters* (Durham, NC: Duke University Press, 1995)
> A theoretical and historical study of diverse representations of monstrosity from the Victorian period to the late twentieth century

Hendershot, Cyndy, *The Animal Within: Masculinity and the Gothic* (Ann Arbor: University of Michigan Press, 1998)
> Examines the relationship of cultural and literary forms of Gothicism to constructions of masculinity from the nineteenth to the late twentieth century

Hurley, Kelly, *The Gothic Body: Sexuality, Materialism and Degeneration at the Fin de Siècle* (Cambridge: Cambridge University Press, 1996)
> A study of diverse representations of the body in Gothic fiction of the late Victorian period in terms of their political, cultural and scientific contexts

Sedgwick, Eve Kosofsky, *Between Men: English Literature and Male Homosocial Desire* (New York: Columbia University Press, 1985)
> A wide-ranging study of representations of relations between men, and of the male body in nineteenth-century fiction

Showalter, Elaine, *Sexual Anarchy: Gender and Culture at the Fin de Siècle* (New York: Viking, 1990)
> A historical, cultural and literary analysis of formations of gender identity in the late nineteenth century that contains discussions of some key Gothic fictions of the period

Nation, Empire and Postcolonial Readings

Arata, Stephen, *Fictions of Loss in the Victorian Fin de Siècle: Identity and Empire* (Cambridge: Cambridge University Press, 1996)
> A study of *fin de siècle* fiction, including some key Gothic works, in the contexts of British imperialism, colonialism and related political and cultural practices

Bratlinger, Patrick, *Rule of Darkness: British Literature and Imperialism, 1830–1914* (New York and London: Cornell University Press, 1988)
> Examines the influence on late Victorian fiction of the expansion of empire and changing conceptualisations of nationhood at the *fin de siècle*

Brogan, Kathleen, *Cultural Hauntings: Ghosts and Ethnicity in Recent American Literature* (London: Macmillan, 1998)
> A study of the extent to which Gothic tropes and themes in contemporary American fiction reflect and interrogate cultural constructions of racial and national identity

Davison, Carol Margaret, *Anti-Semitism and British Gothic Literature* (London: Palgrave, 2004)
> Examines the Gothic's complex engagement from the eighteenth to the late nineteenth century with anti-Semitism and British national identity

Edwards, Justin D., *Gothic Passages: Racial Ambiguity and the American Gothic* (Iowa: Iowa University Press, 2003)
> A study of the relationship in nineteenth-century America between the language of the Gothic and the construction of categories of racial difference across a range of literary and cultural discourses

Khair, Tabish, *The Gothic, Postcolonialism and Otherness: Ghosts from Elsewhere* (London: Palgrave, 2009)
> Examines contemporary discourses of difference and identity and their relation to forms of colonial and postcolonial Gothic

Malchow, Howard, *Gothic Images of Race in Nineteenth-century Britain* (Stanford, CA: Stanford University Press, 1996)
> An analysis of representations of race in nineteenth-century Gothic and their relation to developing ideologies of imperialism and empire

Winter, Kerri J., *Subjects of Slavery, Agents of Change: Women and Power in Gothic Novels and Slave Narratives, 1790–1865* (Athens: University of Georgia Press, 1992)
> Explores the relationship in early Gothic between gender and slavery and the narrative connections between slavery writing and Gothic fiction

Index

Index

Acknowledgements

Extracts from:

MILLENIUM PEOPLE by J. G. Ballard. Copyright © 2003 by J. G. Ballard. Used by permission of W. W. Norton & Company, Inc. and HarperCollins Publishers Ltd

Iain Banks, *The Wasp Factory* (London: Macmillan, 1984), reproduced by Abacus, an imprint of Little, Brown Book Group

Angela Carter, *The Magic Toyshop* (1967, London: Virago, 1981). Copyright © Angela Carter. Reproduced by permission of the author c/o Rogers, Coleridge & White Ltd, 20 Powis Mews, London W11 1JN

Bret Easton Ellis, *Lunar Park* (London Picador, 2005), reproduced by permission of ICM Talent

T. S. Eliot, *The Waste Land* (1922), reproduced by permission of Faber and Faber Ltd

Sigmund Freud, from 'The Uncanny', *The Standard Edition of the Complete Psychological Works of Sigmund Freud* (S.E.), Vol. 17, pp. 234–5 (London: The Hogarth Press, 1955), reproduced by permission of Sigmund Freud Copyrights/Paterson Marsh Ltd

Alasdair Gray, *Poor Things* (London: Bloomsbury, 1992), reproduced by kind permission of the author

The Woman in Black by Susan Hill, published by Vintage. Copyright © Susan Hill, 1992. Reproduced by permission of Sheil Land Associates Ltd

Beyond Black by Hilary Mantel (Copyright © Hilary Mantel, 2005). Reprinted by permission of A. M. Heath & Co. Ltd

Fay Weldon, *The Life and Loves of a She-devil* (London: Hodder and Stoughton, 1983), reproduced by kind permission of Capel & Land Ltd on behalf of the author

H. G. Wells, *The Island of Dr Moreau* (1896, New York: Barnes and Noble, 2004), reproduced by permission of A. P. Watt Ltd on behalf of the Literary Executors of the Estate of H. G. Wells

YORK NOTES **COMPANIONS**

Texts, Contexts and Connections from York Notes
to help you through your literature degree ...

The best books ever written

PENGUIN CLASSICS

SINCE 1946

20% discount on your essential reading from
Penguin Classics, only with *York Notes Companions*

The Castle of Otranto
Horace Walpole
Edited with an Introduction and Notes by Michael Gamer
Paperback | 208 pages | ISBN 9780140437676 | 28 Sep 2001 | £5.99

The Mysteries of Udolpho
Ann Radcliffe
Edited with an Introduction by Jacqueline Howard
Paperback | 704 pages | ISBN 9780140437591 | 26 Apr 2001 | £9.99

Northanger Abbey
Jane Austen
Edited with an Introduction by Marilyn Butler
Paperback | 288 pages | ISBN 9780141439792 | 27 Mar 2003 | £6.99

Frankenstein
Mary Shelley
Edited by Maurice Hindle
Paperback | 352 pages | ISBN 9780141439471 | 30 Jan 2003 | £6.99

The Strange Case of Dr Jekyll and Mr Hyde and Other Tales of Terror
Robert Louis Stevenson
Edited with an Introduction and Notes by Robert Mighall
Paperback | 224 pages | ISBN 9780141439730 | 27 Feb 2003 | £5.99

Dracula
Bram Stoker
Edited with an Introduction and Notes by Maurice Hindle
Paperback | 560 pages | ISBN 9780141439846 | 27 Mar 2003 | £6.99

To claim your 20% discount on any of these titles
visit **www.penguinclassics.co.uk** and use
discount code **YORK20**

188179